CULINARY NUTRITION
FOR FOODSERVICE
PROFESSIONALS

Carol A. Hodges

VAN NOSTRAND REINHOLD
New York

Copyright © 1989 by Van Nostrand Reinhold

Library of Congress Catalog Card Number 88-17168

ISBN 0-442-22686-1

Printed in The United States of America

Van Nostrand Reinhold
115 Fifth Avenue
New York, New York 10003

Van Nostrand Reinhold International Company Limited
11 New Fetter Lane
London EC4P 4EE, England

Van Nostrand Reinhold
480 La Trobe Street
Melbourne, Victoria 3000, Australia

Nelson Canada
1120 Birchmount Road
Scarborough, Ontario, M1K 5G4, Canada

16 15 14 13 12 11 10 9 8 7 6 5 4 3 2

Library of Congress Cataloging in Publication Data

Hodges, Carol A.
Culinary nutrition for foodservice professionals.
  Bibliography; p.
  Includes index.
  1. Nutrition. 2. Foodservice. 3. Foodservice
employees—Nutrition. 4. Culinary & cooking. I. Title.
QP141.H5117 1989 613.2 88-17168

ISBN 0-442-22686-1

Contents

Part I
SCIENTIFIC ASPECTS OF NUTRITION

Part II
LIFE-STYLE IMPACT ON FOOD
CONSUMPTION AND PRODUCTION

Part III
NUTRITION APPLICATIONS IN
FOOD SERVICE

Forewords

Nowhere in the archives of history can circumstances be found where diets, eating patterns, and nutritional requirements have played such a significant part of everyday lives as in today's society. Professional foodservice management and personnel are actively seeking resources and training that will guide them in adapting their recipes and menus to accommodate their customers' dietary and nutritional desires.

The dining preference of today's customer is changing the thinking of and bringing new challenges before the foodservice professional. Whether the meal is to accommodate a special occasion, a specific diet, or physical and mental health, or just fill a hunger void, the food must be appealing and pleasing to the visual, olfactory, and taste senses. The primary techniques for attaining satisfaction of these three critical human senses are as follows:

1. *Visual.* In the presentation include varying natural shapes, sizes, textures, and colors. Have only one focal point in each presentation. Make portion sizes small, yet fulfilling. If volume is needed, use variety. Never crowd a presentation.
2. *Olfactory.* Make each product distinguishable from the other; complement products with herbs, spices, and accompaniments as appropriate only to enrich the natural aromas.
3. *Taste.* Let each item on the plate have its own flavor personal-

ity and each personality compliment the others. Have no domi-
nating or offensive flavors. Use cool and palate-cleansing foods
to remove a strong aftertaste whenever appropriate.

Although the three senses and techniques are familiar to most professionals
in planning, the means of stimulating the senses simultaneously is challeng-
ing to all. That challenge is compounded substantially when planning and
preparation considerations must also take into account the new factor of
nutritional and health care needs. This text helps formulate this new factor
for practical use and provides the direction to integrate and enhance the
methods used in satisfying customers.

Culinary Nutrition for Foodservice Professionals takes a practical and
systematic approach in delivering the nutritional essentials to help foodservice professionals at all levels develop a philosophy about healthful eating,
as well as in providing the necessary guidelines for recipe adaptation and
menu planning. Hodges' combined culinary arts and dietetic education and
experience have earned her the recognition and authority to author this
text, which is designed specifically for the foodservice professional. Whether
that professional is a novice or more experienced, the text will increase his
or her practical and theoretical knowledge, facilitating the long overdue
marriage of nutrition and the culinary arts in the commercial kitchen.

To say I am impressed with the content of this book would be an
understatement. It is, in my opinion, right on target with what every
foodservice professional needs to know to adapt his or her recipes and
menus to meet the changing needs of today's customers. It is written at the
level and in the vocabulary of a chef, foodservice manager, and other
foodservice professionals.

As the Certification Chairman of the American Culinary Federation
Educational Institute, I wholeheartedly endorse this publication. I would,
without reservation, encourage our members to use this volume as an
option toward meeting their certification requirements.

Jeff Larson, CEC
Certification Chairman
The Educational Institute of
the American Culinary Federation
Blaine, MN

*   *   *

This book will certainly be useful to all of us. Healthy eating does not mean we must continually restrict our pleasure in food. That would make a very dull and unhappy existence, since eating well and enjoying good meals with friends are certainly two of life's joys. I think a good approach is to have a symbolic shelf labeled *Indulgence* upon which reside those delicious temptations like butter, heavy cream, sausages and pâtés, prime porterhouse steaks, rich chocolate desserts, and cakes filled with buttercreams. We are allowed a limited amount of them, and each of us should know our personal maximums. Then when we indulge we can freely enjoy every mouthful.

"Moderation in all things, a great variety of food, exercise, weight watching, and satisfaction in one's life work"—this is the rule for gastronomes to live by. You can't overdo on indulgences if you practice moderation. You won't miss out on essential nutrients if you eat a little something of everything. Exercise maintains the body politic, and a satisfying life makes for good digestion.

Julia Child
Trois Gourmandes Productions, Inc.
Cambridge, MA

Preface

The American public is becoming increasingly interested in food and cooking, while at the same time hectic life-styles are dictating that more meals be purchased or eaten outside the home. Regardless of where people eat, the type and quality of food consumed has become increasingly important—particularly in terms of nutritional value.

Scientific reports linking diet to many life-threatening diseases and degenerative conditions have created a more knowledgeable, health- and fitness-conscious consumer. This consumer is looking for creative, high quality food that is both delicious and nutritious. The foodservice industry is responding to this trend by focusing on fresh foods and healthful menu options. This book shows students and working professionals how to facilitate and promote healthful food choices by patrons, assists them in preparing and serving foods high in nutritional value, and encourages foodservice employees to achieve a healthful life-style.

The book can be used as both a classroom text and a professional reference. Students as well as professionals will learn about the characteristics of the major nutrient groups, their relationship to diet and health, and the foods in which they are found. They will then be able to apply these principles to menu planning; marketing; and food purchasing, preparation, and service activities. The importance of hands-on applications in both academic and professional settings should not be overlooked.

The concept for the book was established in 1983, when I was asked to design and teach a nutrition course that would meet the needs of students in the then new Culinary Arts Department at Newbury College in Boston, Massachusetts. In thinking about the course outline, I realized that a traditional approach would not meet the special needs of these students. My own culinary background suggested that they would benefit most from a course (and a text) that stressed the application of nutrition principles to all aspects of foodservice and to most settings in which they would be working. The book grew along with my lecture notes. And through observation, discussion with students and chef-instructors, and feedback, the conversational tone was established and the book took shape.

To begin, the book discusses the scientific basis of nutrition in combination with applications in food preparation. There is special emphasis on interactions among menu planning, food selection, and handling and preparation techniques in meeting current nutritional guidelines in the kitchen. The book also discusses the nutritional quality of foods in terms of processing, handling, and preparation, as well as current health concerns as they relate to dietary practices and the foodservice industry. It addresses concepts of consumer behavior and marketing response and presents practical applications in menu planning, recipe modification, nutritional evaluation of recipes, and wait-staff training. It examines physiological stresses confronting food preparation workers and presents nutrition- and fitness-related suggestions for helping staff increase productivity and cope with the demands of the job.

Although the book is intended for the wide audience of culinary and restaurant management students and working food professionals, it is also useful for nonprofessional cooks and consumers who are concerned about the nutritional quality of foods purchased, prepared, and consumed. This audience is varied in educational background and scientific knowledge. For this reason, the book presents scientific concepts in simplified ways, using familiar analogies. Scientific terminology is minimal. References have been carefully selected to be relevant to the interests of the audience.

Creative, fresh, healthful food that tastes good is the challenge for food professionals today. The nutritional quality of food is affected from soil to plate — which may mean from farmer to line cook. It is important for food professionals to remember that the same factors necessary for good food from a culinary standpoint are also necessary for the nutritional quality of that food: carefully conceived menus, freshness of product, proper storage and handling, appropriate preparation techniques, and balance of foods in presentation. This book will become a useful resource for foodservice industry professionals in developing a nutritional philosophy and guidelines for menu planning.

Acknowledgments

I would like to acknowledge the many food and nutrition colleagues, friends, and students who have asked questions and offered comments and advice that have influenced the direction and scope of this book. Special thanks go to Mary Tabacchi, associate professor, School of Hotel Administration, Cornell University; Ruth Palombo, director, Department of Nutrition, Massachusetts Department of Public Health; and Henry Ogden Barbour, adjunct professor, Department of Hotel and Food Administration, Boston University, for reviewing the manuscript and offering suggestions and encouragement along the way. I am also extremely grateful for the professional and expedient word processing of the manuscript by Connie Nordahl.

About the Author

Carol A. Hodges received a B.S. degree from Ohio State University, an M.A. degree from Virginia Polytechnic Institute and State University, and an M.S. degree from Boston University. She is a Registered Dietitian and holds a professional diploma in the culinary arts.

Hodges is an adjunct instructor in the Graduate Nutrition Division at Boston University and is a food and nutrition consultant. Before joining the faculty at Boston University, she taught nutrition in the Culinary Arts Department at Newbury College in Boston. In addition to teaching in the areas of food and nutrition, she has worked in private industry, in restaurants and in catering, and for the federal government, and has authored and contributed to numerous papers and publications.

Hodges is chairperson of the American Heart Association (Greater Boston Area) Restaurant Heart Health Nutrition Education Program, author of the AHA Chef/Manager Workshop Training Manual, and recipient of the AHA Outstanding Leadership Award for Community Programs. She is a member (and past president) of the Women's Culinary Guild of New England. She is also a member of the American Dietetic Association, the Society for Nutrition Education, and the American Institute of Wine and Food.

Part I

SCIENTIFIC ASPECTS
OF NUTRITION

Chapter 1

NUTRIENTS, THEIR CHARACTERISTICS, PHYSIOLOGICAL ROLES, AND IMPORTANCE IN FOOD PREPARATION

Nutrient Functions in the Body

Nutrition is a buzz word in the food industry now, making it seem as if the scientific aspect of eating is a new phenomenon. Actually, the study of food in relation to its physiological role in the body is not new. But since major discoveries regarding the biochemical processes of nutrient utilization have occurred over the past several decades and continue to develop at a rapid pace, scientists regard this field as still in its infancy.

Nutrition is a biological science that addresses our need for nutrients, the sources of these nutrients, and their teamwork in maintaining body health and well-being. Because the body is so complex, a breakdown in one of its processes can impair others. Thus, nutritional deficiencies can impair physical and mental capacities, attitudes and outlook, which in turn can affect us physically in an ongoing cycle. It is the same in foodservice: A smoothly functioning operation depends upon teamwork. If one station is not functioning properly, for example, service for an entire shift can be hampered.

Nutrients are chemical substances in foods that act as a team to provide energy, to support growth, maintenance, and repair of tissues, and to regulate body processes. To better visualize nutrients as components of foods, they are classified into six groups—carbohydrates, fats, proteins, water, vitamins, and minerals—each with its own characteristics. Next, it is important to understand that all nutrients are composed of atoms, which can be thought of as the building blocks of all substances. The composition of food substances, which results in particular characteristics of taste, texture, odor, and color, is dependent upon the arrangement of atoms into molecules. This is how it works. Atoms have an equal number of protons, positive charges, and electrons, negative charges, and are neutral. However, they can gain or lose electrons, becoming either negatively or positively charged. When one atom combines with another of opposite charge to share electrons, they bond to form a molecule. An example of this is a compound found in most kitchens—salt. The result of the bonding of one atom each of the elements sodium (Na) and chloride (Cl) produces salt (NaCl). Thus, salt gets its taste and texture from its molecular composition.

Another way to visualize nutrients is to classify them by size and weight. Carbohydrates, fats, and proteins are called macronutrients (the prefix *macro* means large); a single molecule of one of these nutrients can contain thousands of atoms. Macronutrients are consumed in larger quantities than

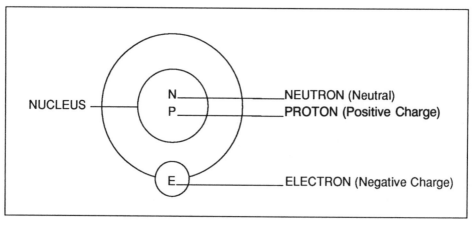

FIGURE 1.1 The atom.

vitamins and minerals, which are called micronutrients (*micro* means small). These are much smaller and are consumed in minute amounts. A day's requirement of vitamins and minerals fills only a fraction of a teaspoon. Water, although consumed in macro quantities, is a small molecule, containing only three atoms (Chapter 3). Macro- and micronutrients function together biochemically as a team.

Variety and Moderation

Some nutrients are found in many foods; others are found in only a few major food sources. Furthermore, many nutrients depend upon each other to do their jobs. Therefore, to achieve optimal nutrition, it is necessary to consume moderate amounts of a variety of foods. Since all nutrients are not found in every food, eating different foods every day helps provide the body with all the raw materials (i.e., nutrients) it needs to run smoothly. Busy people find it all too easy to make a tuna sandwich or broil a hamburger every night for dinner. Although there is nothing nutritionally wrong with either of these foods as *part* of a meal, having them with only a diet soda day in and day out provides an inadequate balance of nutrients and is monotonous as well. Many popular weight loss diets (see Chapter 2), which offer little choice of foods, are other examples of monotonous and nutritionally inadequate eating patterns. Fortunately, these are not usually adhered to for long. Another advantage of variety is that it reduces the amounts of contaminants that might be ingested when repeatedly eating large quantities of a single food.

In addition to a variety of foods, an appropriate quantity is important. Eating moderately means consuming amounts of food that are sufficient to meet, without excess, the body's energy needs at a particular time. Thus, moderate amounts of a variety of foods will provide most healthy people with adequate nutrition and a sensible dietary lifestyle. Note that adequate, not optimal, is used, because even in the context of variety and moderation, the nutritional quality of food is affected by its form, that is, the way it is processed and cooked.

Major Roles of Nutrients

There are three major roles that nutrients play in keeping the body running smoothly—they provide fuel for the energy needed to do work, they are used for growth, maintenance, and repair of body tissues, and they regulate the biochemical processes in the body.

Nutrients in foods provide the body with energy to fuel physiological processes such as respiration and muscle contraction. Energy that is not used is held in reserve in fat tissue. The macronutrients (carbohydrates, fats, and proteins) provide fuel for energy; vitamins and minerals do not provide energy themselves, but act as catalysts (initiators) in the biochemical reactions required to release and use the energy from carbohydrates, fats, and proteins.

The other functions of nutrients—growth, maintenance, and repair of body tissues and regulation of biochemical processes—are accomplished with the help of hormones, which act as chemical messengers to regulate enzymes (protein substances) in their facilitation of the reactions that transform food nutrients so they can be used by the body. Figure 1.2 categorizes

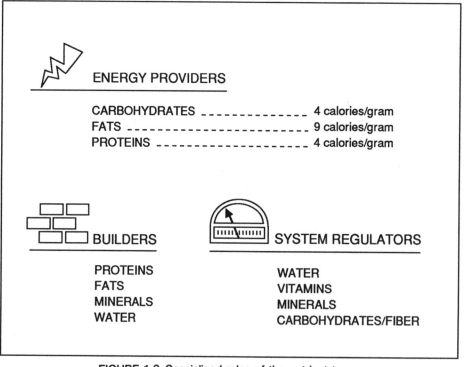

FIGURE 1.2 Specialized roles of the nutrient team.

the functions of nutrients as energy providers, builders, and system regulators. Energy values in calories per gram (calorie/g) have been assigned for comparison, and specific energy contributions of the nutrients are discussed in later chapters.

Macronutrients

Carbohydrates

When asked to identify carbohydrate foods they consume, people most frequently name bread, pasta, potatoes and candy. This is not surprising, since carbohydrates are often thought of as "starchy" or "sugary." But what about fruits, green and yellow vegetables, grains, legumes and milk products? These foods are also sources of carbohydrates. When people talk in terms of sugars and starches, they are actually referring to the two major categories of carbohydrate. The terms simple and complex are also used to describe these categories. Figure 1.3 illustrates the composition of these categories of carbohydrate as food components.

The simple message that comes from this seemingly complex diagram as it applies to food selection, preparation and consumption, is: *sugars are simple carbohydrates, whereas starch and fiber in foods are complex.* Figure 1.3 can be clarified by examining how these different forms of carbohydrate are constructed.

Carbohydrates are composed of atoms of carbon, hydrogen, and oxygen arranged into molecules that vary in size from the single-molecule monosaccharides and the two-molecule disaccharides (*mono* and *di* mean one and two, respectively) to the large molecular chains of the polysaccharides (*poly* means many). Glucose and fructose, for example, are single-molecule sugars used in commercial cooking and baking. The word dextrose, often seen on food labels, is a technical term for glucose. Through chemical combination, glucose and fructose can combine to become sucrose, a two-molecule disaccharide commonly known as table sugar. The chemical combination of many monosaccharides results in the complex chains called polysaccharides. This linking process is the result of condensation, a chemi-

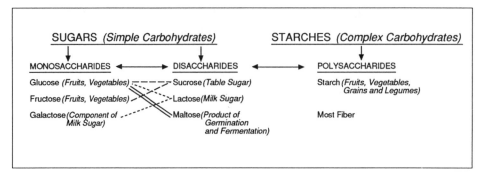

FIGURE 1.3 Composition of carbohydrate.

cal reaction between molecules in which water is a byproduct. Di- and polysaccharide links can also be taken apart by hydrolysis, a reaction in which water is added, thus recreating the original structures. As indicated in Figure 1.3, sucrose is composed of glucose and fructose, lactose of glucose and galactose, and maltose of two glucose molecules.

When we eat carbohydrate foods, sugars and starches are broken down into glucose. This single-molecule sugar (often referred to as blood sugar) is the major source of energy available to cells in our body. When more carbohydrate is consumed than is needed for energy and our glycogen storage areas are full (glycogen is the storage form of carbohydrate), the carbohydrate is converted to fat (as are excesses of dietary protein and fat) and stored as a reserve to be drawn upon at another time. This process ensures a continuous supply of energy.

Importance of Carbohydrates in the Body   The importance of carbohydrates is often overlooked. This nutrient is the *first* and foremost source of energy in the body. Indeed, providing a ready source of ENERGY is their **prime** function. When dietary carbohydrates are low in supply or absent, body metabolism not only slows down but must depend on alternate sources of available energy to sustain life — most of which are provided as the result of a process, gluconeogenesis, in which noncarbohydrate sources of energy from fat and protein are converted to glucose. Glucose is the sole source of energy for the brain and nervous system under normal metabolic conditions.

Carbohydrates also function in the regulation of fat metabolism. They are necessary for the normal breakdown and utilization of fat components for fuel. When supplies of carbohydrates are inadequate, potentially toxic substances called ketones are produced, leading to an abnormal state of body affairs called ketosis. This condition, if not reversed, can be fatal.

Grilling is a popular method of cooking. Think of cooking on a wood-fired grill in a restaurant or backyard as an illustration of how ketones accumulate in the body. Assume that the applewood fuel represents fat to be metabolized by the body. For the wood to ignite and burn properly, kindling is needed to start the fire; imagine the kindling as carbohydrate. Without kindling, the fire will not burn; it will just smoke. The smoke given off by the incomplete combustion of the applewood is representative of the ketones produced in the body when, in the absence of adequate carbohydrate, fats cannot be metabolized properly.[1]

A third function of carbohydrates is their protein-sparing action. An inadequate intake of carbohydrate foods will result in the use of protein to provide energy. Proteins are necessary for many vital body functions, but they are an inefficient source of energy, since they have to be "transformed" before they can be used for this purpose. Wasting protein as an energy source also "wastes" the body, because when dietary carbohydrate is low, protein will be sacrificed from lean body tissue such as muscles in order to provide glucose for brain and nerve function and body metabolic processes. In fact, at least 100 grams (g) of carbohydrates are necessary daily to prevent the sidetracking of protein from its more important roles of builder and regulator to that of energy provider.

A fourth function of carbohydrates is to provide fiber, or roughage, in the diet. Fibers are a class of polysaccharides; their importance in the diet will be discussed in Chapter 3. Figure 1.4 summarizes the major functions of carbohydrates in the body.

Functional Aspects of Carbohydrates in Cooking and Baking   Most cooks would classify sugars as sweeteners and starches as thickeners, which in fact are their primary chemical contributions to the foods in which they are used. They also differ in taste. Simple sugars, such as honey and table sugar,

---

[1]Adapted from *Fit or Fat?* by Covert Bailey. Copyright © 1977, 1978 by Covert Bailey. Used by permission of Houghton Mifflin Company.

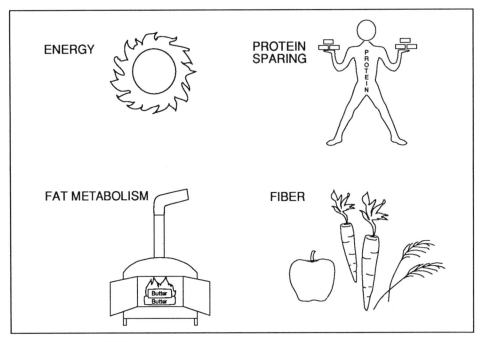

FIGURE 1.4 Functions of carbohydrates in the body.

taste instantly sweet in our mouths, whereas long-chain complex carbohydrates produce a low-intensity sweetness only when chewed.

Therefore, carbohydrates used in cooking differ in their molecular arrangements, which in turn determine their degree of sweetness and, if liquid, their viscosity.

Sugars

For cooking and eating, we use table, or granular, sugar more than any other sweetener. These granular sugars come in different forms: For instance, brown sugar and white sugar differ slightly in chemical composition, but mostly in color, which is provided by a trace of molasses in the brown variety. Confectioner's sugar is finely ground to a powder and mixed with some cornstarch. As its name implies, it is a staple in the bake shop because its characteristics prevent it from caking and make it easy to incorporate into substances in which regular sugar would remain grainy. It is used most often for uncooked cake frostings, candy, and pastry fillings. Bar or super-fine sugar, which is ground fine but not powdered, dissolves fast and is useful in batters and for beverage making. Cubes, once a popular form of sugar for the table, are declining in use in the United States; however, they are still used frequently in Europe, especially in the home.

Beside adding sweetness, sugar can be caramelized, thereby giving a visually pleasing and tasty brownness to sweet baked foods. Another browning reaction, the Maillard reaction, occurs in foods with little sugar content, such as broiled or roasted meats. Here a carbohydrate reacts with protein substances in the food, causing the brownness that contributes to attractiveness and taste. Blackening and charring foods is a popular and tasty method of preparing meat, vegetables, and seafoods. The crisp, flavorful deep brown-to-black parts of foods cooked in this manner, however, may have *potential* carcinogenic effects; as of yet, the evidence is inconclusive (McGee 1984). But remember to exercise moderation when eating intensively cooked smoked and charred foods.

Sweeteners also come in the form of syrups, which include honey, molasses, and corn syrup. Corn syrup, which is a water solution of glucose chains, has unique properties that have made it popular in commercial food production and processing. Its versatility results from being able to control the degree of breakdown of the long glucose chains in one (corn) starch. The relative proportions of one- and two-unit molecules to longer chains alter its taste and consistency. In confectionery and baking, its viscous nature prevents crystallization, which is helpful when a smooth glaze is desired. It also gives foods texture and helps prevent moisture loss, thereby increasing shelf life. Because of the long chains, which do not cause a very sweet taste, corn syrup can be used freely without the product becoming overly sweet, as would be the case with an equal amount of honey, for example (McGee 1984).

In addition to adding sweetness and taste, all sugars help retain moisture in foods, thus extending shelf life. They also act as preservatives, competing for the water that microorganisms need to thrive. Two final points to keep in mind when working with sugars reflect their major functions in determining the quality of sweet baked foods. Sugar helps retain elasticity in gluten, a protein component primarily found in wheat flour. In sweet batters and doughs, sugar prevents the gluten proteins in flour from absorbing water and developing into the stiff, elastic dough characteristic of kneaded breads in which sugar is low or absent entirely. (The kneading itself also contributes to the springy quality of these doughs.) The effect of all this is a tender product. Too much sugar, however, has detrimental effects. For instance, large amounts of sugar in a starch-thickened base such as pastry cream or pie fillings will result in a thin, watery product. In this case, sugar competes successfully with the starch for water, the starch granules cannot swell fully, the sugar and water form a solution, and the result is an undesirably thin, watery product.

Therefore, when using sugar or its alternatives, consider form and sweetening power as well as amount in order to achieve the best taste, moisture content, and texture of the finished product. Also remember that, nutritionally, it does not matter which type of sweetener is used. Although some sugars are absorbed and metabolized slightly differently than others, the net biochemical difference and nutrient content of all sugars are insignificant. In fact, foods containing a high proportion of sugar are often described as being empty calorie, suggesting they contribute calories (and often many) but usually very little in terms of nutritional value.

Starches

Starches are polysaccharides which are produced in plants as an energy store. Starch is found in plants in granular form. The granules contain two types of starch molecules—amylose and amylopectin, which have different structures. To visualize the difference between these, visualize amylose as a long "fence" of linked glucose units and amylopectin as a linkage of glucose units branched in the form of a "tree." Starches vary in the amounts and proportion of these two molecules. This accounts for differences in viscosity, texture, stability, and translucency—all qualities which affect the finished food product. Our food sources of starch include grains such as wheat, corn, and rice (which may be as much as 70 percent starch), tubers such as potatoes and the like, and legumes such as peas and beans.

When cooking with starches, it is important to keep in mind the changes they undergo, especially in their role as thickeners. Sugar stirred into water, for example, will dissolve and disappear in the liquid solution; however, if flour or corn starch is mixed with cold water, they will cause the water to become temporarily cloudy but will then settle to the bottom. However, if the mixture is added to a hot liquid, as in sauce making, the viscosity will increase until eventually a gel is formed. This process is the gelatinization of starch—and one of its primary functions in cooking.

When heated in a liquid, starch granules absorb water and begin to swell like sponges until they lose their tight structure and become intermingled with water, forming gels, or liquid networks of long molecules. It is at this point that suspension of granules can no longer be seen and the mixture becomes somewhat clear—the degree depends on the type of starch. Thickening occurs when the granules are so swollen that their content of starch escapes and binds the liquid (thus reducing the total amount) until a network, or gel, is formed.

A sauce will begin to thicken at about 35°C (95°F), and gelatinization will occur at about 96°C (205°F). To ensure maximum stability, make sure starch-bound sauces come just to the boiling point, 100°C (212°F). Once maximum viscosity is reached, the sauce will start to thin again. Therefore, boiling a thickened sauce or even heating it for a long time will result in thinning, as will rapid stirring—especially with a wire whisk. Overcooking it simply breaks the granule network into small pieces, and liquid becomes more evident.

Foods such as puddings will congeal when cooled even though they are not at maximum viscosity. In the absence of heat, their molecular motion decreases until, in effect, the liquid is trapped in the solids. The same principle applies to starch-bound sauces. As a sauce cools from cooking to serving and eating temperatures, it will gradually become thicker. Too much thickener will therefore create an unattractive and less tasty finished product. Even though starch-bound sauces have lost favor to the lighter-textured emulsified sauces, corn starch or arrowroot is sometimes used to tighten reduction sauces with low gelatinous qualities. Be careful to use appropriate amounts since the same principles apply (McGee 1984).

Wheat flour is the most frequently used starch in U.S. and European cuisine, whereas corn starch and tuber starches are preferred in the cuisines of other countries such as China and in Latin America. Important points to remember when substituting starches concern the quantity and appearance of the thickened sauce. Since flour contains protein, more is necessary to achieve thickening than with corn starch, which is pure starch. The commonly used root starches, potato and arrowroot, will thicken in even smaller quantities. Flour-based sauces will look opaque, whereas corn and root starches give a translucent finish, differing slightly among them. These considerations should be kept in mind when developing recipes or improvising.

When a starch-thickened sauce or filling is frozen and thawed later, it separates and becomes watery. This process is called retrogradation, which can be thought of as an extreme extension of the gelation process. To avoid retrogradation, only freeze foods in which the starch concentration is low or use a chemically modified starch that has been pregelatinized. Pregelatinized dry mixtures, which will gel milk proteins without need for heat, are the base for instant puddings and uncooked or briefly cooked starch-thickened food products (McGee 1984).

Fiber

The dietary importance of fiber, the other food polysaccharide in Figure 1.3, is discussed in Chapter 3. Here, we discuss fiber in terms of its cooking characteristics.

Fiber, which is the structural component of plants, is readily identified by its effect on the texture of both raw and cooked foods. In general, fiber is either partially or completely broken down by cooking, depending upon the type and amount present.

The major fibers found in fruits and vegetables are cellulose, hemicellulose, pectin, and lignin. (Although grouped with the fibers, lignin is a noncarbohydrate, woody substance that is practically indestructible, e.g., the "woody" core of parsnips.) Other types of fibers include gums, mucilages, and algal polysaccharides from seaweed. These are often used as thickening agents in food processing; note the words vegetable gum on many food labels. Other food sources of fiber are wheat bran, which is high in cellulose, and oats, apples, and citrus fruits, which are high in pectin, the familiar thickener in jams and jellies.

In cooking, each fiber behaves differently. Pectins are soluble in water and become viscous; cellulose and hemicellulose are insoluble. These characteristics are being studied regarding their beneficial effects in prevention and control of specific diet-related diseases.

Two easy ways to observe the presence of fiber are to cook batches of brown and white rice simultaneously and to bake a red and a golden delicious apple. The white rice will cook in less time than the brown because the white grains are missing their fibrous bran coating (as well as some nutrients). The red delicious apple will become mushy in baking, whereas the golden variety will hold its shape.

Fats

"Fat" is often used as the general term for a class of nutrients called *lipids.* This group is actually comprised of both fats and oils. In this book the general term fat is used to discuss their chemical characteristics and use in cooking.

As with carbohydrates, fats are composed of carbon, hydrogen, and oxygen. Fats contain more carbon and hydrogen in proportion to oxygen, which accounts for their higher energy value (9 calorie/g; Figure 1.2), making them the most concentrated source of energy of the three macronutrients in foods.

Fats perform many beneficial functions in the body: They transport fat-soluble vitamins and provide energy, pad and support organs, provide insulation, and help keep skin and hair healthy and supple. In the small intestine, food fats are broken down into fatty acids and glycerol before being utilized. As with the other macronutrients, fat can be stored in fat cells in the form of triglyceride as an energy reserve. Bodies have an unlimited capacity to store fat, which can cause overweight and increase risk factors for some diseases.

The predominant form of fat in the body and in food is triglycerides. A small percentage of fat is present in other forms including phospholipids and sterols such as cholesterol, which will be discussed later.

The basic structural element of triglycerides is the fatty acid. Triglycerides are composed of three fatty acids (*tri* means three) attached to a glycerol molecule. All glycerol molecules are identical, but fatty acids vary structurally. It is these differences that are of interest to the cook in terms of food fat characteristics and behavior in processing and cooking. In addition, anyone concerned about the effects of a high dietary intake of fat on health is probably already familiar with the terms "saturated," "monounsaturated," and "polyunsaturated," which are used to describe structural differences among fatty acids and their effects on biochemical processes in the body.

Fatty acids are even-numbered chains of carbon atoms to which hydrogens are attached. Their chemical characteristics in foods and the body are determined by the length of their chains and the number of hydrogens on the chain. Length varies from two carbons, found in acetic acid, the sourtasting compound in vinegar, to fourteen or more carbons, found in fatty acids predominating in meats. Saturation, a key factor in the behavior of fatty acids, is determined by how many hydrogens are attached along the chain.

Figure 1.5 illustrates saturation of three fatty acid chains. Eighteen carbon chains were used for consistency because this is the only length at which all three degrees of saturation are represented. The top chain illustrates a saturated fatty acid (stearic acid) in which hydrogen atoms are attached to all of the carbon atoms in the chain; thus, it is "saturated" with hydrogen. The middle chain depicts a monounsaturated fatty acid (oleic acid) in which two hydrogen atoms are missing on the carbon chain. A double bond is formed at this point. In the bottom chain, a polyunsaturated fatty acid is illustrated (linoleic acid). Four hydrogens are missing, resulting in the formation of two double bonds. Thus, the degree of saturation is indicated by

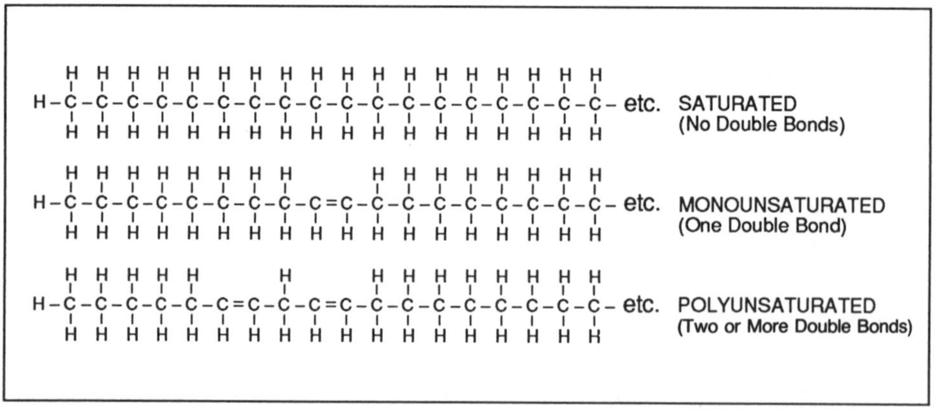

FIGURE 1.5 Illustrations of saturated (stearic acid), monounsaturated (oleic acid), and polyunsaturated (linoleic acid) fatty acids.

missing hydrogen atoms and the resultant number of double bonds on the chain.

Importance of Fats in the Diet   All foods are combinations of fatty acids of various lengths and degrees of saturation. The important point for both cooking and health applications is the proportion of polyunsaturated, monounsaturated and saturated fats in foods.

Saturated fats are found primarily in animal foods such as meat, eggs, and dairy products. Because they are saturated with hydrogen, they are solid at room temperature. Saturated fats have a high melting point. Monounsaturated fats are found primarily in plant foods and vary as to density and melting point. Examples are olive oil, peanut oil, and avocados, and some of the newer specialty nut and seed oils. Polyunsaturated fats are found mostly in plant foods, are liquid at room temperature, and have a low melting point. Examples include corn, soy, and safflower oils. In general, animal fats are mostly saturated, and vegetable fats are high in mono- or polyunsaturates. But there are exceptions; for example, palm and coconut oils, even though of vegetable origin, are highly saturated. They are inexpensive and thus are frequently used in food processing. They can be found in products such as cereals, nondairy creamers, and commercial milkshake mixes. Other exceptions are hydrogenated vegetable fats. When vegetable oils are hydrogenated, missing hydrogen atoms are replaced on the carbon chain, thus increasing saturation to provide a desired texture. Hydrogenated vegetable oils can therefore be as saturated as animal fats. Remember that foods contain a combination of fatty acids even though one type may predominate. Beef, for example, contains more saturated fat than chicken and fish.

Other classes of lipids need to be mentioned here for, although accounting for only a small percent of the fats in our diet, they are important in many ways. Phospholipids are similar to triglycerides; however, instead of three fatty acids attached to a glycerol, a different acid holds the third place. These acids contain phosphorous and nitrogen, as evident in their name. Phospholipids are important components of cell membranes and help keep circulating fats in the body in solution. Lecithin is probably a familiar name, because it appears on food labels frequently as an emulsifier. In this phospholipid, a choline molecule occupies third place along with two fatty acids on the glycerol molecule. Choline is lipotrophic—that is to say it is water soluble, whereas the fatty acids are water repellent. Between them, they function in opposite ways as components of lecithin to stabilize emulsions and to keep fat or oil molecules suspended in liquid. It is the high lecithin content of eggs that gives them their emulsifying properties as in salad dressings and mayonnaise as well as the warm emulsified sauces such as hollandaise, for example.

Cholesterol is actually not a lipid, but a fat-soluble alcohol (sterol). It differs from triglyceride in that its carbons form several rings instead of a straight chain. As shown in Table 1.1, cholesterol is present in foods of animal origin. Since it is found primarily in lean tissue rather than fat, some animal foods, such as shrimp (Figure 1.6), that are low in fat can be relatively high in cholesterol. The body manufactures cholesterol in the liver. It is necessary to the body and plays several important roles. However, elevated blood cholesterol levels contribute to cardiovascular disease. The important point to remember here is that although dietary cholesterol is found only in animal foods, foods high in saturated fats, whether they are animal or highly saturated vegetable fats, are even more effective in elevating blood cholesterol levels.

Functional Aspects of Fats in Cooking   Many types of fats are available for cooking, including lard, vegetable oil, butter, and shortening. Fats are usually selected on the basis of whether they are from animal or vegetable sources; their form, that is whether they are liquid or solid (their degree of saturation); and their taste. Other factors include their smoke point, their stability in terms of spoilage, and their effect on health.

In cooking and eating, the choice between a liquid or solid fat generally depends on use. Will the fat be spread on toast, be used for deep frying, or be included in a salad dressing? Will it be combined with other ingredients, such as creaming it with sugar, or will it be cut into flour for doughs and batters?

Choice of a cooking fat may also be dictated by the necessity of meeting both use and health considerations at the same time. Although highly unsaturated vegetable oils, through the process of hydrogenation, assume the same qualities of plasticity as butter and other solid animal fats, they have become saturated in the process. However, they do not contain cho-

TABLE 1.1   Cholesterol Content of Selected Foods

Food Portion	Cholesterol (mg)	
Fruits, grains, vegetables	0	LOW
Oysters (cooked, about 3½ oz)	45	
Scallops (cooked, about 3½ oz)	53	
Clams (cooked, about 3½ oz)	65	
Fish, lean (cooked, about 3½ oz)	65	
Chicken/turkey, light meat (without skin) (cooked, about 3½ oz)	80	
Lobster (cooked, about 3½ oz)	85	
Beef, lean (cooked, about 3½ oz)	90	
Chicken/turkey, dark meat (without skin) (cooked, about 3½ oz)	95	
Crab (cooked, about 3½ oz)	100	
Shrimp (cooked, about 3½ oz)	150	
Egg yolk, one	270	
Beef liver (cooked, about 3½ oz)	440	
Beef kidney (cooked, about 3½ oz)	700	HIGH

lesterol. Therefore, cooking technique, taste and health factors should *all* be considered when selecting the most appropriate fat for a particular food product.

In addition to firming oils to provide textural control, hydrogenation also protects fats from spoilage and from rancidity. Any food that contains fat can become rancid, which is detected by an acrid, bitter taste and unpleasant odor. Fats become rancid when fatty acid chains break down as a result of oxidation. This produces unstable molecules, called free radicals, that proliferate rapidly and have the potential to be carcinogenic. If cell membranes, which are rich in polyunsaturates and may be vulnerable to attack, become damaged, genetic materials may be altered and abnormal cell reproduction may result.

Hydrogenation, as well as vitamins E and C and synthetic antioxidants, help offset the breakdown of fats. Fats take up oxygen slowly during an induction, or staling, period; however, exposure to heat, light, and additional oxygen speeds up the oxidation process, as do salt, iron utensils, and moisture in foods being cooked. High heat causes rapid breakdown of fats. Excessive foaming of cooking fat before food to be sautéd is added; exposure of fat to flame in grilling; and smoking oils for stir frying—all initiate the breakdown process. Furthermore, each time a frying fat is reused, its quality decreases because of its exposure to heat, oxygen, water, and food particles. Polyunsaturated fats are missing protective hydrogen atoms, making them vulnerable to rancidity. Hydrogenation of unsaturated fats makes them less susceptible to breaking down and becoming rancid.

To lengthen the life of cooking oils, keep them in tightly closed, dark containers away from heat, and refrigerate oils that will not be used quickly —they can become stale within six weeks after they are opened, even under seemingly ideal conditions.

Hydrogenation of polyunsaturated oils also has some disadvantages. Although hydrogenated vegetable oils do not contain cholesterol, they are still saturated fats, which can raise blood cholesterol levels in some people. In fact, some vegetable shortenings contain up to 50 percent saturated fat, although the percentage is usually much lower in margarines. Another disadvantage of hydrogenation is that the change in configuration at the sites of the double bonds that lack hydrogen atoms produces trans fatty acids, which are an anomaly not found in the body or most foods. These abnormal molecules are being studied by research scientists with regard to their being potential cancer promoters.

Another factor to consider when choosing a fat is its smoke point. Smoke point temperatures of cooking fats differ. Fats can be heated to relatively high temperatures to cook food quickly, but each time the same fat is used the smoke point is lowered. The best oils to use for frying are those with smoke points of at least 211°C (400°F), such as safflower, corn, peanut, grape seed, and sesame oils. Animal fats, olive oil, and hydrogenated vegetable shortenings smoke at about 190°C (375°F) or lower. The progression from smoke point to flash point (ignition only) to fire point (continued flame) can occur rapidly.

Fats are important in cooking: They add flavor and, because they take longer to leave our stomachs, give us a sense of satisfaction after a meal.

In cooking, fats can play the role of emulsifier, aerator, tenderizer, flavor enhancer, and texturizer. In batters, fat functions as an aerator, trapping air bubbles, forming pockets for the expansion of leavening agents, and thus contributing to optimal volume and texture. Precreamed shortenings that enhance this process are available commercially.

The tenderizing role of fats is the major key to flakiness, the most desirable quality in pastry, biscuits, and the like. Fat waterproofs gluten in flour, thus inhibiting its development, and providing a tender product. In pastes with many alternating layers of fat and flour such as puff pastry (which is rolled and folded precisely to achieve this effect), heat and steam force the separation of these waterproofed layers, creating expansion. In this case, type of fat is important. A chilled, solid fat is necessary for flakiness, since an oil or warm, soft fat will be absorbed into the flour instead of coating and layering it.

The type of fat also affects flavor; for example, fruitiness of olive oil, the nutty taste of hazlenut oil, or the rich taste of butter is desired. Fats influence the texture of food by inhibiting crystal formation, resulting in a smoother product. Cream with a high fat content, for example, will enhance the quality of ice creams and frozen desserts. In sherbets and other frozen nondairy foods, protein performs this function in the form of egg white or gelatin, which are often included as ingredients to achieve a desired effect. Keep this in mind when developing low fat frozen desserts which would normally include heavy cream.

Proteins

Proteins are the macronutrient group responsible for the synthesis, maintenance, and repair of tissues and the regulation of body processes. They also transport nutrients and regulate fluid and pH balance in the body. Protein is best used for construction and regulatory jobs and should be "spared" for these purposes by adequate amounts of dietary carbohydrate. Proteins are found in the body, in muscle, skin, and bone—all tissues as well as enzymes, hormones, and antibodies that help protect us against disease.

Proteins differ chemically from carbohydrates and fats. In addition to carbon, hydrogen, and oxygen, they also contain nitrogen. Before they can be used by the body for energy, the nitrogen must be removed. It is then excreted in the form of urea as a component of urine. It is this process that makes protein an inefficient source of energy.

Importance of Protein in the Diet   Proteins are structured into chains consisting of amino acids linked together by peptide bonds. There are twenty-two known amino acids, which connect in condensation reactions in which two amino acids bond to form a dipeptide, continuing until a long polypeptide chain is formed. Most proteins are in the form of long chains which, unlike carbohydrates and fatty acids, are twisted and coiled. Unlike the polysaccharides, which are composed of only glucose units—proteins are composed of **different** amino acids. The composition of a protein in terms of both quantity and type of amino acids determines its usefulness to the body.

The body builds proteins from amino acids in protein-containing foods. It also manufactures some amino acids, but not all that are necessary. The eight amino acids that the body can't manufacture must be obtained from the foods we eat to ensure a complete supply of amino acids for the construction of protein by body cells.

Protein foods are usually rated by their biological value, which is the amount of nitrogen they provide that the body can actually use. Protein-containing foods with a high biological value are referred to as high-quality proteins; in other words, they supply all of the essential amino acids in proportions necessary to do their jobs. If the amount or ratio of an essential amino acid is inadequate, use of the companion amino acids will be limited. If amino acids are not used, they cannot be stored in the body for later use but are converted to glucose or fat or are used for energy. In the process, the nitrogen must be removed and excreted. Thus, it is important to have an adequate amount of high-quality protein every day. Too much is wasteful and perhaps harmful; too little may compromise building and regulatory functions.

Functional Aspects of Protein in Cooking and Baking   Changes that proteins undergo during cooking largely result from denaturation, a process in which the protein chains uncoil and change shape. Denaturation is caused mainly by heat and acidity, although salt can also contribute to the reaction.

Coagulation is the most obvious change in protein; it happens, for example, when a poached egg or baked custard becomes firm. During this process, denatured (uncoiled) proteins cross bond, forming a visible mass. If the coagulation is continuous, a gel results. This process occurs daily in many restaurants when a protein is used to clarify stock.

The coagulation of protein occurs at temperatures from approximately 16 to 21°C (62 to 70°F). If temperatures are too hot or the cooking time is prolonged, liquid may be released from the coagulated protein (syneresis) (Campbell et al. 1979). A pockmarked, watery quiche, for example, is an all-too-frequent sign of the overcooking of protein-containing foods in restaurants.

Coagulation of protein is also important in baking. The rigid structure in breads is a result of the coagulation of gluten, the protein developed in flour-based foods during hydration and kneading. Since this structure is not desirable in cakes and pastry, some cooks scale in a proportion of cake flour or cornstarch, which lowers the overall protein content. The same principle applies when using flour to thicken a sauce—the more protein in the flour, the gummier it will be. The use of cake flour, with its higher starch content, will result in a smoother sauce.

Heat also affects collagen, a protein and major connective tissue in meats. Collagen is the white, fibrous tissue protein in tendons. When heat is applied in cooking, the collagen fibers start to contract. When liquid is present, long exposure to a hot, moist environment causes meat collagen to break down into gelatin. An example is seen in the gelatinous qualities of stocks. Elastin is a yellow connective tissue protein in ligaments, which does not break down when exposed to heat. Thus, the amount of connective tissue present, cooking temperature, and method of cooking are all important factors in a moist and tender product.

Tenderizing is one way to combat the high concentration of connective tissue in some cuts of meat. Cutting fibers, such as grinding beef into "hamburger" meat, is the most effective, although not always appropriate. Enzymes, such as papain, tenderize by digesting muscle protein. They don't start work, however, until the meat has been heated to a certain point— approximately 65°C (150°F). Also, these enzymes work only on areas they can reach, which means they are mostly surface tenderizers.

Acids and salt are also tenderizers, denaturing surface proteins in the process. That is why vinegar is a common ingredient in marinades. Aging softens muscle tissue but has little effect on connective tissue protein. It does improve the flavor of meats.

When working with meat in the kitchen, the presence of two other protein substances, hemoglobin and myoglobin, can be easily observed. As the oxygen-carrying proteins in red blood cells and muscle cells, respectively, they influence their color. The presence of iron and oxygen is the key. Muscles that are worked harder and have more need for oxygen, and thus a greater supply, are darker red; for example, red beef is darker than pale pink underexercised veal. Iron is necessary for the formation of hemoglobin and myoglobin. To maintain oxygen contact with meat and therefore redness, most prepackage film is permeable. On continued exposure to oxygen, however, iron present in myoglobin oxidizes and meat surfaces turn brown. During cooking, heat denatures the myoglobin, and oxidation results in the brown surface of cooked meat (McGee 1984).

Another function of protein in cooking is, as with fat, the inhibition of ice and sugar crystal formation in frozen foods such as ice cream and sherbet as well as in candy. Gelatin or plant gums are often used to accomplish this purpose. These are also used to increase viscosity of protein-rich liquids such as sauces and will, when cold, solidify (gel) a liquid when used in appropriate amounts. A protein gel made by using gelatin can be reheated to liquify and then be rechilled to set without altering its characteristics. This quality is important in coating foods so as to seal in an applied surface decoration or to give them sheen, as is often seen in presentations on buffet tables and at food shows.

Micronutrients

Vitamins and minerals are micronutrients, but are considered small in comparison to the macronutrients only because the body requires a small amount, not because they are any less important. As stated earlier, if it were not for the micronutrients, the macronutrients could not do their jobs. They work together as a team to run the body.

Just as carbohydrates, fats, and proteins are essential to the body as energy-containing nutrients, vitamins and minerals are essential as activators, regulators, and providers in the many complex physiological activities continuously taking place in our bodies. A normal, healthy individual consuming a variety of foods, in adequate amounts, can obtain all of the nutrients needed by the body from food—without supplements. But many people take vitamin and mineral supplements just to be on the safe side. Many of these are packaged in megadoses of 10 to 500 times the recommended amounts. High intakes of many of the vitamins and minerals, however, can be toxic, create biochemical imbalances, and are expensive. The key to a healthy diet is variety—lots of colors, textures, and different types of foods. It can be that simple. In fact, it is the same goal chefs aim for when menu planning and cooking. In other words, instead of worrying about providing enough of a particular nutrient in a day, learn to choose foods on a daily basis that have covered all the nutrient bases in a general way. Develop meal planning ingenuity, not vitamin paranoia.

There are a few distinctions between vitamins and minerals that will be helpful to understand. First, vitamins are organic substances (like leaves), and minerals are inorganic compounds (like stones). Second, each falls into two categories: Vitamins are classified as fat or water soluble; minerals are classified as major or trace. (Only tiny amounts of trace minerals are necessary to function in the body.) Third, cooking techniques affect vitamins more than minerals—particularly those that are water soluble. Minerals are not as fragile when heated, even though some are water soluble. A few minerals can be rendered less useful by other substances found in the same foods. In addition, an excess of one micronutrient may inhibit availability of another. This is why single nutrient supplements are not a wise idea.

Vitamins

There are two categories of vitamins—the fat-soluble vitamins, vitamins A, D, E, K, and the water-soluble vitamins, the B vitamins and vitamin C (see Figure 1.6).

Fat-soluble vitamins, as the name implies, are absorbed with the fats we eat. Amounts above what the body needs are stored in fat tissues or the liver. If too much of these vitamins accumulates from oversupply, vitamin toxicity can occur, sometimes with serious consequences. It should be noted, though, that toxicity occurs from the use of high-dose supplements

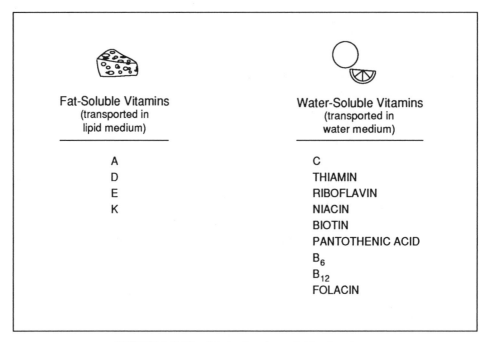

FIGURE 1.6 The fat- and water-soluble vitamins.

and only rarely from food eaten. Water-soluble vitamins, on the other hand, are not stored in the body to the extent fat-soluble vitamins are. When a maximum concentration is reached, they are excreted in the urine. Until recently, high intakes were thought to have little or no effect. Recent research, however, indicates that too much of these vitamins can also have undesirable consequences.

The vitamin content of foods is affected by many things—stage of maturity at harvest, transportation, storage, processing, and cooking—from soil to plate. Water-soluble vitamins are more easily destroyed than the fat-soluble vitamins. However, food processing, preparation, and storage affect all these nutrients.

Claims that foods in the United States lack nutrients because the soil is depleted are unjustified. While it is true that large-scale agricultural practices are damaging to topsoil, it is the plants themselves that manufacture the nutrients that we obtain when we eat them. If the soil did not support growth, the plants would not grow and bear fruit.

Vitamin A   Vitamin A is a fat-soluble vitamin that keeps skin and mucous membranes (inner linings) healthy and enables our eyes to adjust to dim light, such as seeing in a dark movie theater or when driving down a dark road. A deficiency causes skin and membranes to harden (visualize the hard, cracked appearance of a dry river bed) and can cause night blindness. It is interesting to note that protein and zinc deficiency can cause a vitamin A deficiency since zinc-containing proteins are necessary to move vitamin A from its storage place in the liver when needed for biochemical processes. This is another example of mutually dependent teamwork. Excess vitamin A can accumulate in the liver to toxic proportions. This possibility has increased since more foods are fortified with vitamin A and more people take supplements.

People obtain vitamin A in two ways: Retinol, the preformed source, is found in animal foods such as liver, egg yolk, and dairy products; also, skim milk and margarine are usually fortified with A. The other source is provitamin A (*pro* means before), or carotene, a pigment found in deep yellow, orange, and dark green leafy vegetables and fruits. Carotene is converted to vitamin A in the intestine. Fruits and vegetables are our most plentiful source of A. Exceptions include red-purple or white-yellow vegetables such as corn and beets, and pale vegetables and fruits such as green beans or honeydew melon.

Vitamin D   Vitamin D, also a fat-soluble vitamin, actually performs as both a vitamin and a hormone. It is stored in the liver, skin, and bones and is essential for the absorption and use of calcium (a mineral) in maintaining strong bones and teeth. Too little vitamin D results in calcium deficiency and soft, weak bones; too much vitamin D results in an accumulation of calcium, which can form kidney stones and harden soft tissues in the kidneys, lungs, and blood vessels.

Vitamin D occurs naturally only in a few animal foods, with eggs and liver being the most dependable sources. For this reason, milk is usually fortified with vitamin D (be sure to check the label) and is a handy way to get the vitamin from foods. A nonfood source of vitamin D is the sun. A precursor of D, made from cholesterol in the liver, is found in the skin. When we are exposed to sunlight, the precursor is converted to vitamin D.

Therefore, in the presence of ultraviolet rays from the sun, the body can make vitamin D. Most active people who are out of doors a part of each day and consume a variety of foods including fortified milk get all the vitamin D they need. Since many supplements, including some brands of calcium, contain at least 100 percent of the recommended amount of D, a word of caution is in order regarding the possibility of toxicity, which can occur over time even at levels not too far above recommended amounts.

Vitamin E   Vitamin E, another fat-soluble vitamin, is most important in its role as an antioxidant (*anti* means against). Recall the discussion of polyunsaturated fatty acids, which are susceptible to oxidation reactions that produce abnormal molecules called radicals. Vitamin E, acting as an antioxidant, acts as a "mop" trapping and inactivating free radicals.

Vitamin E occurs in many foods, mostly polyunsaturated vegetable oils and foods containing them—a natural protective device. Smaller amounts are found in vegetables and whole grains. In cooking, heat and exposure to oxygen destroy the vitamin; however, this is not an indication for supplements. Disturbances of many body biochemical activities can occur over a period of time at just a little over three times what is recommended.

One final note on E. Cooks often recommend the use of E topically on burns. Vitamin E in pure form may be helpful; however, research has not shown the oil form to be effective in this healing capacity. Indeed, the oily medium of the vitamin may help smooth rough scar tissue in the same manner baby oil or bath oil would work on dry, rough skin. Oils should not be applied directly to burns—this invites infection.

Vitamin K   Vitamin K, also fat soluble, is the star performer in the blood-clotting process. It is manufactured in the intestines by resident bacteria and is found in many leafy green vegetables and milk. In normal adults, deficiency of this vitamin is rare; moreover, since there is no need to supplement this vitamin, toxicity is also rare.

Vitamin C   Vitamin C, a water-soluble vitamin, is important in its role in the formation of collagen, a major connective tissue in the body. It is also, like vitamin E, an antioxidant. And its presence helps the body absorb iron from the foods we eat.

Too little C may result in gums that bleed, small capillaries that break under the skin, and wounds that do not heal. Although deficiencies rarely occur, many people overdose with this vitamin because of highly publicized research by scientist Linus Pauling, who touts the vitamin as a cure for common colds and flu. Current recommendations are for 60 milligrams (mg) of vitamin C per day, but some people take 1,000 to 3,000 mg per day, megadosing in hopes of stalling off disease. What is interesting is that once body tissues are saturated with vitamin C (and this occurs in the 100- not 1,000-mg range), the extra vitamin C is excreted in the urine.

For some people, megadoses of vitamin C have resulted in annoying reactions such as diarrhea and urinary tract irritation. Kidney stone formation is also a possible toxicity effect in susceptible people. As more people take more vitamins in higher amounts, more side effects are likely to appear.

It is simple to get all the necessary vitamin C and more from food. Citrus fruits such as oranges and grapefruit are real boosters—a glass of orange juice at breakfast (or any other time) will meet most if not all of the 60-mg requirement. Other fruits and vegetables, such as broccoli, cabbage, tomatoes, and strawberries, are also good sources. Some companies are adding vitamin C to fortified skim milk, and many fortified cereals contain 100 percent of amounts recommended.

When cooking fruits and vegetables, remember that vitamin C is the most easily destroyed of the water-soluble vitamins. Cook vegetables quickly, in as little water as possible, keeping them intact as much as possible (i.e., minimizing cut surfaces).

B Vitamins The B vitamins are thiamin, riboflavin, niacin, biotin, pantothenic acid, B_6, B_{12}, and folacin (Figure 1.6). Of the B vitamins, the first six on the chart in Figure 1.6 on page 26 are active as members of the team which keeps cell metabolism running smoothly to provide the body with energy from food eaten. The last two are also important as a team working on other important processes at the cell level.

Biotin and pantothenic acid are found in many food sources and are produced by intestinal bacteria; thus, deficiencies are highly unlikely. Both function in the metabolic cycle, during transformation of food components into energy.

Thiamin, riboflavin, and niacin are usually grouped together because of their common function in the release of energy. Thiamin is also necessary for neurological health and riboflavin for healthy skin. A deficiency in any of these three vitamins results in problems ranging from muscle weakness from lack of thiamin to skin disorders from lack of riboflavin and niacin. Taking too much of these singly or as a group, on the other hand, may cause chemical imbalances. Too much or too little of any of the B vitamins is a little like putting sand into the intricate workings of a clock — it will either speed up, slow down, or crunch to a stop.

Variety is the best answer to the question of which foods provide the most thiamin, riboflavin, and niacin. Even though they work together, they do not appear together in necessary amounts in the same foods. Pork is rich in thiamin. Whole grains are also a good source. Milk is the outstanding source of riboflavin, with green leafy vegetables and meats providing a good alternative. Incidentally, ultraviolet rays from the sun destroy riboflavin, so food sources of the vitamin should be protected from light. Peanuts, legumes, and protein foods contribute preformed niacin. This vitamin can also be synthesized in the body from the amino acid tryptophan. This process requires another B vitamin, vitamin B_6. Vitamin B_6 is necessary for the metabolism of amino acid components of proteins. Amounts needed are proportional to the amount of protein in foods being metabolized. Food sources of vitamin B_6 include meats, vegetables, and whole grains.

Vitamin B_{12} and folacin are active in the formation of red blood cells and genetic proteins in the nucleus of all cells. Folacin is particularly important to the normal division of cells, and vitamin B_{12} is necessary to make active folacin, another example of teamwork. Because of this, a B_{12} deficiency will create a folacin deficiency, although the latter can occur separately. Folacin deficiency can cause serious consequences throughout the body, since it affects all cells and ultimately all body systems.

Vitamin B_{12} deficiency results in a condition, pernicious anemia, which if not corrected causes neuromuscular damage. This deficiency may occur through lack of dietary B_{12} or because of the absence of a stomach compound necessary for its absorption. In the latter case, injections of vitamin B_{12} are necessary to prevent damage. Folacin will alleviate the large cell anemia that is a symptom of both B_{12} and folacin deficiency. It is therefore important to accurately diagnose the cause of the anemia to prevent the underlying neurological damage that could occur if it is caused by lack of vitamin B_{12}. In other words, folacin alone could appear to help while obscuring a serious condition.

The reason for emphasizing the interactions of vitamin B_{12} and folacin is that of different food sources. Vitamin B_{12} is found only in animal foods. Aside from organ meats and milk, folacin is found high in foods typically eaten by vegetarians, including dark green leafy vegetables, some fruits, and whole wheat products. Since many people are adopting vegetarian diets or similar eating patterns, it is important when following diets that largely exclude animal foods to include sources of vitamin B_{12}, for example, fortified foods like cereals and soy milk.

Minerals

There are over 20 minerals known to be necessary to body biochemical processes. Their teamwork is varied and complex; and interactions with one another are vital. Imbalances in concentration of minerals that interact can lead to serious consequences in the body. This is why it is important to eat a variety of foods and beware of single-nutrient supplements. Mineral elements familiar to most people are included in this section. They are arranged in terms of their functions and interrelationships with one another.

Sodium and Potassium   Sodium and potassium are important in maintaining water pressure in and outside of body cells; sodium works outside the cells and potassium works inside. This balance between concentrations of sodium and potassium also affects our nerve transmissions and muscle contractions. To understand how different concentrations of these minerals affect fluid balance in the body, consider what happens when we cook and want to extract fluid from a vegetable such as a cucumber or eggplant—we salt it. Water is then drawn out of the food by the salt (which is 40% sodium). Similarly, when we eat salty foods, we get thirsty and drink fluids, thereby increasing the volume in the body to restore balance, and extra sodium and water are then excreted in the urine. For some people, these regulatory mechanisms do not work properly, resulting in fluid retention and abnormally high blood pressure (see Chapter 3).

The important balance between sodium and potassium can also be affected when there is substantial loss of both in body fluid excreted in perspiration during heavy exercise, from diarrhea and vomiting, or as a result of drugs that reduce body fluid retention. After strenuous, prolonged exercise, replace these minerals with food sources rather than salt pills, athletic beverages, or potassium supplements, which can be particularly harmful. Potassium also plays a role in maintaining heartbeat. Too much or too little can cause irregular heartbeat, as well as weakness in other muscles in the body.

Sources of potassium include fruits, such as orange juice and bananas, and potatoes and other vegetables. Foods high in sodium include most processed, packaged, and frozen foods and snack foods. Although some fresh foods are higher in sodium than others, most of the sodium in our foods is added during processing or cooking.

Calcium, Phosphorus, and Magnesium   Calcium, phosphorus, and magnesium work together to build and maintain bones and teeth. In addition, calcium is important for muscle contraction, nerve conduction, and blood clotting. Both phosphorus and magnesium also play a role in energy production. A deficiency in any of these three minerals will cause musculoskeletal problems; also, low calcium intake leads to bone abnormalities in children and bone loss in adults.

Most of the calcium in the body is in the bones. But since some calcium is necessary for other physiological functions, a certain level is maintained in the blood for these purposes. If calcium intake is insufficient, body hormones send signals to remove it from the bones so as to keep blood calcium available as needed. If this occurs over a period of time, bone formation cannot keep up with resorption (calcium withdrawal), and the bones become porous (like a sponge) and deteriorate to the point of breaking even without stress. In other words, blood levels of calcium are maintained even at the expense of bones.

Osteoporosis is the condition in which bone loss progresses to become permanently disabling. It has become a particularly serious health problem for women, whose overall intake of calcium tends to be low because of preference for soft drinks, coffee, or other beverages or because milk and calcium-rich dairy products are perceived as fattening or only for kids. Women also undergo hormonal changes during menopause which leave them without natural bone protective mechanisms, and they usually have a smaller bone mass than men to begin with.

It is important that everyone continue to obtain adequate calcium throughout life. The best common sources by far are milk and milk products; although some green leafy vegetables and fish such as canned salmon and sardines with the bones are also good. For most people, it is more practical to get calcium from milk sources. As mentioned before, vitamin D is essential for calcium absorption, and the ratio of calcium, phosphorus, and magnesium is important. Too much of magnesium and phosphorus can upset the "nutritional applecart," and excess phosphorus may cause bone demineralization. (The typical American diet is high in meat, one of the best sources of phosphorus.) Oxalates in green leafy vegetables, such as spinach and chard, and phytates in fiber-rich whole grains bind calcium in these foods and reduce its availability. Inactivity of bedridden or very sedentary people can also exacerbate bone loss. This same effect has been seen in astronauts when they return from a weightless environment.

Do not forget variety. Although calcium, phosphorous, and magnesium work together, the best sources are found in different food groups: calcium in milk and dairy products; phosphorous in meat; and magnesium in green leafy vegetables, grains, and legumes.

It is best to obtain calcium from foods; however, if the current requirements cannot be met with food, a supplement may be in order. Check with a physician. Supplements should be approached with caution, as they differ. Pure calcium carbonate contains the most elemental calcium. Bone meal and dolomite sources may contain metallic contaminates. Supplements with other nutrients added such as vitamin D or magnesium may cause imbalances.

Iron, Zinc, and Copper Iron, zinc, and copper are mentioned together since the presence of each directly affects the usefulness of the others. Iron is necessary for the formation of hemoglobin and myoglobin, the oxygen-carrying proteins in the blood and muscles that were discussed earlier. It also plays a vital role in the maintenance of the body's immune function. Most of the iron in the body is in the blood; therefore, blood loss will result in iron loss. Iron deficiency, characterized by small, pale red blood cells, is common, particularly in women who eat less than men and lose blood during menstruation. On the other hand, too much iron may cause a toxic buildup in the heart, liver, and pancreas.

Iron from animal foods such as meat, fish, and poultry is better absorbed than that from eggs and vegetable sources such as legumes and dark green leafy vegetables, soybeans being a possible exception. Including a source of vitamin C when eating iron-containing foods aids absorption. Phytates in grains bind iron as well as zinc, copper, calcium, and magnesium. Oxalic acid binds iron in greens, as does tannic acid in coffee and tea.

The importance of a varied, adequate diet is illustrated in the fact that too much iron can decrease zinc utilization, and excess zinc can cause a copper deficiency, which in turn affects iron absorption.

Zinc travels throughout the body attached to proteins and is important in many metabolic processes, cell division, and collagen synthesis. Deficiency may slow wound healing, create vitamin A deficiency, and interfere with calcium absorption. Animal protein foods are the best sources of zinc because fiber and phytates in plant sources render it largely unavailable.

Copper is best obtained from fruits, vegetables, and grains. Copper deficiences are not common.

Selenium　Selenium has received a lot of press as part of an enzyme that functions as an antioxidant and therefore may play a role in cancer prevention. But studies have been inconclusive, and high intakes of this mineral are toxic. Selenium is obtained mostly from animal protein foods. Selenium content in grains depends largely on amounts present in soil. Fortunately, this is not a problem in major wheat-producing areas of this country.

Other Minerals　Other familiar minerals include chlorine, sulfur, iodine, fluoride, manganese, chromium and molybdenum. An excess or a deficiency of one usually affects the body's use of the others. Since these minerals are all found in different food sources, again it is important to eat a variety of fresh, whole foods in moderate amounts rather than rely on supplements.

In reviewing the sources mentioned for the various vitamins and minerals, several food groups, for example, meats and dark green leafy vegetables, stand out as being rich in many of these nutrients. Other groups, such as milk and fruit, represent the only good source of a particular vitamin or mineral. Thus, it is clear that diets that omit specific foods or groups of foods put limitations on the availability of some nutrients. Self-imposed food restrictions warrant careful attention to alternate sources of nutrients that may be lacking or in low supply.

Nutrients are best obtained from foods. Vitamin and mineral supplements, unless well balanced and within recommended ranges, may upset physiological balance. Toxicity is rarely a problem with food sources of nutrients; it is, however, a problem with supplements. Megadoses (over ten times the recommended amount) are really pharmacological doses.

Food Components and Supplements

As people become interested in nutrition and its relationship to health and fitness, they try to improve the quality of their diets by using supplements and so-called ergogenic, or energy-producing, aids in amounts far exceeding recommended allowances. The food supplement – health product business is a billion dollar one fueled by product health claims by manufacturers and promoting practitioners, on the one hand, and a concerned but perhaps gullible consumer, on the other. The result has been a barrage of mixed messages, sometimes pitting unreasonable or erroneous advice against more conservative scientific research.

Seemingly logical arguments derived from manipulating information leads many people to try products for which they have no need. Often this is harmless. Sometimes it is not. Always it is expensive. The First Amendment of the Constitution protects questionable statements about health and nutrition in printed or electronic media from federal regulation.

The best protection against misinformation is to be an informed consumer. Consult with appropriate health and nutrition professionals, such as registered dietitians; read literature written for lay people, such as the health letters printed by the public health, nutrition, and medical departments of universities; ask questions and apply logic; and be wary of extravagant claims.

The following is a list of some popular food supplements and health aids. It is by no means comprehensive. What is "in" today may be off the shelf tomorrow. Use it as a guide to evaluate products. When doing so, be aware of the issue of natural versus synthetic supplements. Many people prefer natural supplements because they wish to avoid ingredients such as coloring and sugar. Chemically speaking, however, the nutrient will be utilized in the same manner, regardless of whether it is natural or synthetic.

Information on many of the following supplements can be found in more detail in an excellent three-part series in the *Journal of Nutrition Education* (Dubick 1983).

Bee pollen is promoted as increasing athletic performance. However, scientific studies do not support this claim. The composition of this expensive product is varied—it may contain up to 55 percent carbohydrate—so would be unwise for persons with allergies to pollen to ingest it.

Brewer's yeast is a mineral and B vitamin supplement, used primarily by vegetarians. It is not ergogenic, however, and ingestion of live organisms occasionally present in yeast products has resulted in yeast infections. Some yeast products can be bitter; others have been processed to enhance taste and facilitate consumption.

Bioflavonoids, a group of compounds widely distributed in plant foods (especially those identified with vitamin C), are not essential to the diet nor do they enhance the effects of vitamin C. Once labeled vitamin P, they subsequently have been deprived of any vitamin status.

Pangamic acid, sometimes falsely referred to as vitamin B_{15}, was originally derived from apricot pits. It is not a vitamin and has no vitamin functions as promoters claim. Moreover, claims of its abilities to dispel fatigue, allergies, and a host of other problems are unfounded. It is now marketed as a mixture of substances.

Ginseng is an herb derived from the root of a plant and is mostly available as tea, although it can be found in tablets and even cosmetics. It is promoted as a stimulant. At levels high enough to produce its desired effect, however, it may be toxic for some people. Also, steroids, peptides, and other substances in ginseng could cause adverse effects if taken in large quantities over a long period of time.

Tryptophan, an essential amino acid, is promoted as a sleep inducer. It is a precursor to brain neurotransmitters that participate in the sleep process. The large dose necessary to promote sedation has the potential to upset natural amino acid balance, and it is most effective when combined with a high carbohydrate meal.

Choline and inositol are claimed to have health benefits even though they are not essential nutrients. Choline is a component of lecithin, a phospholipid discussed earlier in the chapter. Lecithin is a natural fat emulsifier and, as inositol, is active in metabolic processes. Claims that choline (and lecithin) can clear arteries of fatty deposits and prevent heart disease is illogical and misleading. According to Whitney and Hamilton (1984), although pharmacological doses of these have been used as drugs to treat nondeficiency-caused neurological disorders, it does not mean that ingesting supplements will improve memory. In fact, megadoses of these compounds can cause nausea and diarrhea, as well as disturbances of the cardiovascular and nervous systems. Inositol is claimed to reduce fat accumulation, as well as prevent baldness. It is synthesized in the body from glucose and is common in food; therefore the beneficial effects of supplements would be questionable.

PABA (para-aminobenzoic acid) is a component of folacin and is frequently found in topical sunscreen lotions. Internal ingestion can cause physiological problems, including blood disorders, nausea, and vomiting. It is not a vitamin itself and has no nutritional value.

Spirulena is an algae sold as a high-protein, ergogenic food. Other than being high in protein, it contains no extraordinary nutritional content. Seaweed in general has become popular as a food snack, but not all forms of algae are safe to eat. Some are toxic. Spirulena contain high amounts of nucleic acids, which could precipitate crystal formation in joints and the urinary tract. The long-term effects of regular ingestion of these foods are not known.

Fish oil supplements are sold in concentrated capsule and emulsion forms for the purpose of altering blood chemistry and reducing risk of blood clot formation. Some supplements may pose hazards in the form of pesticides and other contaminates that concentrate in the liver and fatty tissues of fish. Vitamins A and D, present in cod liver oil and some other supplements, can be toxic when consumed in large quantities. Also, prolonged consumption of highly unsaturated oils to lower blood cholesterol may result in vitamin E deficiency (Zamula 1986).

REFERENCES

Arizona Department of Education. 1982. *Sports Nutrition.* Tucson, Ariz.: Arizona Department of Education.

Baily, C. 1978. *Fit or Fat?* Boston, Mass.: Houghton Mifflin.

Brody, J. E. 1981. *Jane Brody's Nutrition Book.* New York: W. W. Norton.

Campbell, A. M., Penfield, M. P., and Griswold, R. M. 1979. *The Experimental Study of Food.* Boston, Mass.: Houghton Mifflin.

Dubick, M. A. 1983. Dietary supplements and health aids—A critical evaluation. Part 1—Vitamins and minerals. *Journal of Nutrition Education 15* (2), 47–51.

Dubick, M. A. 1983. Dietary supplements and health aids—A critical evaluation. Part 2—Macronutrients and fiber. *Journal of Nutrition Education 15* (3), 88–92.

Dubick, M. A. 1983. Dietary supplements and health aids—A critical evaluation. Part 3—Natural and miscellaneous products. *Journal of Nutrition Education 15* (4), 123–127.

Hillman, H. 1981. *Kitchen Science.* Boston, Mass.: Houghton Mifflin.

Labuza, T. P., and Erdman, S. W., 1984. *Food Science and Nutritional Health.* St. Paul, Minn.: West Publishing.

McGee, H. 1984. *On Food and Cooking.* New York: Charles Scribner's Sons.

Marshall, C. W. 1983. *Vitamins and Minerals: Help or Harm?* Philadelphia, Penn.: George G. Stickley Publishing.

Meyer, L. H. 1978. *Food Chemistry.* Westport, Conn.: AVI Publishing.

Nickerson, J. T. R. 1980. *Elementary Food Science.* Westport, Conn.: AVI Publishing.

Weiss, T. J. 1982. *Food Oils and Their Uses.* Westport, Conn.: AVI Publishing.

Whitney, E. N., and Hamilton, E. M. N. 1984. *Understanding Nutrition.* St. Paul, Minn.: West Publishing.

Zamula, E. 1986. The Greenland diet: Can fish oils prevent heart disease? *FDA Consumer 20* (8), 6–8.

Chapter 2

NUTRITION AND
BODY PERFORMANCE

Digestion, Absorption, and Metabolism

This section of Chapter 2 is an overview of how the body uses food to provide life-sustaining energy for all of its functions. If one eats a tuna sandwich for lunch, for example, the carbohydrate, fat, and protein are digested, that is, broken down into their smallest components; the components are then absorbed and distributed throughout the body to be used as needed. A major step in the process of food utilization is metabolism, which can be thought of as burning food fuel sources in the cells. The energy derived from this process is necessary to carry out the complex biochemical reactions that keep the body running smoothly.

Digestion occurs in four major areas: the mouth, stomach, small intestine, and large intestine. In the mouth, food is broken up and moistened with saliva, and the starch in the sandwich bread begins to be broken down by an enzyme. Next, the sandwich reaches the stomach, where starch digestion continues, fat is mechanically broken up, and protein digestion begins. Gastric (stomach) juices, which are acidic (hydrochloric acid), help turn the solid sandwich into a liquified mixture called chyme. After the stomach, the sandwich mixture travels to the small intestine. This is where much of the action takes place. Enzymes from the pancreas, gall bladder,

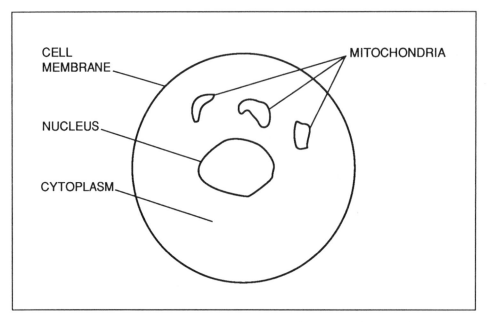

FIGURE 2.1 A cell, indicating cytoplasm, mitochondria, and the nucleus.

and small intestine itself reduce the carbohydrate, fat, and protein in the sandwich to their simple components of glucose, fatty acids and glycerol, and amino acids, respectively. This is also the area where the products of digestion are absorbed into the circulatory system and distributed throughout the body. A function of the large intestine is to collect leftover residues from the sandwich before they are excreted in the feces.

To summarize, digestion occurs in four places—the mouth, stomach, small intestine, and large intestine. Nutrients contained in the sandwich are absorbed in their simplest forms. Although water that might have been consumed with the sandwich does not produce energy, it is also a vital constituent of the body and acts as a regulator in many body processes.

The energy stored in the macronutrients of the sandwich can be used only after their simple components reach the cells. In the cells, glucose, fatty acids and glycerol, and amino acids are metabolized with the help of the vitamins and minerals, and energy is released. The metabolic process is carried out in two areas of the cell, the cytoplasm and mitochondria (see Figure 2.1). It may help to think of the mitochondria as microscopic wood stoves in the body where energy is extracted from sandwich nutrients.

The sandwich contained all three macronutrients. Follow each as they are metabolized to contribute energy (Figure 2.2). The carbohydrate from the bread is broken down into glucose, which is used for energy. Any not needed for energy is stored as glycogen with the help of a compound, glucose-6-phosphate. However, when glycogen stores are filled, extra glucose will be converted to triglyceride and be stored as fat.

Oxygen intake is the key to how far glucose can proceed in the metabolic process and how much energy it can give at any time. Under normal circumstances, when oxygen is sufficient, glucose metabolism will proceed through the pyruvate and aCoA checkpoints to complete oxidation (or complete combustion as you would see in your wood stove) in the TCA (tricarboxylic acid) cycle. (This is also called the Krebs cycle after the biochemist who unraveled this complex series of reactions.) The energy given off in this process is in the form of the compound ATP (adenosine triphosphate), so named because of the high-energy phosphate bonds it contains. Complete oxidation (a roaring fire in the stove) produces a total of 38 energy units of ATP. This whole process first takes place in the cytoplasm of the cell; then after the pyruvate checkpoint, oxidation occurs in the mitochondria (see Figure 2.2). Carbon dioxide and water are produced during the metabolic process.

In the event that oxygen is in low supply, such as what happens after lengthy, strenuous exercise, there will be no roaring fire in the wood stoves. Neither does glucose metabolism proceed very far. It stops at the pyruvate checkpoint, and lactic acid accumulates. This might be visualized as the smoky by-products accumulating from the slow fire. This, as a real wood stove, is reversible, however, and when oxygen supply is increased, complete oxidation will begin. In this oxygenless phase, which is called anaerobic (without oxygen) glycolysis (glucose breakdown), only two ATPs are netted. This occurs in the cytoplasm of the cell. Understanding the importance of oxygen availability and an adequate supply of glucose is important to understanding body functions during athletics (Chapter 4) and the principles behind weight control, which are discussed next.

So what happens to the fat in the mayonnaise and the protein in the tuna in the sandwich? In the case of fats, the fatty acids enter the pathway at the aCoA checkpoint and proceed through the TCA cycle. As discussed in Chapter 1, however, if there is insufficient glucose to keep the cycle going, incomplete metabolism occurs and potentially toxic products, ketones,

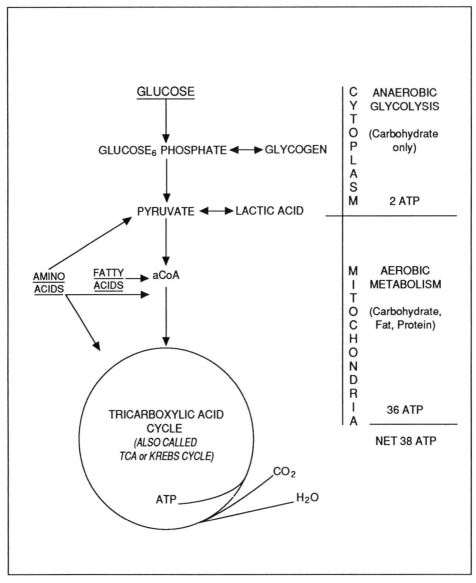

FIGURE 2.2 Cell metabolism.

result. This would be the same as putting big logs of fat in a wood stove without sufficient carbohydrate kindling (Baily 1978). Some fat can be converted to glucose; however, this amounts to only 3 percent found in the glycerol portion. Fat alone, therefore, is a very inefficient source of energy, underscoring the importance of adequate carbohydrate in the diet. Remember, the brain and nervous system normally use only glucose for energy. Depending on the body's energy requirements, some fat components from the sandwich will be reassembled into triglyceride and stored in fat cells.

Protein, unlike fat, can provide a fair amount of glucose. Remember, however, that the primary function of protein is the building and maintenance of tissues, which occurs when carbohydrate intake is adequate. In a normal situation, the amino acids in protein will be used to build body tissues. If carbohydrate and fat are insufficient to meet energy needs, amino acids can provide glucose, which will then be oxidized to provide energy. If energy needs have been met, excess amino acids stop at the aCoA checkpoint and are converted to fat for storage. Thus, the body can become fat if an excess of protein is consumed—a fact many people are not aware of. Whether amino acids are used for energy or stored as fat, the nitrogen-containing amino group must be removed. In this process, ammonia is produced in the liver and converted to a nontoxic product, urea. Urea travels through the bloodstream to the kidneys, where it is excreted. Not only is the use of protein for energy inefficient, but excess protein in the diet can place a burden on organs to remove nitrogen wastes.

Thus, protein and fat can provide glucose. A very small part of fat (glycerol) and about half of the proteins we eat can be converted to glucose by gluconeogenesis (which means "newly formed glucose"), a process in which noncarbohydrates supply glucose. This can be life-saving.

If the sandwich is not eaten and the supply of glucose dwindles, glycogen, fat, and eventually lean protein tissue will be metabolized to restore ATP as energy. During metabolism the release of heat, carbon dioxide, and water accounts for slight rises in body temperature, the exhaling of carbon dioxide (in exchange for oxygen inhaled), and the excretion of water in urine, feces, and perspiration.

It is interesting to note that many acids common to the TCA cycle, such as citric acid and fumaric acid, are also used in food processing. They are either produced by fermentation or made synthetically, and appear frequently on food product labels.

Energy Balance

Aside from politics, weight control may be the most frequent topic of conversation among people of all ages and occupations. Everyone seems to be preoccupied with dieting, including those who need not be.

Despite a current interest in health and fitness, however, many people are having problems with body energy balance. For one thing they eat the majority of meals, ranging from rich haute cuisine to fat-laden fast foods, away from home. For another, the work day has become more sedentary, thanks to labor-saving machines such as power saws, food processors, and—cars!

When food intake provides just the amount of energy needed, fat does not accumulate and energy balance is achieved. For people whose weight never seems to change, food, exercise, and body metabolism are in synch; for others, there is a dilemma: food is necessary and omnipresent in our lives, but so are media messages to remind us of the need to be thin and fit. Unfortunately many people resort to one diet plan after another with little success, but some people do discover how to manage food intake so they can have a bit of cake and a waistline, too.

This section discusses the whys and wherefores of weight gain and loss and provides suggestions for achieving a healthy balance in which food and exercise both play a vital part.

When weight is gained, what happens? Unfortunately, scientists do not know much more about the weight-gaining process beyond the fact that taking in more fuel than your body can burn will result in fat "layaway." This is one reason why so many diets and diet books exist, appearing one after the other. Few plans result in the *successful* loss of weight in terms of maintenance. Most result only in short-term weight loss, which disappears upon completion of the diet plan or the book, when regular eating habits are resumed.

There are many theories that address the biological aspects of weight control. One that shows promise is the set-point theory, which is based on the premise that heredity has programmed the body to function at a certain weight, give or take a few pounds. When a person tries to lower that weight, the body makes adjustments to conserve fat. This might explain why some people maintain a particular weight no matter how hard they try to alter the reading on the scale.

Trying brings up another point. Trying too hard can actually cause a derangement in body metabolism, whereby it shifts to a lower gear to protect the body from the threat of "starvation." Thus, each time someone diets and reduces calories drastically, the body downshifts metabolism until fat is maintained at a considerably lower calorie intake than initially. This is why most health professionals advocate increasing exercise rather than solely lowering calories.

Much scientific research is now focusing on the effects of physical and psychological stressors on brain neurotransmitters that send signals regarding hunger status and possibly causing overeating. What much of this suggests is that we have a weight that is biologically normal for us, and hunger patterns which may be normal for us, and we have to live within these parameters when attempting to regulate our weight. For some persons, this weight may not be their idea of how they want to be. However, maintenance of weight much below this point may be difficult. For them trying to have an angular, thin look can create both psychological and physiological problems—not to mention the expense of attempting to mold unwilling bodies.

It should be made clear that obesity contributes to many degenerative and life-threatening health problems. A firm, fit body is one well able to withstand environmental stresses, illness, and injury. The point is that many people have an unrealistic view of what they should weigh, to the point of becoming obsessed with it. On the other hand, when weight creeps up past a desirable level appropriate for one's body type, it is a good idea to assess and adjust dietary lifestyle and activity levels to stay within an appropriate weight range.

Whatever the biological reasons, the bottom line is that if calories ingested exceed the body's energy needs, fat stores will increase. And bodies have an unlimited capacity to put away fat as an energy store. Unlike bears that need to prepare for a winter of hibernation, people need to develop an eating plan that maintains energy reserves consistently year after year.

A calorie is the amount of heat required to raise 1 gram (g) of water 1 °C. The number of calories in food is determined by burning the food and analyzing the residue. In terms of food energy, carbohydrates and proteins each provide four calories per gram and fats nine calories per gram. Alcohol provides seven calories per gram. The truth is, it's the fried onion rings and not the roll in the bread basket that will add the most calories. Of course, the more butter that is put on the roll, the more it will look like the high-fat onion rings to the body.

For determining the number of calories a person needs, most standards are based on body weight as related to height and frame size; individual weight is then compared with the standard. The Metropolitan Height and Weight Tables, frequently used as a standard reference, are not necessarily appropriate for everybody. Moreover, body weight is not often a reliable indicator of body fat. The most common way to determine percent of body fat is to measure skinfold thickness, a technique often used in exercise and fitness centers and by health professionals.

A quick assessment of ideal body weight can be done as follows. If used, however, it must be understood that this is a "ballpark" method only. With this method, allow 45 kg, or 100 pounds (females), and 48 kg, or 106 pounds (males), per 150 cm, or 5 feet, in height. Then an additional 2.3 kg, or 5 pounds (females), or 2.7 kg, or 6 pounds (males), per additional cm (inch) is added. When this is calculated, add 10 percent of the total for a large frame and subtract 10 percent for a small frame (see Figure 2.3).

There are three other factors in addition to a person's height and frame size that affect the number of calories needed to maintain an ideal weight: basal metabolism rate (BMR), which is the amount of energy required to keep all of the physiological processes such as breathing going at complete rest (nonactivity), physical activity, and body food processing. BMR accounts for the largest part of the body's caloric needs, physical activity accounts for about 30 percent, and body food processing after a meal accounts for less than 10 percent.

To understand the basal metabolic contribution to energy needs, consider that lean muscle tissue is metabolically more active than fat tissue. Lean muscle tissue not only requires more fuel, it burns it faster and more efficiently. Thus, the greater the percentage of lean body tissue and the lower the percentage of body fat, the more efficiently the body burns food eaten. Lean tissue requires more calories to support it than fat tissue. In addition, lean people seem to be active people, which contributes to increased muscle tone. Inactivity hinders attempts to lose or maintain weight.

These factors explain why two people who are the same height, weight, and frame size can look different in terms of body composition and fit of clothes. Think of athletes or dancers who gain weight and change shape after retirement. When muscles are not used, they deteriorate. Inactivity,

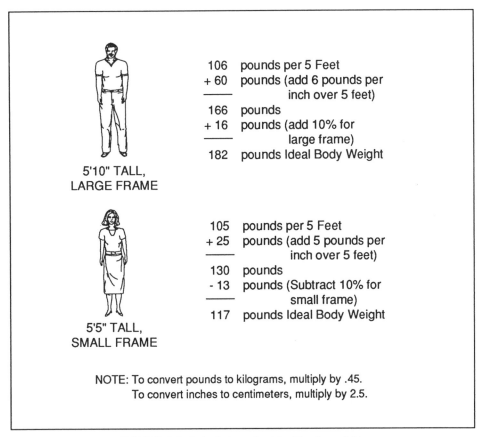

FIGURE 2.3 Calculations for ideal body weight.

coupled with dietary habits that have not been readjusted from more active times, results in these body changes.

Diets

Many fad diets rely on reducing calories alone. But if this method is not combined with an exercise program, it is usually unsuccessful over the long term. Moreover, severe calorie restrictions upset body metabolism and may be nutritionally deficient. And the food choices may be so limited as to discourage compliance.

There are 3500 calories in 1 lb (0.45 kg) of fat. A minimum of 1200 calories is necessary for the average person to spare protein, prevent ketosis, and receive adequate nutrition. Many weight loss diets drop daily calorie intake to 800 or less; however, below 900 the body will probably be using protein to provide energy, thus wasting lean body tissue. Many diets are also very low in carbohydrate, but at least 100 g are necessary to prevent ketosis. The rapid weight loss seen with these diets (usually followed by a lengthy plateau) is mostly water. As carbohydrate is reduced and body glycogen stores are depleted, weight loss occurs through the loss of water stored with the glycogen, not loss of fat! And so it goes, the popular weight loss industry gets richer and the dieters poorer.

The most successful weight loss programs assess a person's biochemical status, body composition, dietary lifestyle, activity level, and psychosocial factors that might contribute to difficulty in maintaining weight. Then a diet that is adequate in calories and nutritionally balanced is planned to fit that person's needs. Exercise is an important component of any weight control program. It tones muscles, improves oxygen consumption, and increases metabolic activity. Weight loss entails reduced portions of foods eaten, emphasis on nutrient-dense foods from major food groups (and fewer high-fat or sugary snacks) and exercise. A registered dietitian can help to prevent overweight from becoming obesity with all of its related health problems. Obesity for most people falls into a range of between fifteen to twenty percent above ideal weight. Athletic activity can boost calorie requirements to as much as 300 extra, and strenuous athletic training to as many as 600 to 900 more. So if exercise is increased even while maintaining caloric intake, it is a step in the right direction. On the other hand, if caloric intake is increased, say 150 calories per day, because of stops at the new ice cream store after dinner, a weight gain of eleven pounds in a year is possible unless activity level is increased accordingly.

Psychosocial and Psychological Aspects of Weight Control

So far, the physiological aspects of weight control have been explored. There are also psychosocial aspects. In other words, lifestyle activity as well as mental attitude can influence reactions to food, which may mean eat, overeat, or undereat. For instance, food is a part of almost every social activity, whether it is a beer with neighbors or butter-drenched popcorn consumed at the movies. Food is also a part of family gatherings such as Sunday dinners or simply a barbecue in the backyard. Incidentally, family food habits also tend to carry over into adult life. Memories of rich foods or the "clean your plate" syndrome may affect one's reactions at mealtime throughout life. Likewise, psychological states influence one's reaction to food. A sense of comfort brings with it special feelings toward food. For example, when one is warm and cozy, food becomes comforting, non-threatening. On the other hand, when one comes in from frigid temperatures and a driving snowstorm, food is also the provider of warmth, comfort, and security.

Food is often relied upon for comfort in times of anxiety or tension, or with celebration or grief. Food may also become a companion in times of loneliness, or a substitute for love and affection. Celebration, grief, social gatherings, and family tradition are all a part of life, and food cues may prompt one to overeat, undereat, or use food beyond what the situation or physiological needs call for. Once these "triggers" are identified, behavior modification is an effective technique for unlearning these food habits. In group approaches, people are placed in control only after observing and practicing appropriate responses to food cues in the group setting. Reinforcement is usually provided to prevent backsliding into previous habits and serves as feedback in terms of progress. There is also the emotional support of others in the group.

The focus is not so much on the restriction of food choices as on the emphasis of alternatives; for instance, instead of watching television and eating potato chips, one might go for a run or knit a sweater. The major advantage to this approach over fad diets is that it establishes sensible, long-term eating habits and avoids the on again – off again fad diet approach that confuses the body and discourages the dieter.

Reducing Calories in the Kitchen

What can food professionals do to help customers watch calories? Offer low-calorie alternatives on the menu, and be prepared to back them with calculations if asked. A daily low-calorie special can be a marketing tool.

When menu decisions have been made, there are things that can be done in the kitchen. Food professionals can provide variety on plates and strive for attractive presentations. These approaches help offset reduced portion sizes and eliminate the need for small or odd-sized plates. Keep in mind the carbohydrate–fat–protein ratio on the plate in terms of their relative calorie contributions.

Remember, most animal protein and regular dairy products contain fat calories. Become creative with low-fat substitutions. Increase the vegetable and starch to meat ratio on the plate; there are far more vegetables and grains than there are animals that provide meat. Use stock or pan juice reductions for sauces (be sure to degrease). Increase gelatin content or add a tiny bit of corn or potato starch for finish. Avoid the use of liaisons such as roux, egg yolks, and butter. Provide fresh, interesting breads, and place a small crock of butter or margarine on the table instead of individual pats. People will eat less when they have to reach for the food and there is less to begin with.

It is not difficult to create interesting, low-calorie dishes. The food exchange list in Appendix B, which is explained in Chapter 8, is a helpful menu-planning tool. Use it to analyze carbohydrate–fat–protein ratios and calories in relation to portion sizes.

REFERENCES

Baily, C. 1978. *Fit or Fat?* Boston, Mass.: Houghton Mifflin.

Fisher, M. C., and LaChance, P. A. 1985. Nutrition evaluation of published weight reducing diets. *Journal of the American Dietetic Association 85* (4), 450–454.

Hamilton, E. M. N., Whitney, E. N., and Sizer, F. S. 1985. *Nutrition Concepts and Controversies.* St. Paul, Minn.: West Publishing.

Katch, F. I., and McArdle, W. D. 1983. *Nutrition, Weight Control and Exercise.* Philadelphia, Penn.: Lea and Febiger.

Pennington, J. A. T., and Church, H. N. 1985. *Food Values of Portions Commonly Used.* New York: Harper and Row.

Tufts University. 1986. Losing weight and making sure you keep it off. *Diet and Nutrition Letter 12,* 3–7.

Willis, J. 1985. How to take weight off (and keep it off) without getting ripped off. *FDA Consumer* (Feb.). Reprint 85–116.

Part II

LIFE-STYLE IMPACT ON
FOOD CONSUMPTION
AND PRODUCTION

Chapter 3

NUTRITION AND THE AMERICAN DIET

Current Dietary Recommendations

Where do nutrient recommendations come from? Who determines them? Which ones should be followed in order to have a healthy diet? The springboard for all dietary recommendations is the Recommended Dietary Allowances (RDAs), which suggest amounts of energy, protein, and selected vitamins and minerals necessary for an adequate diet. The RDAs serve as the scientific standard, or yardstick, against which the nutrient content of individual diets, institutional food programs such as school lunches, and food products are measured.

The first RDAs were published in 1943. Since then they have been updated and revised every 5 years. Prepared by the Committee on Dietary Allowances of the Food and Nutrition Board of the National Academy of Sciences, they are basically estimates of nutrient allowances considered to be adequate to meet the nutritional needs of most healthy persons. As science progresses, new issues arise with each revision of the RDAs. The 1985 (tenth) edition, has been delayed due to ongoing discussion regarding new scientific research that may affect recommendations for some nutrients. Some of the concerns revolved around identifying allowances at a satisfactory level between that of just preventing deficiencies and that above which either no further benefit or even undesirable consequences occur. An overall goal has been to set recommendations at levels that can be easily met using available foods in customary dietary life-styles (Gussow and Guthrie, 1985).

Since the RDAs are set with a wide margin of safety, it is not necessary to become overly preoccupied with meeting recommendations on a daily basis. If someone consistently falls short of obtaining adequate nutrition, however, deficiencies may occur over a period of time. The easiest road to an optimal diet is to eat a variety of foods from all food groups in adequate amounts (this usually means at least 1200 calories per day). Limit empty calorie foods, such as sweets and most packaged snack foods and alcoholic beverages, which are high in calories and low in nutritional content.

Unfortunately, many dietary analyses done in health clubs and other group settings base nutritional assessment on a 1-day recall of foods eaten. Results can be unreliable because of forgotten foods or an atypical day. No overall pattern emerges. If results of an assessment do not reflect normal eating patterns and results indicate an inadequate nutrient intake, the assessment should be repeated. If, on the other hand, the day was typical and the results were unsatisfactory, poor dietary habits may be to blame. A registered dietitian should be consulted when an individual has difficulty obtaining a nutritionally adequate diet.

The USRDAs were developed by the Food and Drug Administration to condense the RDAs for the nutritional labeling of food products and nutrient supplements. They indicate what percentage of the USRDA for selected nutrients consumers get in one serving of that food, or a supplement, and so on.

Other nutrition-related health guidelines developed during the late 1970s and early 1980s are listed below.

1977   Dietary Goals for the United States, Select Committee on Nutrition and Human Needs, U.S. Senate

1979   Healthy People: The Surgeon General's Report on Health Promotion and Disease Prevention, U.S. Department of Health, Education and Welfare/Public Health Service

1980   Dietary Guidelines for Americans, U.S. Department of Agriculture, U.S. Department of Health and Human Services

1980   Promoting Health, Preventing Disease, a report with ensuing National Nutrition Objectives for 1990 and Goals for the Year 2000, U.S. Department of Health and Human Services/Public Health Service

1982 Report on Diet, Nutrition and Cancer, National Academy of Sciences

1984 Recommendations for cancer risk reduction, Reports by the National Cancer Institute and the American Cancer Society

1984 Recommendations for Reducing Blood Cholesterol Levels, National Institutes of Health Consensus Development Conference

1986 American Heart Association Revised Dietary Guidelines (original Guidelines were developed in 1965, followed by revisions in 1968, 1973, 1978, and 1986)

1986 1990 Health Objectives for the Nation: A Midcourse Review, U.S. Department of Health and Human Services/ Public Health Service

1987 National Cholesterol Education Program—the nation's first detailed guidelines for identifying and treating people whose blood cholesterol levels are high enough to require medical treatment. Issued by a panel convened by the National Cholesterol Program, a co-operative effort between the National Heart, Lung and Blood Institute and twenty-three medical associations and health organizations.

1988 Surgeon General's Report on Nutrition and Health. The first nutrition report by a U.S. Surgeon General recommends that Americans consume less fat, particularly saturated fat, and consume more complex carbohydrates and fiber. Office of the U.S. Surgeon General.

Some of the recommendations in the table are in the form of general dietary suggestions; others are more specific in terms of dietary modifications thought to lower risk factors for certain diseases. Thus, formal, scientifically based nutritional standards and more easily understood consumer-oriented, food-related guidelines for food selection, preparation and consumption are available to the public.

The Dietary Guidelines for Americans are a consumer-directed tool to be used in selecting and preparing foods.

- Maintain Desirable Weight
- Avoid Too Much Sodium
- Avoid Too Much Sugar
- Eat a Variety of Foods
- Avoid Too Much Fat, Saturated Fat, and Cholesterol
- Eat Foods with Adequate Starch and Fiber
- If You Drink Alcoholic Beverages, Do So in Moderation

The guidelines are directed toward healthy people; those with diseases or conditions that require special diets need to consult with a physician or registered dietitian. They also point out that good eating habits based on variety and moderation can help maintain health. Keep in mind, however, that health status depends on many factors including heredity, lifestyle, personality traits, mental attitudes, and environment. Diet, therefore, is a major factor, but not the only factor in good health.

The American Heart Association Dietary Guidelines are intended to assist healthy people in preventing cardiovascular disease. These guidelines advise limiting intake of total fat to less than 30 percent of total calories, with less than 10 percent of calories coming from saturated fat, up to 10 percent from polyunsaturated fats, and the remainder from monounsaturated fats. They also advise limiting cholesterol to 300 mg or less per day, sodium to no more than 3,000 mg per day, moderating alcohol consumption, and maintaining appropriate weight.

Advice regarding nutrition and cancer suggests reducing the intake of total fat to less than 30 percent of total calories; including fruits, vegetables, and whole-grain cereal products daily, especially citrus, carotene-rich and cabbage-family vegetables; minimizing consumption of cured, pickled, and smoked foods; and drinking alcohol in moderation.

How can all of this information be easily incorporated into various dietary lifestyles without conscious thought all the time? Choosing foods for a balanced diet should become second nature—a matter of habit. A good way to tackle the framework suggested in the dietary guidelines is to put all foods eaten into an imaginary dietary "pie" consisting of approximately 55 percent carbohydrate, 30 percent or less fat, and the remaining 12–15 percent protein (see Figure 3.1). Some of the special characteristics of a

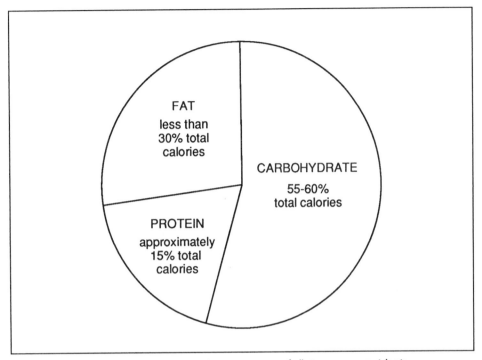

FIGURE 3.1 Recommended percentages of dietary macronutrients.

good diet can be added by filling the carbohydrate slice with mostly complex carbohydrates and the fat slice with up to 10 percent each of saturated and polyunsaturated fats, and the remainder with monounsaturated fats.

But—how is it possible to keep track of all the micronutrients and be sure that the variety of foods eaten covers all nutritional needs? The easiest way to design a balanced diet (and, indeed, a balanced menu) is to choose foods from each of the *four food groups.*

The four groups consist of *meat* and meat substitutes such as eggs, nuts, and legumes; *milk* and milk products; *grains* such as bread, cereal, pasta, rice; and *fruits and vegetables.* The number of servings from each group to include in meals on a daily basis is determined by a simple formula. For adults, the recipe is 2-2-4-4, or two servings daily from both meat and milk groups and four each from the grain and fruit-vegetable groups (Figure 3.2).

Depending on the variety of foods chosen from each group, recommended servings from the four food groups will provide about 1200 to 1600 calories and an adequate nutrient intake for most people. To cover all

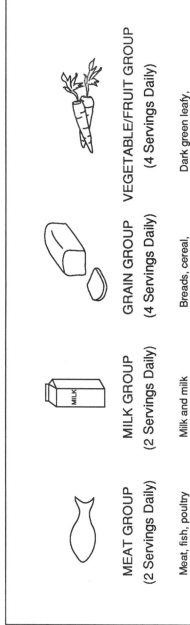

MEAT GROUP
(2 Servings Daily)

Meat, fish, poultry and meat alternatives such as eggs and cheese, or combinations of legumes, nuts, seeds and grains

MILK GROUP
(2 Servings Daily)

Milk and milk products such as cheese, yogurt

GRAIN GROUP
(4 Servings Daily)

Breads, cereal, pasta; grains such as rice, bulgar, buckwheat groats

VEGETABLE/FRUIT GROUP
(4 Servings Daily)

Dark green leafy, deep yellow-orange; light colored vegetables such as cauliflower and cabbage; starchy vegetables such as potatoes, corn

Citrus fruits such as oranges, grapefruit; deep-colored fruits such as peaches, cantaloupe; and light-colored fruits such as apples, pears, bananas

FIGURE 3.2 Four food groups.

nutrient bases, include at least the recommended servings and use mostly whole, unprocessed foods. The more processed the food, the less nutritious it is, and the term enriched does not necessarily mean that *all* of the original nutrients have been replaced. In addition to choosing foods from the four food groups, it is wise to keep tabs on the amount of sodium, fat, and cholesterol present in foods which may be added during processing or preparation. Some foods often consumed on a daily basis do not precisely fit into the four groups. These include coffee, butter, salad dressings, and alcoholic beverages, for example. It is better to think of these extras in terms of the dietary pie than in terms of the negligible amounts of vitamins and minerals they might supply. Nevertheless, the four groups are still the easiest guide to use when assessing variety and general nutrient coverage. They may also help achieve a good macronutrient ratio in terms of the recommended percentages of carbohydrate, fat and protein in the dietary pie in Figure 3.1.

What has just been described is an eating/cooking scheme that includes an adequate number of moderate-size servings from the four major food categories, with specific foods and preparation methods selected with an eye on the macronutrient ratios in the dietary pie. (Use the exchange list in Appendix B to compare the amounts of carbohydrate, fat, and protein in foods.) There will be a chance to practice visualizing foods, individual dishes, and complete menus in terms of their variety and balance in the menu game activity in Chapter 8.

As a food professional, it is necessary to develop food awareness—an ability to visualize, in terms of product, preparation methods, colors, textures and portion sizes, what a dish, a meal, or a whole menu has to offer in terms of nutrient composition and relative balance compared with the dietary pie. To begin, here are a few tips on meeting nutritional guidelines within the four food categories.

When choosing foods, remember that whole grain products increase complex carbohydrate (starches), and are also high in fiber. Fresh fruits provide natural sugars, vitamins, minerals and fiber—better than processed sweets high in refined sugar, sodium, and fats, that have few nutrients and lots of calories. Fresh vegetables also provide natural sugars and are naturally low in sodium compared to processed vegetables. Lean fish and poultry without the skin are better choices than high fat meats or eggs, which should be eaten less frequently. Low fat milk products not only lower calories, but also reduce the amount of saturated fat and cholesterol in a meal and provide high quality protein as well. Replace sweet, salty, and fried snack foods with fresh, natural, nutrient-dense snacks such as fresh fruit and vegetables, low fat milk and yogurt, whole grain breads/crackers and the like. For food professionals, skill and creativity are only as good as the food products selected, and fresh, whole foods are the key to tasty and healthful menu items.

As various food components in the American diet are discussed in the following sections, it should become clear that a few adjustments here and there can significantly improve the nutritional quality of meals. For example, lowering the fat content of a dish will lower the calorie count considerably, because fat is a more concentrated source of energy than either its carbohydrate or protein counterparts. When total fat content is reduced and the ratio of saturated, poly-, and monounsaturated fats is adjusted as suggested by the American Heart Association, the calories and cholesterol-raising potential of that food item are automatically lowered. The key is developing a sense of balance. A rich sauce need not be omitted, but could be integrated into the entire presentation so as to maintain dietary "pie" ratios. This may mean different choices in terms of food to be sauced, amount of sauce, treatment of accompanying vegetables, grains and so forth, and reduced portion sizes for some items. A less rich version of a sauce, or a different sauce, might be prepared to maintain portion sizes, depending on clientele preferences.

Sometimes it is necessary to "rob Peter to pay Paul." However, it is all a part of achieving *balance*—taking some from here, adding there. Cooks do this all the time. Think of it in terms of exercising alternatives. Start with menu planning—include variety in terms of the foods offered in each menu category and balance rich dishes with leaner alternatives throughout.

Composition of the American Diet: An Evaluation

Carbohydrates

The two major sources of carbohydrate in the American diet are the complex starches and the simple sugar, sucrose. Unfortunately, a large part of our total carbohydrate intake comes from sugar. Even though dietary guidelines advise increasing consumption of complex carbohydrates and reducing the amount of sugar in the diet, there has been a decline during this century in the consumption of starchy foods and the natural sugars found in fresh vegetables and fruits. Refined sugars found in processed foods have been favored instead. According to the Center for Science in the Public Interest, the nutritional quality of the American diet dropped considerably when starch-containing foods, which are important sources of vitamins, minerals, protein, and fiber, were traded for sugars, most of which are refined sweeteners devoid of nutrients. The good news is that people are now increasing their consumption of some complex carbohydrate foods, although much of the increase is still in the processed fruit and vegetable category (Brewster and Jacobson 1982).

The shift away from complex carbohydrates has also been accompanied by an increase in fat consumption, most of which comes from animal foods such as meat. In fact for the average American, approximately 40 percent of calories consumed come from fat and another 18 percent from sugar. This means that for many people, nearly 60 percent of their calories come from fat and sugar! Current recommendations, remember, tell us that 55 to 60 percent of total calories should come from complex carbohydrates — *not* fat and sugar! Carbohydrate foods are often thought of as fattening, uninteresting, or merely vehicles in which to transport other foods to the mouth. They have not had the allure, either in the marketplace or on the table, that meats have had. Moreover, when the waistline expands, what foods do most people cut back first? Starches. "Just a steak and a salad for me," says the patron on a weight loss diet, who then consumes a well marbled steak and salad covered with Roquefort dressing. "No roll, it's fattening," continues the dialogue.

Clearly, complex carbohydrates have been relegated to the sidelines. But they have garnered a reputation they do not deserve. Carbohydrates provide four calories per gram, as does protein. The protein in animal foods, however, also contains a good deal of fat, which provides nine calories per gram. Unprocessed carbohydrate foods are low in fat. Of course, if fats such as butter, cream, or cheese are added to them, or processed versions with added fat are used, their calorie content will increase and their nutritional value will decrease. But do not blame it on carbohydrates, which are relatively low in calories and fat. Complex carbohydrates are a major source of important nutrients and dietary fiber. They are also the primary source of energy for body activity.

Fortunately, the health value of complex carbohydrates has been widely publicized, and many people are now rediscovering their merits—not only in terms of nutritive value, but also in terms of taste and general appeal in many dishes as well as alone. Many starch-based dishes from the American repertoire, as well as those of other countries, have become popular. For example, many carbohydrate staples such as baked beans, polenta, corn-bread, and tortillas, are now being offered, often in updated versions, as trendy restaurant fare, not only in their regions of origin, but across the country.

Aside from bread, the two complex carbohydrate foods most frequently seen both at home and in restaurants seem to be potatoes and rice. Although these are fine, nutritious foods, few cooks make use of the vast array of foods from this group that range from grains to beans to starchy vegetables to fruits. In addition, many people obtain most of their carbohydrates from processed foods such as white bread, syrupy fruits, and sweets, including presweetened breakfast cereals, sweet snacks and desserts. Even the popular high-fat croissant has been further embellished with sweet and savory fillings. Others may purchase healthful carbohydrate foods and then prepare or adorn them so as to render them undesirably high in sugar, fat, and sodium.

Advertising in the media and stimuli at the marketplace pit nontraditional foods such as instant scalloped potatoes and sugary cereals against traditional carbohydrate foods such as fresh potatoes and old-fashioned oatmeal. Today, traditional food sources of carbohydrates have been partly replaced by nontraditional, processed forms such as breakfast bars, presweetened and instant cereals, instant rice and muffin mixes, for example. From the four food groups, simple and complex carbohydrates are contributed by fruits and vegetables, legumes, grains, and milk and milk products. They can also be found in processed or prepared foods including the sugar in catsup and some peanut butter; quick breads; and sweets such as cakes and cookies, for example.

Fruits in general contribute fiber to the diet as well as key nutrients, depending on which are selected. Citrus fruits are especially good sources of vitamin C, for example. Vegetables can be divided into two groups. Dark green vegetables are low in calories and provide fiber; vitamins A, C, folacin and riboflavin; and the minerals iron and magnesium. Greens also include broccoli and the salad vegetables watercress, romaine, chicory, curly endive, and escarole, plus other salad components such as lamb's lettuce and arugula, which are growing in popularity. All dark green *and* deep yellow vegetables are good sources of vitamin A, and many, such as tomatoes, broccoli, and peppers, are good sources of vitamin C as well. Vegetables that are good sources of vitamins A and C, as well as those vegetables from the cabbage family, are thought to offer some protection from some types of cancer. Starchy vegetables include fresh and dried peas and beans, corn, potatoes, parsnips, rutabagas, and some vegetables of Latin American origin such as plantain and taro root. These are now appearing in restaurants and in the produce section of many food stores. In addition to starch and fiber, these vegetables are good sources of protein, iron, zinc, magnesium, phosphorus, thiamin, B_6, and folacin, plus other nutrients depending on which are chosen.

Milk and milk products are not usually thought of as carbohydrate foods, but they do contribute simple carbohydrate in the form of lactose. They are good sources of calcium and riboflavin, as well as protein, vitamins A and B_{12}, and, if fortified, vitamin D. Some people cannot digest lactose because of a deficiency in the enzyme lactase, and suffer intestinal discomfort when milk products are consumed. There are, however, several lactose-reduced and lactose-free dairy products now as well as other products that can be added to milk foods to predigest the milk sugar.

Sugary foods and sweet beverages also contribute carbohydrate in the form of simple sugars. Too often nutritious complex carbohydrates are processed with sugar (e.g., presweetened cereals), thus adding calories and detracting from nutritional value. Therefore, it is easier to control the amount of sugar ingested by avoiding presweetened processed foods and sweetening to taste, if necessary. When buying packaged foods, be sure to read the label to see if any of the following sweeteners appear: sugar, sucrose, dextrose, fructose, corn syrup, honey, molasses, or invert sugar. Sometimes they are scattered throughout the ingredient list in the order of amount added. It is surprising to see sugar in foods not normally thought of as sweet, such as catsup and peanut butter. Remember, this group of sweeteners contributes carbohydrate only from simple sugars, which provide calories, but give no nutritional benefits in return.

Grain products are the major nutrient-providing source of carbohydrate in our diets. Breads, cereals, pasta, and other grain-based foods are usually made from whole or enriched grains and are important sources of complex carbohydrates (starch and fiber), as well as thiamin, riboflavin, niacin, and iron. Whole grain foods also provide B_6, magnesium, and zinc, among other nutrients. Again, highly processed versions of grain products may have undesirable amounts of added fat, sugar, or sodium, not to mention additives and preservatives and ersatz (imitation) ingredients. Moreover, even though most refined grain products are enriched, all of the original nutrients are not replaced.

In the early 1900s, white flour became popular. People eschewed the darker, whole wheat variety and the dense, chewy baked products it produced. The softer and whiter the bread, the better. Then widespread deficiency of iron, thiamin, riboflavin, and niacin was discovered. In the process of producing the refined white flour, many nutrients were lost during the milling process. Technology took a giant step backward.

Whole grains contain nutrients from the entire kernel of wheat, that is, the bran, endosperm, and germ. Milling removes the bran and germ, both rich in nutrients, leaving the endosperm, which consists primarily of starch and proteins. The bran layer also provides fiber, and the germ contains important vegetable oils. In 1942, the Enrichment Act provided for the return of four nutrients—iron, thiamin, riboflavin, and niacin—to flour. This eliminated the major deficiencies that were occurring from the use of unenriched refined flour products; however, enrichment does **not** replace the fiber nor all original vitamins and minerals, including E, folate, B_6, zinc, and chromium. The more refined processed foods are, the less nutritious they become because enrichment does not replace all that is lost. Who would want to buy at full price something that has lost its original value? Yet consumers pay full price every day for secondhand nutrition. On the other hand, many foods, especially cereals, are being fortified with nutrients beyond what existed in the food to begin with. Of course, the consumer pays for this, too. As public demand for whole foods increases, more and more whole grain products are hitting the market. The pendulum is swinging ever so slowly toward consumers who vote with their purchasing dollars for foods in their natural state. A popular and expanding grocery company in the Boston area, Bread and Circus, now uses the slogan "The Food, the Whole Food, and Nothing but the Food."

The choice of whole, natural complex carbohydrates available to cooks is extensive. There are many more food choices in this macronutrient group than from protein and fat predominant foods combined. And many complex carbohydrate foods are also good sources of protein. Better yet, these foods are thought to assist in the prevention of heart disease, cancer and stroke. The following products are the major sources of complex carbohydrates available to the cook.

Flour can be milled from any grain. Now that the merits of whole grain flours have been established, should all white flour be discarded? What about pastries? White, enriched flour does have a place in the kitchen, particularly in pastries and some breads and doughs. As a daily staple at the table or in the lunch box, whole grains are more nutritious. However, some products are more acceptable than others when made with white flour. Many professional—and home—cooks produce acceptable pastries using whole wheat pastry flour from soft winter wheat; however, the finished products are not the same in texture or taste as when made with white flour. They are still high in fat and may be filled or otherwise embellished with not-so-nutritious glazes, fillings, creams, etc. One does not eat cakes and pastries for their nutritional value per se. It is fine to have a treat occasionally. In the restaurant, offer flaky napoleons, tarts, or genoise. Then offer alternatives to give people a choice. Offer alternatives in the bread basket, too—a variety of whole grain and white breads and rolls. There is nothing better than a crusty white baguette with some cheeses, whereas whole grain and savory nut breads are better companions for other cheeses. The point, again, is to offer *options*. A garlicky croute cut from a loaf of crusty white bread may be preferable with bouillabaisse for example. Again, it is a matter of being able to choose from a variety of foods to achieve a personal balance, and to exercise a bit of moderation in terms of type, amount and frequency of foods eaten. Those who bake their pies with whole wheat crusts and eat whole wheat croissants every day, for example, are just kidding themselves nutritionally speaking. If the taste and texture of the whole wheat version is enjoyed, fine. But the fact that it is whole grain shouldn't be an excuse to overindulge in these high fat foods.

Cereals have certainly changed from the time Mr. Kellogg first packaged Corn Flakes. This grain-based staple has been processed, puffed, sugared, colored, and over-fortified. Most presweetened cereals contain more sweetener than most people are likely to add at the table. And many contain highly saturated palm and coconut oils. Unfortunately, these adulterated versions of a wholesome food have sold better than plain Grape Nuts, All Bran, and Shredded Wheat. Fortunately, media and product package information regarding the health benefits of dietary fiber have salvaged the more nutritional cereals from extinction and their popularity is on the rise. Granola, although theoretically a wholesome, fiber-rich breakfast or snack food, is usually high in simple sugars and fat, and thus calories. Check the recommended serving size on the package label—is this how much you pour into the bowl? Chances are you add more. Why not make your own? Then you have control.

The amount of pasta eaten in this country over the last decade has soared. This fact alone should provide a boost to complex carbohydrate consumption statistics. Some reasons for its popularity are low cost, ease of preparation, and versatility. Pasta, in its most common version, is either made from durum wheat which has been refined and ground into semolina flour, or regular, all-purpose refined and enriched flour. Flavor treats abound in filled versions, as well as plain pasta which can be made with whole wheat, buckwheat, rice, and corn flours among others. A rainbow of colors can be achieved through the use of vegetable purees, saffron, and even squid ink. It can be combined with simple vegetables or exotic ingredients, all important factors in competitive creativity, which is surging through the foodservice industry at this time.

In the restaurant, pasta provides endless possibilities for hot and cold dishes. It recycles leftovers. It can display truffles and caviar. When tossed with a little oil and garlic or with any of a repertoire of sauces based on tomatoes, or with low fat versions of meat, seafood, and herb- or nut-based sauces, pasta is a nutritious meal in itself. Unfortunately, it is all too easy to finish a pasta dish in butter, cream, and cheese. Offer sauce alternatives and half portions. Pasta dishes low in fat are a good way to provide healthful menu alternatives, and they have customer appeal. Unfortunately, trendy foods usually peak in popularity, then interest recedes. But perhaps pasta will remain as a staple food in this country long after tortellini salads with pesto disappear from take-out shops. Perhaps, as our interest in sports and fitness continues, pasta will hold its place in the kitchen along with other complex carbohydrate foods, which are the number one providers of fuel for muscular energy.

Pasta is often thought of in terms of the Italian version. Actually, many Italians refer to their pasta as noodles. Noodles have also existed in this country for centuries. Yellow-tinged from egg, they are most often cut into flat shapes. Italian pastas, which can be found in a myriad of shapes, are usually made with high-protein semolina flour and rarely contain eggs.

Asian and Oriental noodles are made from a different variety of ingredients including rice flour, mung beans, root vegetables, and seaweed. This accounts for their different textures and appearance. They vary in form from long, yarnlike strands to flat wrappers used in dishes such as Chinese egg rolls and Vietnamese spring rolls. They further extend the culinary possibilities of this category of carbohydrate foods, and may be used in a number of non-Asian dishes as well.

Other flour-based staples include Mexican flour and corn tortillas, which are used as wrappers, underpinnings, and separators much the same as wonton and lasagna noodles. Most cuisines have flour-based food staple(s), including crepes, Indian poppadums, Ethiopian injera, and Middle Eastern phyllo. All of these can add variety and interest on the plate, whether cooking from that country's repertoire or not.

Whole grains, including rice and its grassy cousin, wild rice; corn; barley; millet; triticale; buckwheat groats, better known as kasha, and wheat grain products such as bulgur (cracked wheat); wheat berries (the whole kernel); and couscous (finely cracked wheat that has usually been steamed and dried), offer an extensive array of culinary possibilities. Each of these have different tastes, textures, and appearance and are inexpensive and easy to prepare. They lend themselves to creative menu development. Although basic cooking instructions call for water, they can be prepared with stock, juice, or any liquid. They are tasty by themselves as well as with added ingredients such as the vegetables and herbs in tabbouleh (usually made with bulgur); the vegetables and meats in the Moroccan national dish that takes its name from couscous; the seafoods in paella; and the meat and spices in jambalaya. With recipe adjustment, they can become low fat croquets and fritters; they can be added to breads and batters; they can be used to thicken soups and stews; they can be combined with each other, such as couscous and wheat berries or rice and kasha. Instead of using plain white rice, substitute another grain for variety and interest.

Other than potatoes, starchy vegetables such as dried beans and peas, sweet potatoes, parsnips, and rutabaga hardly ever find their way onto the plate unless they are a component of a dish such as chile or cassoulet or sweet potato pie. Only recently have some restaurants experimented with the use of exotic root vegetables—sometimes as a variation on the potato chip. This category of carbohydrate foods should be explored. Most contribute significant amounts of protein, and they do not require refrigeration.

Certainly, the hour or two it takes to cook most dry legumes is not a problem for most restaurants. Think twice before buying canned versions. Not only are they slightly higher in sodium, but the texture simply leaves something to be desired.

Sugar

According to the USDA, national consumption of food sweeteners in 1982 was 143 pounds per person, with table sugar alone accounting for 68 pounds per person per year. These are averages, however, and may not be typical for some persons. However, for sugar not consumed by one person, there are plenty of others consuming not only their own quota, but part of the quotas for others, too. Some people deny having a sweet tooth. Maybe so, but they probably eat more sweeteners than they realize. This applies to everyone. Try to tell someone in the process of squirting catsup on their hamburger that they are sugaring their meat! What they may not realize is that one tablespoon of catsup has one teaspoon of sugar in it.

More than two-thirds of the sugar people eat comes from processed foods, less than one-third is added by consumers themselves, with the remaining percent obtained from foodservice settings. Food manufacturers use sugar to sweeten, prevent spoilage, retain moisture, and to enhance a product's popularity. Sweetness sells. Take cereals, for instance. If they were not popular, the presweetened versions would not be littering the shelves. However, all of those "sweet tooths" (unfortunately, many of which are in children) have created a market for them. Some cereals contain half their weight in sugar. Maybe they should be labeled breakfast candies.

In the days of the traditional carbohydrate, most of the sugar produced went directly to the consumer—to be used at will. Now, the reverse is true—more sugar goes to food and beverage manufacturers. The result is that people have increased their intake of nontraditional carbohydrates and hidden, nutrient-void sugar calories from beverages, bakery, and confectionery products and processed foods such as catsup.

The problem is not over the existence of refined sweeteners in some foods such as desserts, but in the amount put into foods, the overall amount people ingest, and, worst of all, the indiscriminate sweetening of foods that do not really need to be sweet. When a lot of sugar is consumed, the calories become substantial. And remember, these are empty calories, with little nutritional value. Empty calories not only replace nutritious foods in the diet, but also contribute to obesity and tooth decay. For someone who requires only 1200 to 1800 calories to maintain a desired weight, sweets frequently can use up the calorie allotment before an adequate amount of nutrient-dense foods is eaten. Moreover, people really do not need simple sugars in their diets since complex carbohydrates when broken down to glucose provide energy necessary for body functions. And, of course, many foods, such as fruits, are naturally sweet. Sweets, however, have become an inherent part of the diet. The bottom line here is moderation. Savor a sweet or two but keep an eye on overall nutritional balance. Sweets should accentuate, and not predominate in meals, for a day, a month, or a year.

Sweeteners are used in the kitchen in both crystallized and liquid forms. The most common crystal variety is sucrose. Other forms of sucrose include brown sugar, maple sugar crystals, "raw" sugar, sometimes called turbinado, and fructose. Raw sugar is prohibited from sale by the FDA because of contaminants present, including mold, lint, fibers, and soil. Therefore, sugars billed as "raw" have been cleaned up to remove contaminants and are actually processed.

Fructose is becoming popular both in home kitchens and restaurants. High-fructose syrups produce a lot of sweetness (about 75 percent more than sucrose) per amount used. In home kitchens, fructose is popular because it produces more sweetness for fewer calories. Many proponents see it as a more natural sweetener and others maintain that it does not cause rapid blood sugar fluctuations. The facts are that when fructose is purified and processed into crystals, it is about as "natural" as white and brown and turbinado sugars.

Liquid sweeteners include honey, molasses, corn syrup, invert sugar, and maple, barley, and sorghum syrups. The latter two, which are regaining popularity, are found primarily in health food stores. Honey is formed from flower nectar gathered by bees. Its composition varies depending on the source of nectar and can predominate in either glucose or fructose. It may also contain maltose and sucrose. Honey is up to 50 percent sweeter than sugar, but also contains more calories (64 calories per tablespoon as opposed to 46 calories for one tablespoon of sugar). In fact, with the exception of molasses (43 calories per tablespoon) and fructose (46 calories per tablespoon), other commonly used sweeteners contain more calories per unit than sucrose.

Molasses is the dark liquid that is the result of sugar refining. The more sucrose extracted, the darker the molasses. It is the only sweetener with any nutritive value, albeit small. Iron is the most important of the few minerals it contains, and only frequent consumption of the syrup would make a worthwhile contribution. Corn syrup, another liquid sweetener, is often used in commercial food processing. Look for it on labels, as it is often combined with other sweeteners, such as maple syrup, which then becomes "pancake" syrup. Other sweeteners found on food labels are levulose and dextrose, the technical names for fructose and glucose; and invert sugar, a combination of glucose and fructose that is sweeter than sucrose. It is useful in candy making since it inhibits crystallization.

Sweeteners can be reduced considerably in cooking and baking, with the exception of some items such as angel food cake and genoise, babas, and meringue-based pastries and the like. Most basic cookie, cake, and muffin recipes work fine with as little as half the amount of sweetener specified.

The sweeteners just discussed are collectively referred to as natural sweeteners, even though they are processed to some degree. Another group of sweeteners can be categorized as artificial sweeteners. These sweeteners are popular additions to the kitchen and dining table. The three artificial sweeteners most frequently used in this country are saccharin, aspartame, and a group called polyalcohols (sorbitol, xylitol, mannitol). However, food chemists are constantly on the lookout for safe, low-calorie sweeteners, so people can satisfy their sweet tooths without adding calories and a new sweetener was approved by the FDA in 1988. Acesulfame-K, which is less expensive and more stable than aspartame, has nevertheless generated controversy over its safety. Saccharine, however, is the major sugar substitute in use, but has been under scrutiny because laboratory studies found it to cause bladder cancer in animals. A proposed ban in 1977 was overturned, and a decision was made to study the substance further, placing health warnings on product labels. Aspartame has been approved by the FDA; however, some side effects from its use have been reported. It changes chemically and loses sweetness when heated, so is not a good choice for cooking. Of the polyalcohols, xylitol is under review by the FDA. Side effects of all three, experienced when large amounts are ingested, include diarrhea, gas, and bloating. Sorbitol is used frequently in sugarless chewing gum and chewable vitamins. There are disadvantages to all artificial sweeteners—some major, some minor, and some unknown. Is any potential risk of using them worth sparing the 18 calories a teaspoon of sugar provides? Obviously, sugar substitutes are helpful to diabetics. Whether they really help with weight loss is a matter of debate. It may be advisable for people to reeducate their palates to prefer foods less sweet, and to substitute flavored seltzer waters or fruit drinks for artificially sweetened beverages, for example. To avoid artificial sweeteners altogether, be sure to read labels. They are present in many beverages and foods including cereals. If people who wish to reduce calories eat aspartame-sweetened cereal and then pour cream in their coffee, they are not aiming at the right culprit. They would be better off calorie-wise and health-wise with a teaspoon of sugar on their cereal and skim milk in their coffee.

Fats

The average American diet contains approximately 40 percent fat. Most of this fat comes from meats, eggs, dairy products, desserts, snacks, and the fats and oils added to foods when preparing or eating them. Why the concern over the amount of fat consumed? Why are the media and health professionals pointing their fingers at this macronutrient? The issue at hand is the health implications of a diet that is high in fat. Of course, meat, eggs, and dairy products are nutritious foods that supply important vitamins and minerals. The problem is the amount of high fat foods people eat and the health problems created when these foods are consumed in excess. One solution is choice—choosing prime rib or a marbled steak over leaner cuts of meat or grilled chicken or fish, for example. High fat foods need not be eliminated entirely, but should be consumed infrequently and in moderation. Many people adore ice cream, high-fat cheeses and meats, and pastry and consume these and other high fat foods freely and frequently. Many people, however, are unaware of the amount and type of fat in various foods. The result is that society pays for this excess consumption of high-fat foods with cardiovascular disease, which smolders, in many cases, in the very young, only to strike suddenly during the prime of life.

Cardiovascular disease is the primary cause of death in the United States, and high dietary fat intake—saturated fat in particular—is a major risk factor for this disease. Not only is the relationship between heart disease and fat consumption well documented in the scientific literature, but data is now being gathered which suggests links between high fat intake and some types of cancer.

The Dietary Guidelines for Americans recommend avoiding too much fat, saturated fat, and cholesterol. But, what is the relation between fats and cholesterol in food and fat and cholesterol in the body? And how much is too much?

High consumption of saturated fat and cholesterol results in high levels of blood cholesterol, although this varies considerably from person to person. The body produces cholesterol, and it is present in many foods. And in some cases, the body just does not process cholesterol very well. Heredity is largely responsible for these differences. At any rate, high levels of blood cholesterol can lead to the accumulation of fatty deposits along the arteries, rendering them hard and unexpandable as well as narrowing the passage-way that blood flows through. This is called atherosclerosis, which is the basic underlying problem in most heart and blood vessel diseases. Thus, high blood cholesterol equals greater risk for heart disease, but other risk factors include high blood pressure (especially if present with atherosclerosis), obesity, family history, inactivity, smoking, and reaction to stress.

Foods high in saturated fat and cholesterol tend to raise blood cholesterol levels undesirably high. Excessively high caloric intake also contributes. Although dietary cholesterol may be an important factor for people whose bodies do not handle it properly, for most people, saturated fat is the major food component that raises blood cholesterol levels.

Let us review how the body uses fats in foods people eat. In the intestine, fatty acids with short carbon chains leave through cell walls to enter the circulatory system directly. The long-chain fatty acids, however, reform back into triglycerides. Since these are insoluble in water, they are com-bined with proteins in order to be transported in body fluids. This combina-tion of fat and protein is called lipoprotein. Two forms of lipoprotein, the low-density lipoproteins (LDLs) and high-density lipoproteins (HDLs), and the manner in which they carry cholesterol, play a large role in cardio-vascular health (Figure 3.3). LDLs contain the greatest percentage of cho-lesterol and may be responsible for depositing cholesterol on artery walls. For that reason they could be referred to as "bad" cholesterol. HDL, or high-density lipoprotein, contains the greatest amount of protein and the smallest amount of cholesterol. They are believed to take cholesterol away from cells and transport it back to the liver for processing or removal. High

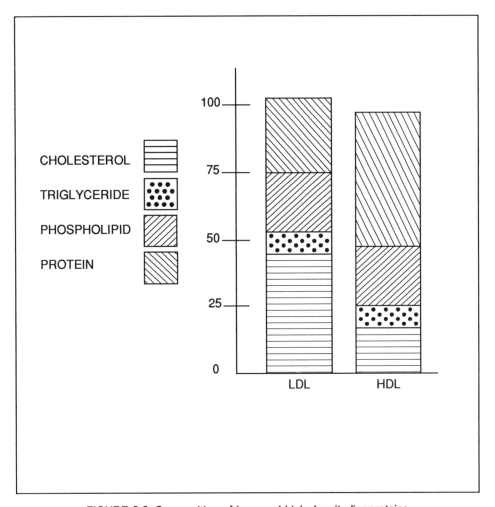

FIGURE 3.3 Composition of low- and high-density lipoproteins.

levels of HDL lower risk factors for heart disease. Thus HDLs could be referred to as "good" cholesterol.

A health goal would be to reduce blood cholesterol levels by reducing the "bad" cholesterol. How can this be done? Blood cholesterol levels can be reduced by decreasing the total amount of fats in the diet and, most importantly, lowering the amount of saturated fats by replacing some with polyunsaturated fats up to 10 percent of total calories. There is now increasing scientific interest in the effect of monounsaturated fats (such as olive oil) on blood cholesterol. Studies indicate that they are as effective as polyunsaturated fats in lowering blood cholesterol. In fact, monounsaturates appear to lower LDLs without affecting HDL levels, whereas polyunsaturated fatty acids lower the beneficial HDLs along with the LDLs. Fish oils, which contain highly unsaturated omega-3 fatty acids, also appear to offer protection from heart disease. They are discussed later with respect to the role of fish in the diet. Another factor that helps fight "bad" cholesterol is exercise, which, when pursued regularly, tends to raise HDLs.

How much fat is too much? It is generally agreed that the amount of total fat in our diets should be lowered to 30 percent or less of the dietary "pie." Of that 30 percent, intake of both saturated and polyunsaturated fats should be less than 10 percent each. Monounsaturated fatty acids would then account for the rest. As for dietary cholesterol itself, a daily limit of approximately 300 milligrams (mg) has been recommended by the American Heart Association, with concurrence by other scientific groups.

Recall from Chapter 1 that cholesterol occurs only in animal foods. Of these foods, some are especially high in cholesterol such as organ meats, eggs, and some ocean foods such as shrimp and squid. Shellfish and shrimp are actually not as high in cholesterol as once thought—only slightly higher than meat and poultry. And they are low in saturated fat. Dr. Richard Wolff, a Boston cardiologist, professor of medicine at Harvard Medical School, enthusiastic cook and cookbook author, maintains that regulating cholesterol becomes automatic once total fat is reduced and saturated, polyunsaturated and monounsaturated fat ratios are acceptable. In other words, if the total fat content of a dish or a meal can be reduced to recommended percentages, acceptable cholesterol levels will probably be met. Dr. Wolff goes on to say that what matters most is not so much the cholesterol and fat in any one dish, but the balance of that dish in a day's intake (Giobbi and Wolff, 1985). It is, in other words, the overall balance of one's diet for a day, a week, a month, and throughout life, that is important. Again, variety—including treats—but also moderation. This is why it is important for the restaurateur to offer low-fat menu alternatives. As people continue to eat more meals away from home, they need to be given opportunities to make healthful food selections.

In the kitchen try relating food selection to the four food groups (see Table 3.1). Remember that foods from the cereal and grain and fruit and vegetable groups are low in fat (avocadoes are the inevitable exception).

Most milk and dairy products are high in fat and saturated fat. Low fat versions of milk and dairy products, ranging from evaporated skim milk to reduced-fat cheeses and low fat or skim milk, however, are plentiful. No cheese is really low fat, however. Most have at least half their calories as fat. With "regular" cheeses coming in at two-thirds to three-fourths of their calories as fat, some low fat versions only reduce these numbers to approximately half while other "low fat" versions can have as much as 80 percent of calories as fat! And many of the low fat versions do not measure up tastewise. When using cheese in cooking, it is best to compensate elsewhere in the dish or the meal. Natural cheeses with less fat include cottage cheese, part-skim mozzarella, feta, and part-skim ricotta. However, a $1\frac{1}{2}$ ounce piece of feta cheese contains approximately 9 grams of fat. This amounts to 81 calories from fat, and over 60 percent of total calories from fat! It is also high in sodium. But cheese is a nutritious food, providing substantial amounts of calcium and riboflavin, in particular; therefore, the answer again is balance and moderation.

As far as the meat group is concerned, fish and skinless chicken contain less fat and much less saturated fat than red meats, even lean cuts. Processed meats such as cold cuts, weiners, and most deli meats are very high in fat.

Fish, especially the oily varieties, now appear to furnish some protection against cardiovascular disease. The polyunsaturated oils in fish contain Omega-3 fatty acids and are different in chemical composition from the polyunsaturates in vegetable oils. They seem to affect our blood platelets, making them less sticky and reducing the likelihood of their clumping together and adhering to artery walls, forming blood clots that can lead to heart attacks and strokes. They also have a positive effect on lowering blood cholesterol. The exact mechanisms by which they work are not yet fully understood. The supplement industry has picked up on the beneficial effects of fish oils; however, taking supplements may be risky, especially since the oils change blood chemistry. It is better to include seafood in the diet two or three times a week. Fish that contain the highest amounts of Omega-3s are the dark-fleshed, fatty ones such as salmon, mackerel, bluefish and tuna. Thus, most fish are relatively low in fat (a four-ounce portion of lean white fish tallies less than 100 calories), and the fat that is present seems to be beneficial.

Fats not found in the four food groups include those in butter, lard, shortening, oils, and nondairy products that substitute for milk and cream.

TABLE 3.1 Selected Nutrient Composition of Frequently Used Fats and Oils

	Serving Size	Total Fat (g)	Saturated Fatty Acids (g)	Mono-unsaturated Fatty Acids (g)	Poly-unsaturated Fatty Acids (g)	Cholesterol (mg)	Food Energy (cal)
Peanut butter	2 tbsp	16.0	3.0	7.4	4.6	0	190
Bacon (cooked crisp)	2 slices	6.2	2.2	3.0	0.7	11	73
Bacon, Canadian (unheated)[a]	3¼ oz	6.4	2.0	2.9	0.6	46	145
Butter	1 tbsp	14.2	7.1	3.3	0.4	31	102
Lard	1 tbsp	12.8	5.0	5.8	1.4	12	115
Tub margarines: Safflower oil, liquid[b,c]	1 tbsp	11.4	1.3	3.3	6.3	0	102
Corn oil, liquid[b,c]	1 tbsp	11.4	2.0	4.5	4.4	0	102
Stick margarines: Corn oil, liquid[b,c]	1 tbsp	11.4	2.0	5.5	3.4	0	102
Stick or tub margarines: partially hydrogenated or hardened fat[b,c]	1 tbsp	11.4	2.2	4.9	3.7	0	102
Imitation margarine (diet)[c]	1 tbsp	5.5	1.1	2.2	2.0	0	49

Mayonnaise	1 tbsp	11.0	1.6	3.1	5.7	8	99
Vegetable shortening (hydrogenated)	1 tbsp	12.8	3.2	5.7	3.1	0	113
Polyunsaturated oils: corn oil	1 tbsp	13.6	1.7	3.3	8.0	0	120
Cottonseed oil	1 tbsp	13.6	3.5	2.4	7.1	0	120
Safflower oil	1 tbsp	13.6	1.2	1.6	10.1	0	120
Sesame oil	1 tbsp	13.6	1.9	5.4	5.7	0	120
Soybean oil	1 tbsp	13.6	2.0	3.2	7.9	0	120
Soybean oil (lightly hydrogenated)	1 tbsp	13.6	2.0	5.9	5.1	0	120
Sunflower oil	1 tbsp	13.6	1.4	2.7	8.9	0	120
Monounsaturated oils: olive oil	1 tbsp	13.5	1.8	9.9	1.1	0	119
Peanut oil	1 tbsp	13.5	2.3	6.2	4.3	0	119
Saturated oil: coconut oil	1 tbsp	13.6	11.8	0.8	0.2	0	117

[a]Canadian bacon is much leaner than was previously reported in Agric. Hb. 8, 1963.
[b]First ingredient as listed on label.
[c]Summary of available data. Composition of margarine changes periodically. Follow guidelines in section on shopping tips when purchasing margarine.

SOURCE: Reprinted with permission from *The American Heart Association Cookbook*, 4th ed., Copyright by The American Heart Association. Published by David McKay, Company, Inc., 1984.

Some nondairy products contain highly saturated coconut, palm and palm kernel oils. While most oils and some nondairy products are cholesterol free, it is saturated fat that is of greatest concern in raising blood cholesterol levels. Become a label reader. It may be better to offer customers milk or even half and half. Some nondairy creamers are made from soy oil, which is cholesterol free, and while not as high in saturated fat, has more total fat than milk. The best thing to do is offer customers a choice and let them decide. Chances are, many of them do not realize the benefits of switching from nondairy creamers to plain old milk.

Protein

A large steak, a baked potato with sour cream, and an iceburg lettuce salad with Roquefort dressing—this is still a popular meal that can be found in many restaurants and homes. Americans have had a long-lasting love affair with meat, particularly beef. Meat has been seen as a body builder and cure-all. Over the years, however, it has been learned that there are drawbacks to a diet that is too high in protein, emphasizing large portions of meat to the exclusion of other foods, including nonmeat sources of protein. Of course, people need protein, and meats provide important vitamins and minerals as well, but many people tend to go overboard and consume far too much.

There are drawbacks to eating excessive amounts of protein. Most protein in meat is packaged with fat, and well marbled meats can be up to 80 percent fat. Chicken and fish are exceptions, with some fish having as little as 10 percent fat. Many red meats are high in saturated fat as well as total fat, whereas chicken and fish are not only lower in fat, but the fat they do contain is mostly polyunsaturated. Vegetable protein sources, on the other hand, are very low in total fat, contributing most of their calories as starch. What this really boils down to is type of protein food and amount. The popular meal described earlier provides more than enough protein. And it is high in fat—from the steak, sour cream, and the salad dressing. This is not a balanced meal, and fat comprises the lion's share of the macronutrients. This meal would not fit into the dietary pie. Another long-standing popular meal, the ubiquitous restaurant "diet" platter consisting of hamburger, cottage cheese, and peach half, is another high protein, high fat meal that is still found on menus far too often.

A high protein diet may contribute an excess of fat. In addition, a lot of protein causes the kidneys to work harder to excrete nitrogen wastes from protein metabolism. High protein intakes are also thought to negatively influence calcium loss from the body. Most athletes do not need extra protein either. An excess will be used for energy or be converted to fat, but it will not be used to build more muscle. Clearly, consuming enough protein is important; overdoing it, however, could lead to health problems, especially if the protein foods are high in saturated fat.

How much protein is enough? The RDAs allow 0.8 grams (g) of protein for each kilogram (2.2 pounds) of body weight. Therefore, a 120-pound woman would need 44 to 46 grams per day (depending on age), and a 154-pound man would need 56 grams per day. These amounts are easily exceeded with typical American meat-centered meals, which may account for over 100 grams of protein a day! The steak in the popular meal just described was probably over 10 ounces and provided over 40 grams of protein. The amount of protein in the dietary pie should ideally measure 12 to 15 percent if fats contribute 30 percent or less and a 55 to 60 percent wedge is devoted to carbohydrates. One way to achieve these ratios is to choose protein foods that are lower in fat. This means using more lean meats and removing all excess fat from meat. It also means eating less. Smaller portions of meat are more acceptable to customers if portions of accompanying foods such as vegetables and grains are increased. Fish and chicken are good alternatives to red meats and can be more versatile in terms of preparation options. Another alternative is to obtain protein from nonmeat sources. Many people are reducing the amount of animal protein in their diets and are substituting plant protein foods. People who consume meat can certainly have a healthful diet; however, some people are abandoning meat altogether for a vegetarian diet. The reasons for the switch are varied: some do it for health reasons, switching to avoid the fat that accompanies most meats; others do it for philosophical or religious reasons; many do it out of economic necessity; and some prefer to eat foods low on the food chain, thus avoiding many of the accumulated contaminants in foods high on the chain, such as meat (Chapter 5). Contaminants may include antibiotics, hormones, and other chemicals which are added to animal feed or are given directly to the animals themselves, e.g., veterinary drugs.

There are several categories of vegetarians. A vegan, or total vegetarian, eats only foods of plant origin; lacto-vegetarians also eat milk and other dairy products; lacto-ovo vegetarians include eggs. Some vegetarians exclude land animals but will eat fish. Others exclude only red meats but eat chicken. Those people who really like meat, but wish to cut back for health purposes, may have two meatless meals per day or three meatless days per week, for example. Some people follow a macrobiotic diet, which is based on a philosophy regarding the chemical balance of foods eaten in a meal and was traditionally a series of progressively restrictive regimens resulting in a diet consisting only of brown rice. A more liberal version, practiced by most macrobiotics now, may be quite adequate for most adults but, as with vegan diets, may be problematic for pregnant women, infants, and growing children. Many macrobiotics include fish or chicken in meals, although the emphasis is on grains.

Vegetarian diets are usually high in fiber and complex carbohydrates, low in fat, and adequate in protein. But fat can become excessive for vegetarians if they rely heavily on high fat cheeses, sour cream, nuts, and nut butters. Also, since the protein in plant foods is not complete (see Chapter 1), vegetarians have to make sure they eat a variety of these protein foods so that amino acids not provided by one are provided by the other. This means combining the major sources of vegetable protein—grains, legumes, nuts, and seeds. Legumes, for example, could be included with either grains or seeds. If dairy products and eggs are used, this makes it easier, since they contain complete or high-quality protein. Many ethnic and American regional and traditional food combinations provide a complementary balance of proteins such as cereal and milk, peanut butter on whole grain bread, baked beans and brown bread, succotash, tortillas with beans, or black beans and rice. The word complementary simply describes two incomplete protein foods, each of which provides amino acid(s) the other is missing, thus providing a complete protein between them when combined.

Grain-based foods are a staple of vegetarian diets. Because these foods are filling, vegetarians as a group seem to consume fewer calories and have fewer weight problems. Some vitamins and minerals may be in short supply; these include B_{12}, D, calcium, iron, and zinc. Vitamin B_{12} may be a particular problem for vegans, since they must rely on sources such as fortified soy milk, meat analogues, or cereals. Fortified soy milk can also be a source of calcium, as can tofu, depending on the brand. Maintenance of adequate iron stores may be difficult for vegan athletes.

The typical American diet is high in fat, sugar, sodium, and calories. It is also low in fiber. There are many health advantages to vegetarian diets that are low in fat and high in complex carbohydrates and fiber. Perhaps it is time to rethink food choices, particularly meat. Many restaurants offering healthy menu alternatives compensate for smaller portions of meat with an assortment of creatively prepared vegetables. In fact, there is actually far more choice of vegetables over the seasons than there are types and cuts of meat. In the past, overcooking and lack of attention have lowered the appreciation of vegetables; now, fortunately, vegetables are reappearing on a grand scale — mostly as a result of customer demand. As people become more health-conscious, the composition of the plate will become more balanced.

Fish is increasing in popularity as a low-fat meat substitute. But a word is in order concerning possible health hazards associated with partially cooked or raw fish, particularly shellfish. Severe gastroenteritis, with its accompanying diarrhea, cramps, and vomiting, as well as hepatitis, cholera, and typhoid, can result from consuming raw or undercooked "filter feeding" shellfish such as clams, oysters, mussels, and scallops from sewage-contaminated water. (Scallops are usually safe in the United States because only the muscle is eaten.)

Shellfish-harvesting areas are monitored using bacterial tests, and state agencies then classify shellfish-growing areas according to sanitary conditions. It is still risky, however, to eat raw shellfish, since the consumer cannot be absolutely sure of the source. Steaming, a popular way to cook clams and mussels, can be problematic since the shells open before the internal temperature rises high enough to inactivate viruses. This takes 4 to 6 minutes.

Other contamination problems include industrial compounds, heavy metals such as mercury, pesticides and other water-quality problems, and worms and parasites. Problems related to parasites are a concern only when raw or marinade-cured seafood is eaten. Cooking and freezing destroys the critters, and seafood processors make every effort to detect their presence. In general, most of the common ones are not harmful to humans. Cooking raw fish for 10 minutes at 140°F (60°C) or freezing it for 24 hours below −4°F (−20°C) will kill any worms (Faria, Massachusetts Division of Marine Fisheries, 1984).

Seafood contaminants vary with the species, food habits, size and age, fat content, and water of origin. In general, the larger and fatter the fish, the more contaminants may accumulate. The U.S. Food and Drug Administration monitors and sets contaminant levels (Faria, Massachusetts Division of Marine Fisheries, 1984); and local public health departments will know if any problems exist in their area. Meanwhile, enjoy a variety of fresh seafood for its health benefits. The hazards are small in comparison, when commonsense precautions are taken in selection and preparation.

Salt

Ordinary table salt is composed of 40 percent sodium and 60 percent chloride. It is liberally sprinkled into foods both during cooking and eating to enhance flavor. The problem is that people consume too much and high intakes have been linked to hypertension, which in turn can increase the risk of heart and kidney disease, and strokes. Only about 20 percent of the population is sodium sensitive, or reactive to even small amounts of it, but there is no way to tell who is and who is not until problems begin to appear. Since studies have shown that population groups with a high incidence of hypertension (high blood pressure) also consume a lot of sodium, recommendations for intake have been established at a maximum of 3,000 milligrams per day, slightly more than 1 teaspoon of salt. Most people consume three or more times this amount.

Salt is an acquired taste. Social and dietary customs have traditionally included reaching for the salt and sprinkling liberally. It is true—not everyone is affected by this habit, and other factors are being examined in relation to hypertension, such as calcium deficiency and blood lipid levels. But in light of the consequences, it would not hurt to cut back to recommended levels. An easy way to measure how much salt is added during or after cooking is to place a piece of waxed paper over the pan or the dish and season as usual. Then measure the amount of salt on the paper. The amount may be surprising. It is not difficult for individuals to control the amount of salt added to foods. However, most of what is ingested has been added by others to processed foods or foods eaten away from home. Even products such as over-the-counter medicines, baking powder, food preservatives, MSG, saccharine, tap water, and water softeners contain sodium. Fortunately, some product manufacturers are offering low and no-salt alternatives.

In July 1986, the FDA put regulations into force that require food manufacturers to list the milligrams of sodium per serving on all nutrition labels. A product labeled low sodium must not contain over 140 milligrams of sodium, those labeled sodium free must contain less than 5 milligrams of sodium, and reduced sodium food must have 75 percent less sodium than the product it replaces. No salt added means only that no salt has been added during processing; it does not account for naturally occurring sodium. Very low sodium indicates 35 milligrams or less, and although no manufacturer would want the words high sodium on the product label, anything over 150 milligrams is getting into the high range.

Most fresh foods are low in sodium, and plain frozen vegetables are usually processed without added salt. Frozen dinners, frozen diet meals, and prepared foods can be extremely high in sodium. However, consumers can read labels to determine more accurately which products are high in sodium. Foods to be used in moderation include condiments, sauces, commercial baked goods, cheeses, canned vegetables, meats, mixes, soups, snack foods, and fast foods. Cured meats and fish are also high in sodium.

To reduce sodium in the kitchen, remember that fresh foods taste good by themselves. Flavor enhancers that add zip to foods include onions, garlic, peppers, dry mustard, lemon juice, and herbs. Experiment with other products such as aromatic bitters or vinegars. Concentrating natural food flavors is a key. Whichever technique or ingredient is used should enhance the food, not overwhelm it. Freshness of product is important in this regard. The fresher it is, the less it is necessary to add flavor.

Salt substitutes are available. Most are mixtures of ground herbs and spices; however, some may contain other flavoring substances as well. Flaked salt is not really low in sodium. Because of its flat flakes, as opposed to crystals, it takes up more space in a volume measure, thus requiring less to fill it. By weight, though, these flakes have the same amount of sodium as regular salt. Some substitutes contain potassium salts and should not be used without a doctor's approval. They are certainly not appropriate for restaurant use. Appendix A lists the sodium content of many common foods. Be sure to compare the values between fresh and processed foods.

Beverages

Beverages might be defined as liquids for drinking. They are, however, usually thought of in more specific terms such as coffee and tea, soft drinks, juices, and alcoholic drinks. Only recently have bottled waters been added to menus in this country.

Plain water, the best drink to satisfy the body's fluid requirements, is no longer obtained only from taps. However, many people are drinking their water from bottles. For some, taste is a factor. Because water differs in its composition from area to area, it also varies in taste; chemical purification can alter its taste. But concern over the purity of groundwater supplies is the major reason people have switched to bottled waters. Chlorination has pretty much eliminated infectious disease organisms from water, but chemical pollution has created a new breed of contaminant. This pollution comes from various sources, including runoff from paved surface areas, pesticides, industrial pollutants, natural gas, and toxic waste storage and disposal areas. Another reason many people are drinking bottled waters is that they have become a low calorie substitute for alcoholic beverages. Some are flavored with fruit essences, and although domestic waters have not become as prestigious as their European counterparts, sales of bottled waters to Americans are steadily increasing.

Bottled waters fall into three general categories: mineral waters, soda waters, and bottled waters. Most mineral water comes from government-regulated springs. Be sure the label contains the words "natural spring water" and "bottled at the spring." Avoid those that say "spring type" or "spring pure;" they could contain water from anywhere. Since all water contains minerals, almost any bottled water could legally be labeled as such, so read the label carefully if it is from a regulated source.

Soda waters are defined by the U.S. Food and Drug Administration as "beverages made by absorbing carbon dioxide in potable water" (U.S. Food and Drug Administration, 1983). They include colas, club soda, seltzer, and sparkling waters, all from a tap source.

Bottled waters other than mineral and soda waters fall under a set of quality standards set by the FDA, which include maximum tolerance levels for various substances as well as bacteriological, chemical and radioactive substances standards. Most bottled waters come from local supplies and contain the same substances as those found in the tap. The bottom line is to avoid serving or ingesting any water that is murky, discolored or odorous. Choose waters bottled directly at the spring; a statement on the label regarding source is the best assurance that the water is actually from that spring. If cost is a concern, local tap water may be the best choice, since local bottled waters are most likely the same thing. All tap water must meet the Environmental Protection Agency's (EPA) national standards for drinking water.

Coffee and tea are both popular beverages; however, caffeine has come under fire in reports linking it to several health concerns. Again, used in moderation, coffee and tea can add variety to beverages consumed. Caffeine acts as a stimulant, and many people consume large quantities to keep going throughout the day. One or two cups should be the limit. Incidentally, two cups of tea provide as much caffeine as one cup of coffee of equal volume. Many cola drinks also contain caffeine. It would be wise to tally all of the sources of caffeine in the diet to avoid possible side effects of restlessness or increased heartbeat.

Many people are switching to decaffeinated coffee and herb teas. Water extraction methods of decaffeination are available for those concerned over chemicals used in the process. This method is definitely preferred if coffee is consumed regularly. Herb teas have their separate set of problems. Read the labels, as all are not caffeine-free. Think of herb teas as being made from plants—the source of many drugs on pharmacy shelves. Although their concentration of chemicals is low, caution and moderation should be exercised when drinking any herb tea. Some herbs, such as senna, comfrey, lobelia, and licorice root, for example, can be toxic in large amounts. Others, like chamomile and marigold, can cause allergic reactions. Also, some loose teas may contain contaminants that have probably been eliminated by well-known packaging companies. Read the label and choose herb teas with fewer, more familiar ingredients rather than those with a multitude of unfamiliar ingredients. Consult a pharmacist or pharmacy department of a hospital or university when there is doubt about potential side effects of an herb.

Alcoholic beverages are mood-altering drinks that anesthetize the mind and are toxic to the body. The effects of the drink depend on its concentration of alcohol, how much is consumed over a period of time, body weight and emotional state. The amount and kind of food consumed before or during drinking, if any, also has an effect. Blood alcohol level determines its effects; the speed at which you drink, coupled with food and body size factors, determine this level.

Alcohol is rapidly absorbed from the stomach and small intestine into the blood stream. The faster you drink, the faster alcohol reaches the brain, resulting in impaired judgment and muscle coordination, and speech impediment. When alcohol levels rise to the point where brain centers that affect breathing and heartbeat become impaired, they can become lethal.

There seems to be a general consensus in the scientific literature that moderate alcohol consumption amounts to one, perhaps two drinks daily. Above this, one moves into the lower end of the heavy scale.

Alcohol negatively affects every cell in the body. Brain cells die and are not replaced; liver cells die and are otherwise altered, resulting in liver disease and cirrhosis, an accumulation of fat in liver cells that can lead to death. Even a little alcohol alters body metabolism processes. Alcohol also acts as a diuretic by suppressing the hormone responsible for retaining body water, resulting in dehydration and loss of important minerals needed for physiological reactions. More recently, alcohol has been implicated with breast cancer. Alcohol contains no significant amounts of nutrients and, in fact, inhibits absorption and utilization of several vitamins. At 7 calories per gram, it eats away at total calorie requirements, perhaps edging out foods providing necessary nutrients.

If too much alcohol has been consumed, there is no way to get rid of it—except to wait out the slow metabolic process. In fact, some studies have indicated that physical impairment may linger to some degree even after blood alcohol has disappeared. Congeners, substances produced during the distillation and fermentation of alcohol, contribute to the unpleasant effects of overindulgence. It is thought that darker alcoholic beverages, such as bourbon, contain more of these substances than white ones, such as gin. But much of the effect is caused by dehydration and the disruption of physiological processes.

Should everyone stop drinking? The answer again is moderation. There is nothing wrong with a drink or two at a social gathering or some wine with a meal. These beverages can enhance the pleasure of these occasions. There are, however, situations in which people should not drink, such as when driving or operating machinery. Also, drugs (whether medicinal or recreational) and alcohol do not mix, and the combination can be fatal. Alcohol can also reduce or negate the effectiveness of certain medications. Pregnant women should refrain from drinking, since alcohol reaches the bloodstream of the fetus and even at low levels can be harmful. The same goes for nursing mothers, since alcohol passes into the mother's milk.

There have been reports regarding the health benefits of one or two drinks a day, especially with regard to preventing cardiovascular disease. In the case of the latter, it is now known that alcohol does increase the levels of one kind of HDL cholesterol; however, it is the wrong one. The right kind is increased by exercise, which is much healthier and is an established protective indicator. In general, the health risks associated with drinking alcoholic beverages far outweigh any unconfirmed beneficial effects.

In the restaurant, offer a wide variety of nonalcoholic beverages, ranging from cider and sparkling fruit juices to assorted waters, alcohol-free wines and beers, and mixed concoctions. Customers will appreciate the choice.

Fiber

Fiber, a complex carbohydrate, comes from plants. It is not digestible by humans, which is perhaps why it has also been referred to as roughage. Foods high in fiber include grains, legumes, nuts, fruits, and vegetables. All contain a mixture of fiber types; however, fruits, vegetables and oats contain more water-soluble fiber, whereas whole grains and the skins of fruits and vegetables are higher in water-insoluble fiber. Cellulose, hemicellulose, and lignin fall into the water-insoluble category, pectins into the water-soluble. This is becoming an important distinction. Insoluble fiber, such as that in wheat bran, absorbs water, increases stool bulk, and helps move food through the intestines. This is thought to help prevent some gastrointestinal problems including constipation, diverticulosis, hemorrhoids, and colon cancer. Soluble fiber such as that in oat bran, fruits, and vegetables — particularly dried beans and peas — now appear to have a beneficial effect in lowering blood cholesterol levels.

The food industry has seen these links between dietary fiber and disease as a marketing tool. Cereal manufacturers are touting the health benefits of their products on labels, and oat bran now has its own shelf space among cereals and grains. Other manufacturers are offering fiber in pill form and high fiber cookies. Retail food stores are pushing raw wheat and oat bran by the bagful. To increase fiber intake, eat more whole grain foods, legumes, and fruits and vegetables. In the restaurant, emphasize these foods in the breadbasket as well as on the plate. Fiber recommendations suggest about 25 to 35 grams per day; the average person probably consumes less than 11. There are, for example, 8 grams of fiber in ½ cup of cooked dried beans, peas, or lentils or ⅓ cup of 100 percent bran cereal. There are 5 grams in 1 cup of whole wheat pasta, a medium orange or banana; 3 grams in ½ cup of broccoli or corn or 1 small potato; and 2 grams in 1 slice of whole wheat bread or ½ bran, corn, or oat muffin. Cooked legumes can provide up to 9 grams of fiber in ½ cup.

Too much fiber also can be problematic. Overdoing it may cause minerals in foods to become unavailable, since fiber binds them so they are merely excreted in the stool. Constipation or even blockage may result from very high intake if water is insufficient. So obtain adequate fiber from natural food sources. (Processing, such as the refining of grain and canning of fruits and vegetables, eliminates much of their fiber content.)

REFERENCES

Brewster, L., and Jacobson, M. F. 1982. *The Changing American Diet.* Washington, D.C.: Center for Science in the Public Interest.

Brody, J. 1985. *Jane Brody's Good Food Book.* New York: W. W. Norton.

Faria, S. 1984. *A Manual of Seafood Products, Marketing and Utilization.* Boston, Mass.: Massachusetts Division of Marine Fisheries.

Giobbi, E., and Wolff, R. 1985. *Eat Right, Eat Well—The Italian Way.* New York: Knopf.

Gussow, J., and Guthrie, H. A. 1985. On withholding the revised RDA's. *Journal of Nutrition Education 17* (5), 191–196.

Lappe, F. M. 1982 *Diet for a Small Planet.* New York: Ballantine Books.

Leaf, A. 1986. Fish story. *Harvard Medical School Health Letter 10* (8), 5–7.

Tufts University. 1985. Benefits of eating fish. *Diet and Nutrition Letter 3* (5), 1–3.

Tufts University. 1986. Your nutrient needs: The facts behind the numbers. *Diet and Nutrition Letter 4* (2), 3–7.

U.S. Department of Agriculture. 1985. *Dietary Guidelines for Americans.* 2nd ed.

U.S. Food and Drug Administration. 1983. The water that goes into bottles. *FDA Consumer* (May), 5–7.

University of California. 1986. Artificial sweeteners compared. *Wellness Letter 2* (4), 3.

Winston, M., and Eshleman, R. (Eds.). 1985. *American Heart Association Cookbook.* New York: David McKay.

Chapter 4

FOOD CHOICE CONSIDERATIONS FOR SPECIAL GROUPS AND PLACES

Food Choices for Children and Teens

School Foodservices

School foodservices may be responsible for providing the most nutritionally balanced foods students eat all day — regardless of whether the dining facility is an elementary lunchroom or a high school or college cafeteria. The word may is used because not only would the meals have to be planned and prepared with good nutrition in mind, but the students would have to have eaten the foods offered. These two factors describe challenges found in many institutional food service settings — achieving or maintaining quality food with taste appeal and high nutritional value, and mitigating plate waste.

School meals can have an important influence on eating habits that may persist long after schooling is completed. Unappetizing meals can send students off to snack machines and fast food places or cause them to simply skip the meal entirely. On the other hand, if food is nutritionally balanced, tasty, and attractive, they are most likely to develop an appreciation for these attributes and rely less on popular fast food items as substitutes.

The challenge of working in school foodservice is to offer simple, colorful, carefully prepared meals that are still within the bottom line budgetwise. Although difficult, it is not impossible to provide good-tasting fresh food even when saddled with high employee turnover, a tight budget, and a less than desirable physical plant.

One way to tackle the problem of food appeal — and plate waste — is to establish a line of communication with both students and parents. An advisory committee, or even something as simple as suggestion or survey cards, will indicate concern about their feelings toward the food.

The school cafeteria or lunchroom environment also influences attitudes toward food. It may or may not be changeable; however, there are several approaches to food service that can improve the quality and appeal of the foods. Many of these principles have been discussed, such as variety, balance, freshness of the foods, and care in preparation. Plan menus for nutritional balance using the four food groups as the basis for incorporating individual food items into the menu cycle. Make sure menus include foods with varied textures and colors. Even random selection should provide some textural and visual interest. Also see to it that hot foods are hot and cold foods are cold. Provide a balance between strong flavors and aromas and less assertive items. Keep empty calorie sweets at a minimum, offering instead choices such as frozen yogurt, fruit juice bars, fresh fruit, homemade custards and puddings, and oatmeal cookies. Use fresh foods in lieu of processed and prepared items. Offer a variety of natural fruit juices and low-fat and skim, as well as regular, milk. Salad bars, which include variations on macaroni and potato salads and coleslaw, cottage cheese, fruits, and rice- and grain-based salads in addition to the usual lettuce toppings offer more interest and variety for older children. Make salad dressings from scratch, using buttermilk or yogurt as a base. Include whole-grain breads and rolls as well as made-from-scratch soups. Introduce new salad and soup recipes every week as substitutes for regular items. Keep in mind, however, that extensive salad bars are not appropriate for young children, who are better off with a preplated meal, finger foods, or sandwich choices with fruit and milk.

Many schools participate in the federally subsidized school lunch program. The program has guidelines for amounts and types of food served, which include 2 ounces (oz) of meat or meat substitute such as eggs, cheese, dried beans or peas; two or more servings of fruits and/or vegetables; the equivalent of a slice of bread (which could also be pizza crust, noodles, pasta, grains, etc.); 2 teaspoons of butter or margarine and 1 cup of milk. If students eat all the foods offered, they will obtain one-third of the RDAs for almost all nutrients. An amendment, however, has been added to the program requirements to decrease waste. It allows students to choose foods from three out of the five groups. In other words, any two items can be omitted if they do not appeal. Therefore, a student could end up with a cup of milk, a roll, and an orange, or a hot dog on a roll and milk, for example. Vegetables, usually because of overcooking, are often avoided.

But it is possible to offer popular foods and still meet program requirements. A vegetable and cheese calzone, fruit, and milk would appeal to high school and college students. And the guidelines offer ample room for creative combinations and for the comfort foods and finger foods appropriate for young children (Food and Nutrition Service 1975).

Because of the wide range of abilities of food preparation workers in most institutional settings, it is up to foodservice professionals to make a work plan that carefully spells out everything that has to be done, when to do it, and who will do it. Standardized recipes will result in products that are nutritionally consistent if directions are followed. They should also include variations. Provide precise information regarding weights and measures of ingredients, method of combining ingredients, proper cooking utensils that are the correct sizes, temperature and length of time for cooking, number of servings and size of servings. Careful attention to preparation techniques not only contributes to the nutritional quality of the meal but also to its palatability and attractiveness, assuming food products are of good quality to begin with.

Alternatives to the school lunch program include brown bag lunches brought from home. Perhaps schools should prepare brown bag lunches that students could purchase to eat in the lunchroom or outside; this might be more appealing than the structure of a cafeteria line. A suitable brown bag lunch includes a protein source, fresh fruits and/or vegetables, bread or starch, and a beverage, preferably milk, or alternatively fruit juice, much the same as the food in federal lunch programs.

Protein foods do not always have to go into sandwiches. Instead, offer cold baked or barbequed chicken, roast beef, or hot soup or stew in a thermos from home. Other homemade brown bag choices are yogurt; leftover pizza; vegetables such as celery and peppers stuffed with cottage cheese, other cheese, chopped veggies or rice; or "crepes" in which meat, cheese and other fillings are wrapped in lettuce leaves and secured with a toothpick. Desserts can be nutritious also; consider fresh and dried fruits, perhaps combined with a few nuts, seeds, or homemade oatmeal, granola, raisin or nut cookies. Remember, sugar and butter can be reduced in most cookie recipes without harming the finished product. Stuffed dates or small peanut butter or cream cheese balls rolled in wheat germ or toasted seeds are good for young children. Prepackaged mixes add saturated fat, sugar, and additives but little nutritive value (Giant Foods 1983).

Restaurant Food for Children and Teens

Another alternative to school lunch is the fast-food restaurant. Unfortunately, this type of eating establishment also accounts for a high percentage of all meals consumed by teenagers and children. And fast-food franchises are taking over many school foodservice operations, thus narrowing food choice options considerably.

Whole categories of foods can be lacking in a steady fast-food diet: Intake of fruits and vegetables, whole grains, and milk usually falls short. Moreover, drinking soft drinks instead of milk can lead to calcium deficiencies. The typical meal of a burger, fried chicken, or fish accompanied by french fries and a soft drink or shake is high in saturated fat, cholesterol, sodium, and refined carbohydrate. Pizza and other ethnic fast foods may have a slightly different nutrient composition, but most are still high in fat and sodium. Even though some companies are now providing salad bars and have switched to vegetable oils for frying, the fat, sugar, and sodium—not to mention calories—remain high. The calories, in fact, could amount to over 60 percent of the daily requirement for most people—and this is just one meal! The high calorie content may make it difficult for teenage females, who have lower calorie requirements than teenage males, to maintain weight without sacrificing other more nutritious foods.

Fast foods appeal to both children and adults in general. Most advertising, however, is aimed at children, emphasizing that fast foods are fun, quick to eat, and easy to eat—all appealing qualities to this age group, not to mention busy parents. It would therefore be beneficial if more fast food operations attempted to improve their fare nutritionally by offering choices such as whole-grain rolls, salad bars containing raw vegetable sources of vitamins A and C, baked and grilled chicken and fish, oven-roasted potatoes, milk and fruit juices, and desserts such as frozen yogurt and fruit ices and fresh fruit parfait cups. Children who grow up on a diet of salty, fatty foods will most likely follow that pattern of food preferences throughout life. (Center for Science in the Public Interest 1986). Despite the increasing adult interest in nutrition as it relates to health, this interest does not seem to be filtering down to children and teens. Nevertheless, the fast food industry should continue to improve its efforts to offer healthful choices and product nutrition information.

It is important for restaurants in which families dine with small children to be aware of children's food preferences and their ability to handle food. Most restaurant portions—even from children's menus—are too large. Small children do not eat very much. They like eye appeal and foods which retain their familiar identity. Finger foods are especially appropriate. Small plates and glasses are easier for them to handle. Straws may be difficult for the very young. Foods which are hard to chew, or which might be choked on, should be avoided. Nuts, seeds, raisins, and hard meats such as pork chops or some cuts of beef fall into this category.

Offer a choice of appropriate food in small portions from the regular menu, or develop a children's menu. Keep it short, though, as too many options make it difficult for them to decide. "Fast foods" which can also be easily eaten, such as cereal-coated, baked boneless chicken breast strips or grilled cheese on whole wheat bread, or for older children, muffin or pita pizzas, are usually well liked. Soups are sometimes messy. Finger food, such as apple slices or banana chunks, make good dessert items. Use imagination in presentation, but keep the food itself simple—no mushrooms in the peas, no sauces. Kids like recognizable, individual foods—exceptions may be pasta such as macaroni and cheese, or lasagna, if they are used to it at home. Avoid highly spiced foods. Make the child feel at home and instruct servers to quickly remove food that obviously won't be eaten.

As more and more families dine out, and food away from home provides a regular source of their diet, it is important to keep in mind that the nutritional quality of meals for young patrons is an important consideration.

Food Choices for the Elderly

Americans are living longer. A child born in 1982 can expect to live to about 75 years of age, and a person who was 62 that year could expect to average another 17 years. The aging process is just now being studied to find out why certain physiological changes occur, many of which are degenerative in nature. It is thought that many of these changes are the result of life-style "disuse" in terms of diet and exercise. Diet and exercise habits can be changed, and research continues on what types of dietary changes are most beneficial and how much exercise is enough.

Eleven percent of the U.S. population is over 65 years old. By the year 2030, this number is expected to increase to 23 percent. What this means for foodservice professionals is that they will be feeding an increasing number of elderly people, in both institutional and commercial settings. It is, therefore, important to be familiar with food-related changes that occur during the aging process in order to better provide appropriate food choices for this age group.

The rate at which the body uses energy decreases with age, although this can be offset to some degree by exercise. In the elderly, lean body tissue decreases and body fat increases. Even if a person were to weigh the same at 70 as at 30, the body would be fatter. Also, body metabolism rates decline about 10 percent after age 50. Food intake, therefore, is generally lower for the elderly, to maintain desired body weight or perhaps because of physical or socioeconomic factors.

Other changes may include a decreased sense of smell and taste, which often affects appetite; dental problems, which result in chewing difficulty; and changes in the gastrointestinal tract, which may cause food-related discomfort and result in reduced absorption of nutrients. Other factors influencing the eating habits of elderly include economic status, loneliness, physical inability to shop and prepare food, and general health status (see Figure 4.1).

When planning menus for elderly people, whether in government programs, institutions, commercial restaurants, or retirement facilities, apply the following guidelines: Emphasize nutrient-dense foods from the four food groups, with an eye to keeping calories down. Make sure the presentation is attractive and the food is tasty, especially when sensory perceptions are diminished. For many elderly, eating may be one of the few pleasures

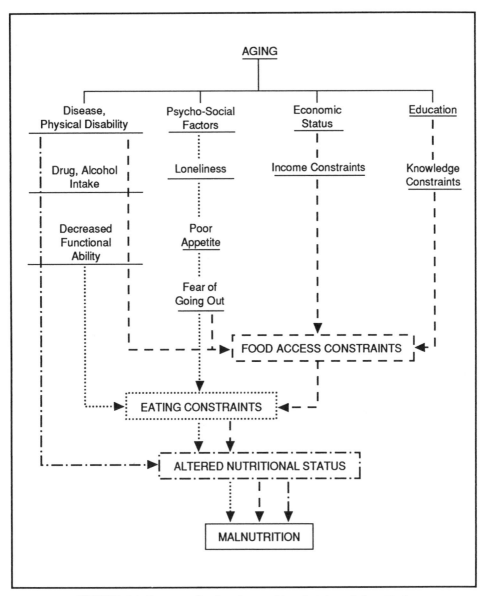

FIGURE 4.1 Factors affecting the nutritional status of the elderly.

they have, so it is up to the foodservice operation to offer appealing foods for this group.

Select and prepare foods in ways that minimize sodium, fat, and saturated fat. Avoid convenience foods—they are costly and usually high in fat and/or sodium. Calcium intake is generally low for the elderly as a group. Therefore, try to incorporate calcium-rich foods such as low fat milk and milk products into meals whenever possible. Dried skim milk powder is inexpensive and can be added to many foods, including breakfast cereals, soups, meat loaf, scalloped potatoes, and desserts. If lactose intolerance is a problem, offer alternatives such as cultured milk products. Emphasize whole-grain breads and cereals and fresh fruits and vegetables.

Provide variety in food textures. Many elderly persons dislike pureed foods and these are usually unnecessary. Offer chopped or grated foods, which are preferable. Cooked vegetables should be tender—never mushy, watery, or colorless. Avoid very hard foods or those with hard crusts that are difficult to chew; bite-size pieces help. Also avoid sticky foods. Very ripe or cooked fruits or naturally soft fruits such as bananas, papayas, and nectarines are a good base for desserts. Sherbets, fruit ices, and low fat frozen yogurts are usually popular.

Seat those who dine alone next to a window or near a fireplace if possible. Do not banish them to a far corner of the dining room. Chances are they eat most of their meals alone and welcome some activity. Ask if they wish to be seated with another elderly person if the situation presents itself. If outdoor dining is available, perhaps they would enjoy being outside. Many restaurants are offering early specials, both in price and menu selection, to those dining in the late afternoon or early evening. This can be helpful in terms of cost as well as the sociability, since they would be with others of their age group. It also helps fill tables during off-hours.

A Special Meal Program for the Elderly

The sociability of eating, whether with family or friends, is missing for many elderly people. This may account in large part for poor food habits and perhaps poor health. Special and group meal programs not only provide a social experience, they provide a nutritious meal for little or no cost.

The Nutrition Services Program for Older Americans, administered by the Administration on Aging, a part of the U.S. Department of Health and Human Services, provides both congregate and home-delivered meals. It provides low-cost nutritious meals as well as nutrition education. Although its major objective is as a nutrition program to decrease health costs and not as a feeding program per se, it is especially valuable to those with economic and social needs.

The service provides at least one hot meal—which provides at least one-third the RDAs—five or more days a week to people 60 years and over. Participants contribute all or part of the cost of the meal, according to ability. In 1987, there were approximately 14,000 lunch sites in the United States at which 240 million meals were served to the elderly. There are 6-week cycle menus developed by menu committees, whose members attend training programs to learn creative menu development, sanitation, food preparation, and so on. All meals are prepared without salt, and desserts may be substituted for those with health problems. The program strives for interest and taste appeal; for example, "meat loaf" goes by other names according to the different versions and is garnished attractively. At approximately $1 raw food cost per meal, portion control is extremely important. Unlike school food service, however, there is virtually no plate waste (Administration on Aging 1980).

In general, a well-balanced diet including a variety of foods with emphasis on nutrient-dense selections over empty calorie foods will provide most older men and women in good health with the nutrients they need to remain healthy. A good diet is based on the four food groups, with food preparation minimizing sodium and fat. Foods should be tasty and attractively presented so as to encourage consumption of adequate calories. Portion sizes should be kept in line with lower calorie requirements and budget constraints.

Food Choices for Athletically Active People

Interest in fitness as a vital component of personal well-being has escalated over the past decade. Recreational exercisers as well as athletes have become aware of the important role of good nutrition in achieving desirable fitness goals. As exercise is integrated into all aspects of daily routines from work to play, public knowledge of nutrition is keeping pace. Food professionals working in hotel, school, or college foodservice, in fitness centers, in corporate cafeterias, or in spa resorts have to plan menus reflecting the needs of customers, ranging from elite athletes, overweight executives, and health-conscious vacationers. Whether it is preparing for a visiting sports team, developing a "spa" cuisine or working with corporate dietitians, a knowledge of the relationship between nutrition and exercise is important to avoid the pitfalls of the myths and misconceptions regarding food for sport. This knowledge will also help you to anticipate the specific needs of these customers.

As discussed in Chapter 1, carbohydrate is the most important source of fuel to meet body energy requirements. It is stored as glycogen to fuel immediate muscle activity, and it is necessary for the efficient use of fat as a fuel. It spares the use of protein for energy so amino acids can perform their vital role of biosynthesis. The fact that the body can switch metabolic "gears" to burn different food fuel ratios depending on physiological demands is important to remember. Therefore, the combination of diet plus activity (in terms of intensity and duration) determine the predominant fuel and the metabolic processes used to provide energy.

Foods as Body Fuel

Foods fuel body activity. After digestion and absorption, the simplest forms of the three energy nutrients are metabolized, or burned, forming the high-energy compound ATP (Adenosine Triphosphate) and releasing heat, carbon dioxide, and water in the process. ATP is the direct energy source for muscular activity. It provides power, for instance, to sprint over to the salamander to remove smoking food. After only a few seconds, however, ATP must be replenished by oxidation of glucose, fatty acids, and amino acids. A little ATP is constantly formed by anaerobic glycolysis in the cytoplasm of cells, and a lot is formed in the aerobic energy release of the Krebs cycle (see Figure 2.1). This is how body energy needs are met.

During very intensive activity, when oxygen supply cannot meet muscle demand, glucose is broken down anaerobically into pyruvic acid, which is converted to lactic acid (see Figure 2.1). As lactic acid accumulates, it causes muscle fatigue. The anaerobic "gear" uses glucose exclusively, however, and when carbohydrate stores (glycogen) are depleted, exercise must discontinue. This is known among marathoners as "hitting the wall." When exercise intensity decreases, oxygen again becomes available and the aerobic "gear" enables the use of fat for energy. Usually, both aerobic and anaerobic systems operate simultaneously. The intensity and duration of activity and availability of food fuel sources, however, dictate which system will predominate.

The amount of oxygen available to the cells depends on one's capacity for oxygen consumption. As the intensity of activity increases, oxygen consumption by cells increases. Maximum oxygen consumption is $\overset{\circ}{V}O_2$ max — a term heard frequently in fitness centers. If exercise intensity increases above oxygen consumption abilities, the anaerobic metabolic "gear" is used. During constant activity such as walking, jogging, or biking, a balance between energy required and that supplied, or a steady state, is achieved. Just as walking was used as an example of steady-state aerobic exercise, the lifting of heavy weights or sprinting can be used as an example of anaerobic exercise. The "gears" used in any exercise, however, depend on the fitness of the person and when he or she might become out of breath.

Amino acids can be oxidized in muscle cells along with carbohydrates and fats. This occurs only on a very low calorie diet when the body cannot get enough fuel from fat or carbohydrate. Then protein is used as a backup fuel instead of building tissue. The result is lean tissue loss.

From all of this discussion, it probably seems that low- and moderate-intensity activities take place in the aerobic "gear." Here, fat is the predominant fuel used to produce ATP, although some glucose is also used. As intensity and oxygen consumption increase, "gears" shift from aerobic to anaerobic. At maximum oxygen consumption (high intensity) the anaerobic "gear," using glucose only, is the source of energy to replenish ATP. If intensive activity lasts only a few seconds, such as jumping up and down violently after burning an arm reaching into the oven, ATP provides sufficient energy.

When someone is not exercising, most energy needs are supplied by fat and a small amount of glucose. Although they are used simultaneously, fat contributes the most energy. Thus, in long-distance endurance exercises, those with the enzymatic capacity to burn fat longer will spare limited glucose resources. If resources in the form of glycogen can be spared, performance will be better for a longer period of time. Fit bodies are not only capable of storing more glycogen, they have the enzymatic capacity to burn fat more efficiently—hence better performance and less trouble keeping body weight in check.

To see how to plan menus for athletes and serious recreational exercises, first consider requirements in terms of food components. Both athletes and casual exercisers are no different from anyone else as far as the basic principles of good nutrition are concerned. Athletes, and everyone for that matter, should choose a variety of foods from the 4 food groups, practice moderation in order to balance the dietary "pie," and rely on wholesome foods, even for snacks. But most athletes can consume considerably more calories than a sedentary or even moderately active person. The energy cost of athletic activity depends on the intermittent or continuous level of intensity as well as the total amount of time one is active. The 2–2–4–4 "recipe" for number of servings from the four food groups will provide approximately 1200 calories. However, if additional calories required by the athletically active for energy needs come from junk foods they will *not* help performance. A diet high in fat and refined carbohydrates is not a healthful diet and may increase risk factors for some diseases.

Consuming an adequate amount of a variety of foods from the four food groups will probably cover most, if not all, of an athlete's micronutrient requirements. Nevertheless, many athletes like to take supplements, hoping to gain an edge. But food supplements will not increase performance by providing more strength or energy or increasing muscle size. In fact, since the athletically active person can—and usually does—consume more calories than less active people, he or she may even be taking in an excess of vitamins and some minerals. The psychological value of certain foods and supplements, however, can be very real. If one feels mentally that they help, one may also feel physically that they do. There is no harm in taking supplements if foods are also part of an overall balanced diet and the supplements are not excessive (Clark 1981).

Athletes should choose carbohydrate foods with naturally occurring sugars, such as those in fruits, vegetables, and fruit juices, rather than refined simple sugars found in soft drinks, candy, cakes, and pastries. In keeping with the dietary "pie," most carbohydrate foods, however, should be of the complex variety found in pasta, dried beans and peas, whole-grain bread and cereal products, oats, corn, rice, and so on. Remember, glycogen, the athlete's prime source of quick energy, is the storage form of carbohydrate.

Contrary to popular belief, physical activity does not increase the need for protein, especially since most persons in this country consume more than the recommended daily amount. Extra protein is converted to fat or energy and it doesn't make sense to load up on meat or protein supplements. In fact, too much protein can decrease athletic performance by increasing body fat and contributing to dehydration due to an increase in protein metabolic wastes that the kidneys must excrete.

Choose animal protein sources wisely, for many come packaged with fat. Remember, fat leaves the stomach slowly. A fatty source of protein would not be a good choice for a pregame or preactivity meal. To put it into perspective, exercise may not increase the need for protein, but it does increase calorie needs from carbohydrates—that number one energy source. Do not forget carbohydrate sources of protein in the active person's diet; they provide energy with little fat.

Vegetarian diets are okay for active people. But it is important to select foods that ensure adequate nutrient intake. Also, vegetable protein sources should be combined so as to provide high-quality protein in meals, such as meatless chili with kidney beans and corn bread.

Beverages for Athletes

It is important for people who are exercising to have frequent access to fluids. This is particularly crucial in warm and hot weather. During strenuous activity, a lot of water is lost from the body in sweat. When large amounts of water are lost, circulation to muscles is slowed, and the body loses its ability to dissipate heat through the skin.

The best beverage is cool water because it is absorbed more quickly than any other drink. Juices and soft drinks that contain sugar and other ingredients may taste thirst quenching, but they are absorbed far less quickly. During the activity or event itself, quick rehydration is necessary; however, when exercisers relax after they finish, juices, milk, iced tea, and other nonalcoholic drinks are fine.

Since alcoholic beverages inhibit release of a body hormone that helps maintain body water, athletes would be better off drinking water to replace fluid losses. Beer and other alcoholic beverages only speed up body fluid loss at a time when it is important to retain water or replace that lost in sweat.

Because heavy exercisers can sweat off 6 pounds or more, replacing fluid weight loss after exercise is the most important immediate nutritional concern when the activity concludes. Thus, providing a selection of appropriate beverages is important: Provide cool water in locker rooms and fitness centers and water, juices, soft drinks, tea, and other beverages in lounges and relaxation areas.

Sports drinks are often consumed during or after exercise. However, electrolyte beverages that contain sodium, potassium and glucose are not necessary. Salt in foods normally eaten will replace body sodium losses and fruit juices will replace potassium losses from sweat. These beverages concentrate solutions that are not readily absorbed, as is water, and in some cases may even cause diarrhea. If they are offered at all, they should be diluted with half the amount of water.

When sweating heavily, the amount of sodium in the blood temporarily increases because electrolytes concentrate as more water is lost. Construction workers who guzzle down whole quarts of OJ on a hot day are the smart ones. A cup of OJ replaces 25 times as much potassium as a cup of Gatorade. Likewise, salt tablets are taboo—water is the most important replacement concern during athletic activity.

New glucose polymer sport drinks consist of chains of sugar molecules, known as polymers. Since glucose polymers are larger in size but fewer in number, they leave the stomach more quickly than traditional sports drinks with many, many molecules of glucose. They, therefore, show promise in long endurance events by replacing carbohydrate without delaying absorption. Still, for the casual exerciser, water is the best and only replacement that can be provided for them.

What about coffee? The caffeine in coffee can reduce the rate at which glycogen is burned by stimulating the release of fatty acids, theoretically enabling you to exercise longer before glycogen runs out. However, as with everything, there is that inevitable "catch." Too much caffeine can make athletes so jittery they cannot perform well. It also greatly reduces iron and thiamin absorption in the same meal—important nutrients to athletes.

Menu Planning for Athletes

There are several guidelines, based on the preceding discussion, that are helpful in terms of menu planning for athletically active people.

With the exception of calories, nutrient needs are not particularly different from nonexercisers. An athlete, however, can easily consume 4000 or more calories per day. It is up to foodservice personnel to see that foods provided are sufficient and nutritionally balanced in terms of the food groups and dietary "pie." Calories beyond those necessary to provide optimum nutrition should come from wholesome foods in the fruit, vegetable, and complex carbohydrate groups. Carbohydrate is the most important fuel for athletes, and protein should be adequate but consumed according to dietary "pie" ratios. Remember, protein will be also supplied by complex carbohydrates, so an excess of meat is not necessary. High-fat foods, including high-fat protein foods, pose certain health risks and leave the stomach more slowly, making them poor choices, particularly for a pre-event meal. Ample low-fat vegetable protein alternatives should be provided, and preparation techniques should not result in high-fat dishes. Therefore, the recipe for menu planning should read high carbohydrate, low fat, and moderate protein. But remember that individuals' food preferences will vary, and the choice is the customer's, even if it is steak for breakfast!

When feeding exercisers before an event, plan to have meals at least 3 hours ahead so that there is no food in the stomach or upper intestine at the time of the event. Provide plenty of cool liquids for body hydration, avoiding those with high sugar concentrations. Keep spices to the minimum needed for taste. Provide familiar foods, appropriate to ethnic tastes.

After an event, high-carbohydrate foods are important to restore glycogen. Optimally, increase the carbohydrate wedge of the dietary "pie" to about 70 percent.

People in the bed-and-breakfast business have asked for help in planning meals for travelling athletes practicing carbohydrate loading. In general, this practice is decreasing in use. Replacing this regimen has been a decrease in training before the event coupled with a high-carbohydrate diet. Traditionally, carbo loading has involved a high-fat, high-protein diet for 3 days, followed by a low-fat, moderate-protein, high-carbohydrate diet for 3 days, followed by a high-carbohydrate diet up to 12 hours before an event, followed by more carbohydrate calories 4 hours before the event. (This diet should be used only for endurance events longer than 1 hour.) Since this process is not tolerated by many athletes and the high fat component is considered a health risk, a high-carbohydrate, reduced-exercise pregame regimen is being used instead to maintain glycogen stores.

Often breakfast will be the pregame meal. To increase carbohydrates and lower fats, emphasize whole-grain breads, muffins, and hot and cold cereals. When preparing and serving pancakes, waffles, and french toast, reduce the amount of whole eggs, substituting whites, and bake french toast to decrease fat content. Offer fruit and yogurt toppings instead of butter and syrup, which are sources of fat and concentrated sugar. When offering pasta dishes at other meals remember meat, cheese, and cream-based sauces add lots of fat. Tomato and vegetable-puree-based sauces add color, flavor, and little fat. Plan menus around starchy vegetables and legumes. Use egg whites or powdered or evaporated skim milk to bind ingredients instead of whole eggs. Bake, broil or poach instead of frying foods (Clark 1981).

Food Choices for the Worksite

Many businesses are hiring individual chefs or those working with contract foodservices to provide meals for corporate dining facilities. Moreover, the foodservice operations at these worksites are increasingly becoming involved with company-based employee health programs. Cafeterias and executive dining rooms are the focus of nutritional aspects of these programs, which may include point-of-purchase nutrition education; alternative menus or selections that are low in fat, saturated fat, cholesterol, sodium, and calories; or specific menus, such as one tailored to fit an in-house employee cholesterol-reduction program.

Foodservice professionals may be required to work with company or consultant dietitians to plan meals to fit program objectives. This will involve changes in approach to menu planning, product selection, and preparation techniques. Perhaps the worksite will not have an organized program as such, but employees may express an interest in healthful options such as entree salads or choices of more fresh fruit and vegetables.

The wellness approach to food planning for companies involves a focus on fresh foods with relatively simple preparations. Attractive garnish and presentation are important. In the absence of a structured wellness program, increase employees' opportunities to eat healthily on the job by making minor—or major—changes in foods available to them on a daily basis.

One area in which food service can play a major role is in recipe development. This could include employee taste-testing sessions and, if staff time and ability permit, cooking demonstrations for employees, which include tasting and evaluating the products. Food service-oriented events can also reinforce existing nutrition education such as employee lectures and classes, individual consultation, messages on table tents, and flyers at point of purchase in cafeteria setups (*Journal of Nutrition Education* 1986).

Thus, nutrition knowledge is important for food service employees. A firm understanding of nutrition will enhance professional mobility and facilitate working with a company nutritionist and/or food service manager, as well as making menu changes on their own. An employee who is knowledgeable enough to conduct training workshops for other food service employees about the nutritional aspects of food preparation has a marketable skill.

Detailed, academic knowledge of nutrition is not necessary for foodservice professionals. Rather, it is necessary to know the contributions of the major food groups in terms of macronutrients and micronutrients, as well as understanding the nutritional principles behind eating for wellness: lowering consumption of foods high in fat, sugar, and salt; eating more complex carbohydrates; and consuming everything in moderation.

What this translates to is the development of a set of nutritional guidelines for the kitchen—perhaps based on the Dietary Guidelines. Rationale for individual guidelines that are developed at the worksite should be outlined for all employees so they understand why one product or technique is preferred over another. Operational guidelines for the use of fresh foods, substitution of vegetable oils, and so forth, should be developed. Established guidelines and procedures are necessary and the staff must understand why they have been developed in terms of health benefits to employee customers and themselves. They must be familiar with the nutritional composition of food products they are working with and be knowledgeable about alternative preparation techniques such as trimming meats, using less fat and oil, and omitting salt. The menu game in Figure 9.1 (Chapter 9) is a good learning tool which can be placed on a chalkboard so food service workers can check appropriate categories for each ingredient in a dish. If the principles are kept in mind, recipes will be executed more accurately. If standardized recipes and a central ingredient room are used for operational control, then accurate interpretation of nutritional guidelines rests in recipe development and nutrient calculation procedures. A computer is helpful for these activities.

A business plan should also be developed so that alternative menus or food selections maintain operating costs. It is important to track sales and revenues from these items to establish and respond to employee demand for nutritious foods in worksite dining facilities. If there is a problem with product acceptability, look at the attractiveness and tasteworthiness of the foods. Focus groups and taste panels can provide feedback on employee opinions. Accessing opinion can also take the form of table tent surveys, depending on the worksite setting. If employees generally bring lunches, provide healthy accompaniments and nutritious alternatives in vending machines (*Journal of Nutrition Education* 1986). This can be important to the success of the effort.

REFERENCES

Administration on Aging. 1980. *Nutrition Service Assessment: A Report on Region VII's Elderly Nutrition Program.* Kansas City, Mo.: U.S. Department of Health and Human Services.

American Alliance for Health, Physical Education, Recreation and Dance. 1984. *Nutrition for Sports Success.* Reston, Va.

American Dietetic Association, Society for Nutrition Education. 1986. *Worksite Nutrition—A Decision-Maker's Guide.* Chicago, Ill.: The American Dietetic Association.

Arizona Department of Education. 1982. *Sports Nutrition.* Tucson, Ariz.

Bailey, C. 1978. *Fit or Fat?* Boston, Mass.: Houghton Mifflin.

Center for Science in the Public Interest. 1986. Fast food and kids. *Nutrition Action Health Letter 13* (3), 8.

Clark, N. 1981. *The Athlete's Kitchen.* Boston, Mass.: CBI Publishing.

Food and Nutrition Service. 1975. *Food for Youth.* FNS-140. Washington, D.C.: U.S. Department of Agriculture.

Giant Foods. 1983. *Bag It! A Guide to Packing Nutritious Lunches.* Form 148. Landover, Md.: Giant Supermarkets.

Hsu, J. M., and Davis, R. L. (Eds.) 1981. *Handbook of Geriatric Nutrition. Principles and Applications for Nutrition and Diet in Aging.* Park Ridge, N.J.: Noyes Publications.

Journal of Nutrition Education. 1986. *Nutrition at the Worksite* (supple.) *18* (2). Oakland, Calif.: Society for Nutrition Education.

Katch, F. I., and McArdle, W. D. 1977. *Nutrition, Weight Control and Exercise.* Boston, Mass.: Houghton Mifflin.

McArdle, W. D., Katch, F. I., and Katch, V. L. 1981. *Exercise Physiology— Energy, Nutrition and Human Performance.* Philadelphia, Pa.: Lea & Febiger.

Mayer, J. 1976. *A Diet for Living.* New York: Pocket Books.

Society for Nutrition Education. 1980. *A Guide for Food and Nutrition in Later Years.* Berkeley, Calif.

Unklesbay, N., and Unklesbay, K. 1978. An automated system for planning menus for the elderly in Title VII nutrition programs. *Food Technology 32,* 80–83.

Wurtman, J. J. 1979. *Eating Your Way Through Life.* New York: Raven Press.

Chapter 5

NUTRITION AND INDUSTRY

Food Processing

Of the thousands of foods available to Americans on a wholesale or retail basis, the majority have been at least minimally processed, depending on how broadly the term is defined. As more food products appear in the marketplace, many consumers have become increasingly concerned about how processing affects nutritional quality and general composition of food-stuffs. Thus, there is growing demand for "natural" foods.

Processing can be described as a series of actions or changes that lead to a particular result; in other words, special treatment of something. If this were widely construed to mean all treatments of all foods from soil to plate, then almost everything we eat is processed to some extent. But many consumers go out of their way to obtain whole foods. A 1986 Gallup survey done for the National Restaurant Association revealed that health-conscious consumers (19 percent of the adult population) are more likely than other consumers to avoid foods that have been processed (Mills 1986). Moreover, at a Food Marketing Institute (FMI) Conference, jointly sponsored by the FMI, the Society for Nutrition Education, and the Public Voice for Food and Health Policy, FMI stated that results of its 1986 Trends Survey of Supermarket Shoppers revealed that the buzzwords of the food marketing industry are light, white, and fresh (white refers to color of meats, wine, and liquor) (Food Marketing Institute 1986). These words also reflect choices being made by restaurant customers (see Chapter 6).

Foods are processed for a number of reasons, including convenience of preparation (i.e., instant mashed potatoes), and new product development, such as meat and fish analogues. The latter have become popular in the form of imitation crab meat, "formed fillets," and even lobster. They are known as surimi in the trade, which is processed and colored white fish paste shaped to mock whichever seafood it is imitating.

Just as some consumers are expressing a distaste for processed foods, others are demanding more quick-to-prepare, instant versions of pantry staples, and industry responds with more processed products, such as instant brown rice. This would seem to satisfy consumer demands for both whole and convenience foods.

Food professionals keep one eye on labor costs and the other on convenience. But there are issues surrounding the effect of processing on food and natural versus processed foods which food service professionals should be aware of. Anyone who has been to a food trade show knows how many products are out there — many foods highly processed or composed of ersatz ingredients. One need not even boil an egg for garnish! A growing percentage of consumers, however, are demanding and are willing to pay for fresh foods. Of course, others do not care. It is up to food professionals to assess and address customer preferences.

Functions of Food Processing

Prevent Disease   A major function of food processing is to prevent the growth of disease-causing microorganisms. Many purists advocate natural products such as raw milk; however, raw milk can be unhealthful. Risks of consuming raw milk range from diarrhea to serious bacterial diseases such as salmonella and even tuberculosis! Although the aging process used for raw milk cheeses (60-day minimum) renders these bacteria inactive, there have been an increasing number of reports of infections caused by bacteria in improperly handled cheeses, most of which have been imported.

Extend Shelf Life   Extended shelf life is another reason for food processing. Degradation can occur in foods even before they are harvested (or in the case of animal foods slaughtered). In fact, most foods have a relatively short shelf life in their natural state. Since we are mostly an urbanized society, most of us do not run out to the back lot for a chicken or a basketful of vegetables for dinner. Although home vegetable gardens and urban gardening plots are on the rise, most of us go to a store for our foods. Long distances from major food-producing centers necessitate some sort of processing to preserve food and extend shelf life. Therefore, with the increase in long distance transport comes an increase in processing. Of course, this does not have to be the case. Air freight can avail anyone of any fresh food from anywhere in the world—anyone willing to pay the price, that is.

Provide Convenience and Variety Socioeconomic changes have contributed to an increase in processed foods. Convenience, for example, is an important reason for processing. With more women in the workforce, less time is devoted to food preparation in the home. Also, in many cases, dual incomes provide the monetary means to rely on costly convenience foods —either prepared fresh foods (which may be processed) or packaged/frozen products. More sophisticated palates have also created a new demand for processed packaged ethnic foods, particularly Mexican and Oriental products, and specialty items known as "fancy foods." So, there are people who would prefer bottled salad dressing to making it themselves and others who prefer fresh unprocessed ingredients but will nevertheless buy a bottled dressing for convenience if the ingredients are all "natural."

Food Processing and Nutrition

Some food processing removes insects, microorganisms, and other contaminants from products. Other unstable food products must be dehydrated, frozen, or packaged so they can survive being transported and stored in urban/suburban areas where they will be consumed. In many cases, food processing reduces the nutritional value of food. But new processing methods are directed toward minimizing these losses, and agricultural experiments with genetic engineering are creating plants with higher initial nutrient content, which would help offset some of the effects of processing. Also, minerals such as zinc and selenium are being added experimentally to fertilizer to produce plants containing more of those nutrients. These same experiments are increasing yields, size, color, and other visible attributes that make food more marketable to the public (Harris and Karmas 1977). Thus, if consumers are interested in nutrient content, they must make their wants known to plant breeders and agricultural engineers. By the time food is marketed, industry, not the consumer, will have influenced how it was produced and processed.

It is interesting to note that a new cottage farming miniindustry has spontaneously occurred in recent years in response to requests by restaurateurs for food products that meet their specifications. In Massachusetts, the State Department of Agriculture is helping bring together food producers, chefs, and caterers. The department produces three publications, has instituted several programs, and puts out a newsletter, *The Fresh Connection,* that mentions growers and their products. Lists of producers of specific foods and brochures with maps indicating farms and sources of farm products are also available. The Agriculture Department also helps organize and promote farmers' markets, is encouraging farmers to grow products that are in demand, and helps sponsor Massachusetts specialty food producers to food trade shows (Schumacher 1986). Thus, there is an increasing trend for foodservice operators to opt for fresh foods when locally available.

As processing can affect nutritional content of foods, many environmental factors, including light intensity, temperature, season of the year, and geographical location, affect the nutritional content of fresh foods, particularly edible plants. Although soil fertility and fertilization affect the yield more than the nutritional qualities of plants, soils deficient in trace minerals can affect the amount of these nutrients in plants. Most people, however, eat a variety of foods from different areas, which helps assure consumption of a variety of nutrients. The addition of fertilizer to soils already containing sufficient nutrients in order to support the growth of plants, on the other hand, has no additional effect on nutrient content (Harris and Karmas 1977). In fact, the addition of one nutrient may adversely affect the availability of another.

This brings up the controversy of organic versus manufactured fertilizer. Speaking strictly from a nutritional standpoint, if the soil can support the growth of plants, nutritional content will, all other factors being equal, be the same whether the fertilizer is organic or nonorganic. The principal effect of soil improvement is to increase the yield rather than the nutritional quality of plants. The exception is mineral content of plants, which is affected by the mineral content of the soil (Harris and Karmas 1977). In the market, there is no way to tell, except through trust in the greengrocer, whether or not food is organic.

The Food Chain and Processed Foods

The food chain is actually composed of three natural links and one man-made link (see Figure 5.1). The lowest link is composed of foods of plant origin. In a process called photosynthesis, green plants use energy from sunlight, plus carbon dioxide in the air and water, to make their own carbohydrate. They give off oxygen in the process. Because they are the first source of nutrients, many people feel that plants are the purest form of food. The next link is made up of meat from food-producing animals who consume a diet of carbohydrate from plant sources. Foods produced by the animals themselves, such as milk from cows and eggs from chickens, provide the third link. At the top of the chain is the link composed of foods processed from the natural foods on the three lower levels of "natural" food: jam from fruits; cold cuts from meats; and cheese from milk. Then all cheese is processed? No, the FDA defines processed cheese products as those which contain ingredients in addition to milk. Cows do not make cheese — man does. Cheeses are considered natural unless otherwise stipulated on the label.

Methods of Food Processing

There are seven commonly used methods of food processing:

1. Altering moisture content such as freeze-drying
2. Heating such as pasteurization
3. Freezing
4. Control of pH such as fermentation, pickling
5. Use of chemical additives such as nitrites used in curing
6. Physical processing such as milling
7. Irradiation

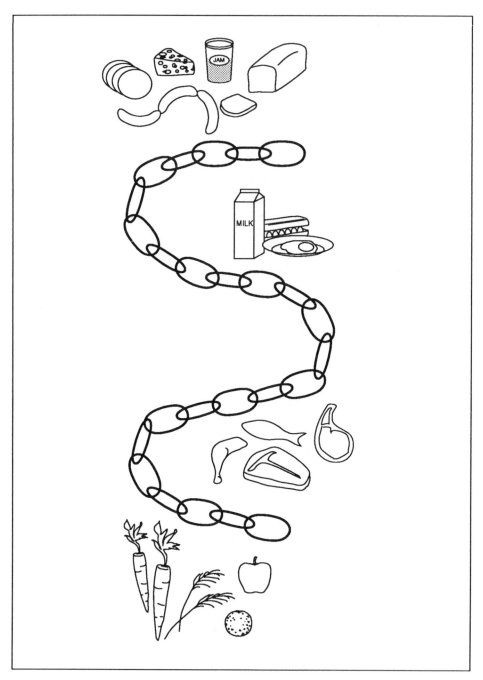

FIGURE 5.1 The food chain.

All of the methods affect the nutrient content of foods, but some methods have less impact than others. Freezing is the least destructive to nutrients. Altering moisture content also causes little nutrient destruction. The humectants (water-binding substances) in use include sucrose, glucose, fructose, sodium chloride, and propylene glycol. In all processing involving heat, thiamin is lowered considerably. Curing causes the loss of water-soluble nutrients since water is lost from the food product. Physical processing causes loss of fiber as well as nutrients. Irradiation causes nutritional losses similar to those in heat processing (Harris and Karma 1977).

The Food and Drug Adminstration (FDA) has approved the use of irradiation for deinfestation of insects in grain, to inhibit sprouting in potatoes, to use on all fresh fruits and vegetables to prevent enzymatic microbiological deterioration, to sterilize spices, and to control trichinae in fresh pork. Irradiation is also being considered as a means of controlling salmonella bacteria. There is, however, public concern over eating foods that have been exposed to radioactive cesium 137 or cobalt 60. Some see it only as a way to get rid of the nuclear waste products of nuclear weapons and energy industries. Proponents claim irradiation will do away with the need for pesticides and many chemical additives used to preserve foods.

To date, prepared foods containing irradiated ingredients are not required to be labeled. However, from 1986 to 1988 fresh foods must contain the radiation logo, the international symbol of a broken black circle and geometric design, and either the statement "treated with radiation" or "treated by irradiation." After that 2-year period, the FDA hopes people will have become sufficiently familiar with the symbol that wording will not be necessary. Because of the tremendous expense involved in irradiation, its use will probably develop slowly (U.S. FDA, Personal Communication, 1986).

Thus, some foods are minimally processed in a beneficial way to destroy harmful microorganisms and their toxins or to prevent product degradation. Also, processing increases the availability of a variety of foods from all areas, all year round. Many people, however, feel strongly about using only fresh, seasonal products that are locally grown and produced, and there is a strong demand, inside and outside the restaurant, for foods that are fresh. Many foods are highly processed and contain chemical additives. Perhaps it is more a concern over processed foods that fall into this latter category that is fueling demand for whole, natural foods.

Healthful Food Products

What are some of the issues concerning use of the terms "natural" and "whole" foods? An understanding of these concepts is important to food-service operators striving to develop menu/product copy complying with local truth-in-menu requirements.

The sixties term health food is misleading. Health foods, just as any other foods, can contain insects or chemical residues or be rancid—not desirable attributes in something that is eaten. In fact, chemical residues can remain in the soil long after use has discontinued. And contamination can occur from use of chemicals carried by wind and rain, as was the case with the temporary contamination of land in several European countries as a result of the Soviet Chernobyl nuclear accident in 1986.

The new consumer interest in healthy (as opposed to health) foods has given rise to the currently popular term whole foods. The words organic and natural also appear on shelf cards and food packages. The FDA has no official definitions for these terms; however, organic generally implies that the food has not been treated with pesticides, contains no preservatives or synthetic ingredients, and has been grown without use of manufactured fertilizers. Natural implies food products that, for the most part, are in their natural state, unenhanced by flavoring, coloring, or chemical additives. But since there are no legal definitions except in a few states, all products bearing these terms do not necessarily conform to the stipulations. There are several major consumer activist groups, including the Center for Science in the Public Interest and the Public Voice for Food and Health Policy (see Appendix E), which are pushing for stricter standards in terms of nutritional quality, ingredients, and labeling.

At the same time some consumers are asking for fresh, others are buying increasing numbers of highly processed, prefabricated food products. Many are ambivalent—they figure that if the processed bottled salad dressings, cereals, and potato chips are made with all "natural" ingredients they are okay. The major issue seems to be more a concern about potentially harmful additives than the degree of food processing.

Natural foods stores provide health-conscious consumers with many of the food products they seek and have helped heighten nutrition awareness, but some information in the pamphlets and other nutrition-related materials they display may be misleading and of questionable scientific accuracy.

Also, not everything in a natural foods stores is healthy. Greasy, salty, natural potato chips fall into the same junk food category as do potato chips with freshness additives—remove the salt and use safflower oil—and you still have a high fat snack, with few nutritional qualities. In other words, the natural chip is no more nutritious than the regular chip, but it does have an edge in that it has no chemical preservatives and no saturated fat, depending on the oil used for frying. It also has another edge—the word natural has great customer appeal, bringing to mind the terms fresh, unspoiled, unadulterated, and pure. Even supermarkets now carry natural food products such as potato chips.

In the restaurant, opt for foods as close to their natural composition as possible. Select fresh foods with an eye on appearance. If the broccoli stems are limp and the flowerettes yellowed and open, choose another vegetable. If it looks over the hill, then it is less than desirable nutritionally. If it is important to have a particular fruit or vegetable and fresh ones are not available, choose frozen over canned. Frozen foods are closest in nutritional quality to fresh ones. Remember, though, oxidation of fatty acids can occur during freezing, causing food to become rancid. Canned fruits and vegetables bear little taste or textural resemblance to their fresh counterparts. Instant mashed potatoes do not resemble light, fluffy, freshly cooked and mashed spuds.

The extent to which processed or convenience food products are used will depend on the type of food operation and budget, personnel, and clientele. Nutritionally speaking, though, minimally processed fresh foods are best.

Food Additives

In the last section, the addition of additives was included in the list of food processing methods. There are naturally occurring additives in foods, as well as those added by farmers, food manufacturers, other processors, and cooks themselves. Most additives are used to prevent natural or microbial deterioration of foods, to change texture or appearance, to add flavor, or to add nutrients. Many additives are not harmful, but others are harmful or at least questionable. Some harmful additives have been banned by the federal government; others are still in use. Many additives such as pesticides, insect fragments, and antibiotics given to livestock sneak quietly into the food supply.

It is difficult to avoid consuming additives altogether, since sugar, salt, and even vitamins are considered additives. The most commonly used additives are sugar, salt, and corn syrup. Add citric acid, baking soda, vegetable colors, mustard, and pepper, and these account for 98 percent by weight of all food additives used in the United States (*FDA Consumer* 1982). The best thing to do is learn about additives, read labels, and then determine whether the risks of consuming them are worth the benefit in terms of product acceptability. In other words, are artificial colorings worth the pretty but unnecessary effect? Is running a red light and arriving at a destination a minute earlier worth the risk of a ticket or, worse, an accident? Are the aerobic and psychological benefits of jogging with an injured knee worth the risk of permanent damage? People deal with this type of risk-benefit decision all the time, yet may feel unconcerned because "it" involves an intangible risk—one they cannot see at the time. When the FDA attempted to ban saccharine, there was a flood of protests from consumers —they felt that the benefit of reducing calories was worth the possible risk of cancer. Saccharine is still on the market—with a health warning—and it is still under suspicion.

In general, then, avoid additives that are unnecessary or questionable to the extent possible. But it is impossible to avoid all additives. Take a typical lunch—ham and cheese on rye and a soft drink. The ham contains sodium nitrite; the cheese may have coloring and ascorbic acid; the spread may have an emulsifier-stabilizer in it; the bread will probably have been fortified with vitamins and will contain freshness additives. The drink may contain natural or artificial sweeteners, caffeine, artificial coloring, or flavoring. Without these it is just carbonated water. Of course, lunch could consist of a nitrite-free meat on preservative-free, whole-grain bread, and a "natural" soda, which will still have natural sweeteners, coloring, and flavoring added to carbonated water.

In its broadest definition, a food additive is any substance that becomes part of a food, either upon direct addition or indirectly. An example of a direct or intentional additive is the MSG added to the canned soup just opened. An indirect or unintentional additive may, for instance, come from the packaging materials, which leave a residue in the food or from insect parts—both of which were unintentional additions.

Many unintentional additives come from nature and can be toxic. Others, such as rot, dirt, insects, insect fragments and excreta, rodent hairs and excreta, maggots, and fly eggs, just create disgust. The FDA has set levels for permissible impurities in food, called food defect action levels. They are based on the assumption that these are unintentionally added at the farm and initial processing stages and pose few health hazards. This harmless dirt is not to be confused with contamination due to poor sanitation, which is not allowable. Different standards for filth are set by the USDA for meat and poultry.

Other natural additions include molds and aflatoxins, some of which are toxic. Ideal conditions for growth of most molds are warmth and humidity. Even when a food producer or handler follows scrupulous practices to prevent the appearance of the fuzzy stuff, it can still appear on foods in the kitchen, factory, warehouse, and store. Since a product made unfit to eat by mold is a waste of an otherwise perfectly good food, some food preparers tend to overlook health hazards, simply scraping mold off. Too often pieces of cheese with blue dots are found in a salad — or in the market.

Some molds cause illness by producing toxins such as aflatoxin. Aflatoxins are produced by a mold that can grow on nuts, peanuts, and corn and contaminate products made from these foods. They can grow in the field or in storage. Aflatoxins are poisons, and continuous low-level exposure can increase risk of liver cancer; hence, moldy foods should be returned to the market or discarded. Lightly molded foods should be trimmed well. Moldy, shriveled, or otherwise odd-looking nuts in the shell should not be consumed.

Molds are members of the fungi family, which also includes mushrooms and yeasts. Some types of mushrooms are harmful and can cause allergic reactions. Everyone who works with food should be familiar with conditions that encourage mold growth and should take care to observe storage and sanitation procedures that protect foods. If mold is on a food product, remember that what is seen is actually only part of it. The rest of it extends, rootlike, into the center of the food. Small spots of mold should be removed along with a sizeable slice of the surrounding area. Cooking and freezing halt the growth of mold but not of toxins that may be produced. Also, do not sniff moldy foods — spores may be inhaled into the lungs (U.S. Dept. HHS 1981).

Additives intentionally put into foods serve many purposes. Additives for nutritional purposes may supplement vitamins and minerals already in the food or they may consist of different vitamins and minerals. A food whose nutrient content has been enhanced by increasing the amounts of vitamins and minerals present is generally referred to as enriched. A food in which vitamins and minerals other than the ones present have been added is called fortified. Since there are no legal definitions for these terms, they are often used interchangeably. Examples of fortified foods are a cereal with 100 percent of the U.S. RDA for almost every vitamin and mineral for which allowances have been established and milk fortified with vitamin D. All products with added nutrients must state this on the label. (This will be discussed in the next section.)

Additives that maintain freshness protect food from either microbial spoilage or oxidative changes. In the first group are salt, sugar, and chemicals such as sodium propionate and potassium sorbate. Antioxidants include vitamins C and E as well as BHA and the controversial BHT. Additives that are used to make food more appealing include coloring agents, flavors, flavor enhancers, and sweeteners.

Additives used to help prepare or process foods include emulsifiers such as mono- and diglycerides, stabilizers and thickeners, pH control agents, leavening agents, bleaching agents, anticaking agents, and humectants. Appendix C categorizes commonly used additives under each of these uses alphabetically for easy reference. Any food professional should be able to access this type of information quickly when consumers ask what is in a food or food product.

Controversy over Additives

Much of the controversy over additives concerns those that are potentially harmful to humans. A recent case in point is the use of sulfiting agents to prevent spoilage and discoloration in vegetables, seafood, drugs, beer, and wine. Because of the potential of extreme allergic reactions—and death—in those who are sensitive to sulfites, the FDA, after much prodding from consumer activist groups, revoked their "generally recognized as safe" status and eliminated their use on raw fruits and vegetables to be served or sold to consumers. This decision primarily affects salads and salad bars in restaurants and other food service outlets, as well as raw produce in stores and supermarkets. It also established that the presence of sulfites in meat and poultry products must be stated on the label since the use of sulfites in fresh meats and poultry is primarily to mask spoilage. Wine and beer fall under the jurisdiction of the Bureau of Alcohol, Tobacco and Firearms, which has ordered sulfite labeling for alcoholic beverages containing sulfur dioxide levels of 10 parts per million or more by 1988. The decisions do not, however, solve the problem of sulfites in packaged foods that are not labeled, such as packaged potato products or legally treated foods such as olives, potato salad, and shrimp.

Sulfites can be identifed on food labels by the following terms: sulfur dioxide, potassium bisulfite, sodium bisulfite, sodium metabisulfite, and sodium sulfite. Table 5-1 lists foods that may contain sulfites.

TABLE 5.1   Common Foods That May Contain Sulfites[a]

Food Category	Types of Food
Alcoholic beverages[b]	Wine, beer, cocktail mixes, wine coolers
Baked goods	Cookies, crackers, mixes with dried fruits or vegetables, pie crust, pizza crust, quiche crust, flour tortillas
Beverage bases	Dried citrus fruit beverage mixes
Condiments and relishes	Horseradish, onion and pickle relishes, pickles, olives, salad dressing mixes, wine vinegar
Confections and frostings	Brown, raw, powdered or white sugar derived from sugar beets
Dairy product analogs	Filled milk (skim milk enriched in fat content by addition of vegetable oils)
Fish and shellfish	Canned clams; fresh, frozen, canned or dried shrimp; frozen lobster; scallops; dried cod
Fresh fruit and vegetables[c]	Banned by FDA regulation (7/9/86), but fresh pre-cut potatoes excluded from ban
Gelatins, puddings, fillings	Fruit fillings, flavored and unflavored gelatin, pectin, jelling agents

continued

TABLE 5.1   Common Foods That May Contain Sulfites[a] *(continued)*

Food Category	Types of Food
Grain products and pasta	Cornstarch, modified food starch, spinach pasta, gravies, hominy, breadings, batters, noodle/rice mixes
Jams and jellies	Jams and jellies
Nuts and nut products	Shredded coconut
Plant protein products	Soy protein products
Processed fruits	Canned, bottled or frozen fruit juices (including lemon, lime, grape, apple); dried fruit; canned, bottled or frozen dietetic fruit or fruit juices; maraschino cherries, glazed fruit
Processed vegetables	Vegetable juices; canned vegetables (including potatoes); pickled vegetables (including sauerkraut, cauliflower and peppers); dried vegetables; instant mashed potatoes; frozen potatoes; potato salad
Snack foods	Dried fruit snacks, trail mixes, filled crackers
Soups and soup mixes	Canned soups, dried soup mixes
Sweet sauces, toppings, syrups	Corn syrup, maple syrup, fruit toppings, high-fructose corn syrup, pancake syrup, molasses
Tea	Instant tea, liquid tea concentrates

[a]Sulfur dioxide and various forms of inorganic sulfites that release sulfur dioxide when used as food ingredients are known collectively as sulfiting agents. On food labels, their presence may be identified as sulfur dioxide, potassium bisulfide, potassium metabisulfite, sodium bisulfite, sodium metabisulfite or sodium sulfite. *Not all* manufacturers of these foods use sulfites. The amounts that are used may vary. Information from this list should be supplemented by reading the labels of packaged foods.
[b]Use of sulfites in wine and beer comes under the jurisdiction of the Treasury Department's Bureau of Alcohol, Tobacco and Firearms, which has proposed requiring sulfite labeling for wine, distilled spirits, and malt beverages if sulfite levels are 10 parts per million or more.
[c]Sulfur dioxide is used as a fungicide on grapes, a use regulated by the U.S. Environmental Protection Agency.
SOURCE: U.S. Department of Health and Human Services. 1985/1986. Reacting to Sulfites. *FDA Consumer*. Dec./Jan. Rockville, Md.: Food and Drug Administration. Reprint No. 86-2209.

Another controversial additive is sodium nitrite, which is usually mixed with sweeteners, salt, herbs, aromatics, and spices to cure meat and seafoods. Nitrite enhances color, giving ham, bacon, wieners, and deli meats their pink hues. It also protects against botulinum bacteria, which produce a hazardous toxin that, if ingested, may cause death. Some meats are also smoked or dried after curing. Although curing and smoking kill bacteria, mold, and yeast, they do not protect against parasites such as trichina in pork. Cold-smoked meats should be cooked. Of course, much cured meat and fish are eaten raw, such as salmon, for example. This can be risky. The problem with nitrites, which also appear in other foods and beverages, is that they act with amines and ureas in the gastrointestinal tract to form nitrosamines, which can be carcinogenic. Vitamin C has been found to react with nitrites before they form nitrosamines, so some food processors are replacing nitrite with vitamin C–related compounds such as sodium erythorbate and sodium sorbate. Many vegetables contain nitrates, which can follow the nitrite–nitrosamine process in the bodies. People are also exposed to a number of naturally occurring substances that are potential tumor promoters. Using nitrites is a case of risk versus benefit. If foods are handled properly, switching from nitrites to other methods of preserving foods should pose little problem. The USDA allows lower levels of nitrites by plants with USDA quality control programs. As food science technology advances, further safe cutbacks in the use of nitrites will be seen (Nutrition Policy 1986).

Grilling and smoking of foods also produce potential carcinogenic substances. The bottom line here is moderation. Restaurants that offer little other than grilled foods, many of which are partially blackened in the process, should offer alternatives for those who do not want grilled meats or who are repeat customers. There has not been any visible consumer wariness of these foods—indeed, they are very popular. Enjoying them from time to time should do no harm.

Other controversial areas of food additives are hormones and drugs in animal feed and agricultural pesticides. More than a billion pounds of insect killer a year are used in the United States. Also, more than half of the farm animals producing beef and pork for consumer consumption receive antibiotics. For some people, half or more of the food they consume can contain chemical residues.

The use of antibiotics in livestock feed is promoting antibiotic-resistant strains of bacteria, which can then be transferred to people who eat meat that has not been sufficiently cooked. The result has been not only a significant increase in reported cases of salmonella food poisoning, but also an increase in the severity of these infections. Another problem is that antibiotics given to kill bacteria that cause human illnesses must be given in higher doses to be effective, and some are no longer effective at all. The chief offenders in these cases are raw and improperly handled meat and poultry. It is of utmost importance that all food handlers observe proper sanitation and food-handling procedures. They do not want to become a victim, nor do they want their customers to become victims.

Another controversy is the use of veterinary drugs of questionable safety to treat animals, the residues of which end up in meat, milk, and eggs. The result is ingestion of medications that are not needed and that may be harmful to health (Center for Science in the Public Interest 1986; Harvard Medical School Health Letter 1985).

Government Regulation of Food Additives

Consumers rely on the government to assure the safety of the foods they consume. There is, however, always room for improvement of current inspection and enforcement systems, and, of course, there is the noncompliance factor on the part of food producers. Add to that whatever laxity occurs in transportation, storage, handling, and preparation, and it is remarkable that more food-borne illnesses do not occur. But more do occur than are actually reported. Most individual low-grade cases are attributed to a 24-hour bug and dismissed.

The FDA, which is part of the Public Health Service under the umbrella of the U.S. Department of Health and Human Services, addresses the issues of food additives and drug residues. It also establishes food standards. The USDA establishes standards for meat and poultry products and regulates use of drugs and additives in them. FDA and USDA have jurisdiction over foods sold in interstate commerce. Locally manufactured foods are under jurisdiction of local food and health authorities. FDA, USDA, and the EPA share responsibility for regulating pesticides. USDA's Food Safety and Inspection Service enforces EPA's regulations. Note that gelatin and wild game fall under FDA regulations.

Another important consideration for food handlers is the microorganisms and residues present on fresh, raw produce—especially organic produce. Wash *all* produce whether it will be cooked or not. This also helps remove chemical residues. Remember the dirt on those mushrooms is *not* clean dirt.

Most people no longer rely on the family farm for foods whose purity and quality they themselves are responsible for. For the most part, food has been processed in factories and transported far and wide to supermarkets and stores. This has created food safety and quality problems that have necessitated government laws and regulations.

In 1938, the original Food and Drug Act of 1906 was replaced by the Food, Drug and Cosmetic Act. It offers protection to consumers in the areas of safety and wholesomeness; truthful and informative labeling; testing of drugs, colorings, additives, and chemicals; and tolerance limits for chemical residues and other additives in foods, drugs, and cosmetics. As new food safety concerns have surfaced, amendments have been developed such as the 1954 pesticide amendment, the 1958 additives amendment, the 1960 color additive amendment, and the 1970 water standards amendment.

The 1958 additives amendment established the Generally Recognized as Safe (GRAS) list of substances in foods already in use, which although not tested, were generally recognized as safe. But when testing of the items on the list was initiated, the GRAS status was revoked for some, such as sulfites.

The Delaney Clause is a controversial part of the same amendment. It states that no cancer-causing substances can be added to foods. It was responsible for the ban of the artificial sweetener cyclamate in 1970, but when it was invoked to ban saccharine, however, public outcry resulted in a moratorium, which has been extended as further testing is done. There is a movement afoot to take some of the teeth out of this clause because zero risk is unachievable when any chemical enters the body via food—even naturally occurring chemical substances in foods. But opponents say that no benefit of any chemical in the food supply is worth the risk of developing cancer.

As was said earlier, most food safety issues revolve around trade-offs in which benefits are weighed in terms of the risks involved. This is a difficult area for scientists for a number of reasons. Many cancers take many years to develop. Testing of chemical substances is done on animals using doses that are much higher than a human would normally ingest in food, and the levels at which there are no effects from use of the substances are not known in many cases. Then there is also the question, If a lot of the substance causes tumors in rats, can proportionately smaller amounts have the same effects on humans? Many consumers feel a "better safe than sorry" approach should be followed.

The FDA sets tolerance, called action, levels for potentially harmful substances. Individual states, however, can set stricter levels. But because of economic hardships to producers, action levels unfortunately are raised, not lowered, in some instances. So become an active consumer—voice concerns and support consumer advocacy groups that represent those concerns. Names of several of these groups are in Appendix E.

Food Labeling

Reading labels can be a fascinating experience, especially after the discovery that there is more to most packaged foods than most people think. The desired item may be listed two-thirds of the way through all of the other ingredients, which often make up more of the product than the identifying ingredient. Is the product 100 percent orange juice, for example, or has orange pulp been combined with water, sugar, corn syrups, citric acid, tricalcium phosphate, artificial flavors and colors, and xanthan gum to make it look and taste like the real thing? To avoid getting duped, read labels.

Information on Food Labels

Food labels must contain certain basic information: the product name; the net contents or net weight (net weight also includes the liquid in which the food is packed); and the name and address of the manufacturer, packer, or distributor. With one exception, ingredients must be listed on the label in descending order of predominance by weight. The exception is foods falling under a standard of identity set by the FDA requiring that all those with a common name, such as mayonnaise, contain certain mandatory ingredients. These ingredients need not be listed on the label. If, however, additional ingredients are added, they must be mentioned on the label. Additives in most food products must be listed by name, but colors and flavors can simply be listed as artificial color or flavor or natural flavor. A food product label must state whether flavors are artificial. Disclosure of artificial color is not required for butter, cheese, and ice cream.

Nutrition information is required on labels for foods that have added nutrients or make a nutritional claim of any sort. Nutritional labeling must contain the following information: calories per serving; grams of carbohydrate, fat, and protein per serving; milligrams of sodium; and the percentage of the USRDAs for protein, vitamins A, C, thiamin, riboflavin, and niacin, and the minerals calcium and iron. This information can be voluntarily provided on any product, and many food manufacturers see this as an appropriate response to customer requests.

Imitation Foods

There are many imitation foods on the market today. As close as they may be in appearance to the real food, FDA mandates that the word "imitation" be used on labels for products that are not as nutritious as the ones they are imitating or substituting for. Those that are just as nutritious must be given a different name than the product they are replacing. It is not difficult to understand why the FDA defines imitation as nutritionally inferior.

Food imitations are most likely to be found among dairy foods, juices, and processed meats. If the first ingredient on the label is not orange juice, milk, or meat, or whatever the product should be, it is a clue that the food may be an imitation product. Many commercial orange drinks contain as little as 10 percent of the real stuff.

A real problem with fake foods is that their ingredients can be changed by manufacturers at will—there are no standards of identity for imitation eggs or orange juice, for instance. Since there is no consistency among the same products, the consumer is left in the dark as far as content and nutritional quality go.

If a jurisdiction has truth-in-menu legislation, there is some legal recourse against buying a prepared fresh food product that is not what it says it is.

For the price of real shrimp or crab, one should get just that, not an analog. A juice that looks like orange juice but is in reality a drop of orange juice in flavored water, would have to be labeled diluted orange juice drink. The percentage of the real food that is actually in the packaged version may also be required. A flavored food means that it contains an extract rather than the original flavor. Strawberry-flavored ice cream could contain strawberry extract, whereas strawberry ice cream would have to be flavored from whole strawberries (National Dairy Council 1983).

Misleading Labeling

Labeling rules, unfortunately, allow room for cheating. Manufacturers sometimes use loopholes to make misleading statements. For example, the package for a sweetened, sugary cereal may state that it is just as nutritious as Grapenuts. What the package label does not add is that the majority of carbohydrates come from refined sugars, whereas the Grapenuts contains mostly complex carbohydrate.

Many processed, enriched foods do not contain all of the nutrients the whole, fresh food did, but others are fortified with vitamins and minerals far in excess of what the fresh food contains. As the fortification of foods continues, there will be an increase of misleading product advertising. What is in reality a junk food can be made to appear nutritious. For example, the fortification of the diet cola Tab with calcium to encourage consumers to switch from milk to Tab is a public injustice. Calcium or no, Tab is an empty calorie beverage containing only flavored, carbonated water and controversial artificial sweeteners. To substitute this beverage for milk—skim, low fat, or whole—is to be robbed of the numerous beneficial nutrients contained in that wholesome dairy beverage. The uninformed consumer can be misled by product advertising. A nutritionally inferior food can be made to appear healthful by fortifying it with one or more nutrients and emphasizing this in advertising statements. However, if the label were read for this product, it would be discovered that all of the unhealthy saturated fat, sodium, etc., is still in the food—it has not become more healthful through fortification. Moreover, some scientists are concerned that the combined increase in food fortification and intake of high-potency vitamin and mineral supplements will lead to more cases of toxic reactions from this super-overload of nutrients far beyond recommended levels.

The FDA has in the past ruled out any health claims on food package labels. Now, terms such as "fortified," "low calorie," etc., imply health benefits. An even bolder approach has been taken by the Kellogg Company, with its implications that eating bran cereal will help prevent cancer. Currently, the FDA is allowing health messages that emphasize good nutrition but are not misleading. So there has emerged a gray area between the extremes of misleading health claims and of helpful nutritional information on product labels. Once again, the more informed the consumer is, the more easily he or she will be able to analyze food products for their real worth, not an implied or perceived health benefit. Advertising for FDA-regulated food products is actually the responsibility of the Federal Trade Commission (FTC). But if the information or claims are on the product label, rather than in an ad, FDA is responsible.

Labeling Regulations and Standards

Recent regulations and standards set by the FDA and the USDA will result in more nutrient information on labels as well as clearer definitions of the standards—all aimed at informing consumers about products. The U.S. Department of Agriculture, for example, has initiated new regulations for labeling ham and cured pork products in terms of the amount of fat-free meat protein only, rather than in terms of the amount of water and curing solution in the meat. USDA policies would require lean meat and poultry to contain no more than 10 percent fat by weight and extra lean meat to contain no more than 5 percent. State and local requirements may differ, however. It is wise to find out what the terms mean where meats are actually purchased. New USDA standards are also forthcoming for terms such as lite, light, and leaner and lower fat.

Fast foods, which customers purchase in wrappers or other types of packages, fall under the requirements of the Food, Drug and Cosmetic Act to list ingredients in packaged foods on the package labels. It has been up to individual states to enforce the requirements, however. In 1986, the state of New York forged ahead and committed McDonald's, and by now possibly other fast-food chains, to provide ingredient information for the foods they sell in that state. Later in the same year, bills were introduced in Congress that would require all fast-food operators of a certain size in terms of number of outlets to provide a list of ingredients.

Another issue of concern was the use of animal fat for frying. Pressure from consumer activist groups has resulted in a switch to vegetable oils by some fast food operations. Most of the major operations are distributing fliers that give nutrition information for foods in units or are providing them on request. But resistance is high to labeling packages with ingredients, one reason being that consumers would not know what was in the food until after it was purchased.

For product information not on labels, let the consumer beware. False food (and other) product claims can be and are made. The First Amendment of the Constitution guarantees the freedom to speak or write about products. In so doing, it also allows anyone to speak or write misinformation about a food product in terms of health and/or nutritional benefits, as long as the statements do not appear on the label. Books, pamphlets, and verbal media messages can virtually say anything. And studies show that consumers depend heavily on both the written and electronic media for health and nutrition (as well as other) information. Appendix E lists agencies and organizations that are involved in researching and disseminating scientific nutrition information for consumers. The nutrition departments of major colleges and universities as well as hospitals are also trustworthy sources of information.

Keep in mind that anyone can call him or herself a nutritionist. The title Registered Dietitian (RD), however, can be used only by those who have completed an appropriate course of study at the college level and passed a qualifying exam. They must also meet continuing education requirements to retain their RD registration. People with advanced degrees may be highly knowledgeable and professional, but the credentials M.S., Ph.D., and so on, can be obtained by mail order from questionable educational institutions. So check with a local department of education to verify credentials. Also beware of individuals promoting products or cures that legitimate current scientific research does not recognize. The best protection from false or misleading advice is to be an informed consumer.

REFERENCES

Center for Science in the Public Interest. 1986. Animal drugs. *Nutrition Action Health Letter 13* (5), 1–7.

Center for Science in the Public Interest. 1984. Watch those fly parts. *Nutrition Action Health Letter 11* (9), 13.

Cowart, V. 1985. Keeping foods safe and labels honest. *The Journal of the American Medical Association. Contempo '85,* 2340.

Graham, H. D. 1980. *The Safety of Foods.* Westport, Ct.: AVI Publishing.

Harris, R. S., and Karmas, E. 1977. *Nutritional Evaluation of Food Processing.* Westport, Ct.: AVI Publishing.

Harvard Medical School Health Letter. 1985. *Drugs in Animal Food 10* (9), 1–3.

Labuza, T. P., and Erdman, J. 1984. *Food Technology and Nutrition.* St. Paul, Minn.: West Publishing.

Levine, A. S., Labuza, T. P., and Morley, J. E. Food technology, a primer for physicians. *The New England Journal of Medicine 312,* (10) 628–634.

Mills, S. 1986. National Restaurant Association Research Conference, Chicago, Ill. Presentation.

National Dairy Council. 1983. *The Limitations of Imitations.* Rosemont, Ill. Brochure.

Nutrition Policy. 1986. *On USDA's Docket: Nitrites, Lowfat Hot Dogs and Chicken Standards.* Washington, D.C.: Webster Communications Corporation, *1* (6) 9.

Schloss, A. 1984. Smoked, salted and dried meats. *Cook's Magazine* Nov./Dec., 86–91.

Schumacher, A. 1986. Presentation by commissioner. Boston, Mass.: Massachusetts Department of Agriculture.

Stare, F. S., and Aronson, V. 1985. *Food for Fitness After Fifty: A Menu for Good Health in Later Years.* Philadelphia, Penn.: G. F. Stickley.

Stratton, B., and Schlossberg, H. 1986. Color Us Nutritional. *Restaurants and Institutions 96* (19), 151–4.

U.S. Department of Agriculture. 1975. *Nutrition Labeling: Tools for Its Use.* Agricultural Information Bulletin No. 382. Washington, D.C.: Agricultural Research Service.

U.S. Department of Health and Human Services. 1977. A consumer's guide to food labels. Food and Drug Administration. *FDA Consumer* June (Reprint No. 77–2083). Rockville, Md.

U.S. Department of Health and Human Services. 1978. Hazards from nature. Food and Drug Adminstration. *FDA Consumer,* May (Reprint No. 81–2102). Rockville, Md.

U.S. Department of Health and Human Services. 1981. Danger lurks among the molds. Food and Drug Administration. *FDA Consumer* Dec./Jan. (Reprint No. 81–2143). Rockville, Md.

U.S. Department of Health and Human Services. 1982. More than you thought you would know about food additives. Food and Drug Administration. *FDA Consumer* Feb. (Reprint No. 82–2160). Rockville, Md.

Part III

NUTRITION APPLICATIONS

IN FOOD SERVICE

Chapter 6

FOOD CONSUMPTION TRENDS AND MARKETING ISSUES

Traditionally, restaurateurs have seen food trends come and go and products and customer preference change with amazing swiftness. Many of these trends emanate from within the industry itself. These movements influence eating habits across the country. An increase in health consciousness and worldwide travel have made many Americans more aware of the food they eat in terms of health and cultural diversity. Basically, consumers are more sophisticated.

For the food industry, keeping in tune with trends and influences can mean an increase in profits. Some food professionals categorize trends as crossovers; this means new relationships among different ethnic and regional foods, preparation techniques, ingredients, and flavorings. These relationships often result in new food concepts, usually combinations of established products and techniques, perhaps transported to new areas, adapted to meet new preferences, labeled by the industry, and finally promoted as the "new" by the media.

Today's restaurant patron is a more adventurous eater and a more demanding customer. Increasing consumer interest in foods that meet established nutritional criteria is affecting the food service industry, particularly the restaurateur. The importance of nutrition in the restaurant is significant; it is part of a growing trend toward simple, good-tasting, fresh food. This trend is not going to disappear when media promotion declines, especially because of the increased awareness of the effects of diet on health. Neither restaurateur nor patron will totally ignore this relationship. Virtually any concept or style of cooking can be adapted if necessary to reflect scientifically established dietary recommendations without sacrificing taste or presentation.

Changes in Food Preferences and Eating Habits

Interest in the health aspects of food is no longer confined to "health food types" and those on medically restricted diets. Today, an increasing number of healthy Americans have made health-related changes in their eating habits and food preferences. Socioeconomic and life-style changes have also resulted in changes in food preferences and eating habits, and there has been a marked increase in eating out or purchasing prepared foods to eat in. In either case, some people are eating more food prepared by others than by themselves.

National Restaurant Association surveys indicate that the average individual eats out approximately 3.7 times a week and that nearly 80 million customer transactions occur in commercial food service establishments each day. The association estimates that 40 percent of the food dollar is currently spent away from home.

For some people—particularly businesspeople and others who travel frequently—as much as half their nutrition needs might be provided by the food service industry, primarily restaurants. A disadvantage for these people is that restaurant food selection may be limited, with choices being of less than desirable nutritional value. In fact, researchers at Cornell University found that overall nutrient intake was lower for those persons eating meals away from home (Bunch and Hall 1983).

However, consumers are changing food choices rather than their away-from-home eating habits. A Gallup survey conducted for the National Restaurant Association in 1986 found that six out of ten consumers had changed their eating habits at home, basically to conform more closely to the dietary guidelines discussed in Chapter 3. The survey also indicated that four out of ten were changing away-from-home eating habits in a similar manner (National Restaurant Association 1986), by requesting that menu items be prepared without salt or added fat, for example.

A segmentation study conducted by the National Restaurant Association grouped similar types of customers to investigate how attitudes toward health and nutrition issues affect food choices. Four customer groups were identified. Although most people in the groups were aware of diet-health issues, study results indicated that in the restaurant, patrons acted differently according to their groups.

"Traditional" consumers ate out the most and ate the most fast food. Their behavioral descriptions revealed that they are meat-and-potatoes oriented: They eat whatever they like and are not particularly interested in the healthful qualities of food when eating out. Their choices at home reflect their choices out: regular soft drinks, white bread, steak. This group constitutes the primary market segment for the fast food industry.

The weight-conscious and health-conscious groups accounted for a large share of dining occasions in fine-dining and atmosphere restaurants. The groups differed in that the health-conscious showed less concern for calories than with nutritional content and avoided diet drinks, artificial sweeteners, and other calorie-reduced foods favored by the weight-conscious group. Both groups, however, looked for menu items low in fat, sodium, and calories. The weight-conscious group expressed a strong desire to eat out more often and for more restaurants to offer appropriate options.

A fourth group, the uncommitted, represented busy, on-the-go people with mixed attitudes and behavior. They listen to the issues but tend to have erratic eating habits, such as skipping meals and snacking, and exhibited no particular emphasis in menu selection (National Restaurant Association 1986).

It appears that consumers who are most interested in nutrition in restaurants tend to eat in those described as atmosphere or fine dining. This may become a limiting description because of the trend toward casual but upscale establishments that the same groups who eat in fine and atmospheric restaurants will also frequent. Since these people are extremely knowledgeable about the relationship between nutrition and health, restaurateurs in these categories will have to be knowledgeable about nutrition and translate that knowledge to the menu mix in order to attract what may be a major portion of the clientele.

Most people, however, usually rely on a mix of food and dining experiences. For example, those who routinely choose fine or atmosphere restaurants for dinner may take their children to a fast food or family establishment once a week or eat lunch in a sandwich shop. Therefore, healthful menu alternatives in every type of operation would meet the needs of both occasional and regular patron groups.

Consider the fast food business. Even though a majority of customers may not express an interest in more healthful choices at point of sale, pressure from consumer advocacy groups and some individual consumers has encouraged some chains to provide ingredient information, to change cooking oils, and to offer salad bars. Fast does not necessarily have to be greasy, salty, or sugary. Good marketing strategy is revealed in efforts to accommodate all customers as much as possible within the concept/type of operation.

The major problems in restaurants, from a health standpoint, are foods that tend to be high in fat, saturated fat, cholesterol, sodium, and calories and the use of highly processed convenience items that may be high in saturated fat and sodium. Overcooking, cooking and holding/reheating, soaking, and other preparation methods also detract from nutritional value. The entire menu should emphasize good, fresh food prepared in a healthful manner—not just nutritious alternatives.

Consumers tend to pay more for products that reflect their personal concerns and interests: This can be accomplished by knowing your clientele, and individualizing menus by offering choices appropriate for them. Customers will return if the food is not only nutritious but tastes and looks good. Witness, for example, the success of the Spa Cuisine offered at New York's The Four Seasons restaurant. It accounts for approximately 35 percent of menu sales. For patrons, it offers an alternative that tastes and looks just as good as regular menu items. This helps contribute to a pleasant dining experience for both regular and special-occasion customers.

As more restaurateurs develop healthful menu items, it is important to remember that offering a choice is the key. The choices may be a few specific items, variations on a particular dish, or a completely separate menu. Therefore, the nutritional aspects of menu planning, as well as purchasing, preparation techniques, presentation, and marketing, are important operational considerations.

In another survey conducted by Gallup for the National Restaurant Association, 40 percent of those interviewed said they changed their eating habits when dining out by increasing, when possible, choices of fruit, vegetables, and whole grains or by decreasing choices of foods perceived to be high in sugar, animal fat, and salt (National Restaurant Association 1983). This survey was repeated in 1986, with the same statistical findings (National Restaurant Association 1986). As the price of meals increases, however, so do patron expectations in terms of freshness of ingredients, wait-staff knowledge of individual dishes, and kitchen flexibility in preparing special requests (National Restaurant Association 1982).

Restaurants responding to nutrition-related customer preferences may use several marketing approaches. They can emphasize freshness by mentioning regional foods and local products. Menu copy can indicate use of simpler, lighter preparation methods, announce an affiliation with a nutrition program or consultant, or state the availability of nutrient breakdowns on request. Healthful menu alternatives with nutrient analysis of key items might be scattered throughout the menu or listed on a separate menu or flier. Knowledgeable, accurate responses to customers' questions and requests are a vitally important, adjunct to what appears on the menu.

In 1983, the Public Voice for Food and Health Policy issued a report, *Nutrition and the American Restaurant,* which described various restaurant nutrition programs in terms of case studies. Common structural components of these efforts were then described. It was found that restaurants present alternative menu items in various ways, dictated largely by the individual operation. But almost all of the efforts presented in the case studies included the following elements: emphasis on freshness and simple preparation methods; interest and commitment by the chef or restaurateur; a wait-staff training program; new arrangements with suppliers; and technical assistance from health professionals or participation in a health program. Consumer information about and marketing of healthful food alternatives included innovative use of menus, use of table tents, brochures and recipes in the restaurant, and media advertising or promotion through health organizations and consumer groups. Wait-staff training was seen as a very important element in communicating with customers and selling items (Public Voice for Food and Health Policy 1983).

Most restaurant nutrition efforts are in response to customer demand. Concerns expressed by consumers with regard to foods they eat include the amount of fat, cholesterol, additives, processing, and sodium. The biggest changes consumers are making, however, seem to be meat related (read fat and cholesterol) (Food Marketing Institute Conference 1986). There also seems to be a shift to consumers eating things that they perceive as good for them instead of just avoiding what is perceived to be bad. Food professionals can help consumers make appropriate choices by planning menus and using a variety of ingredients that reflect current health concerns. Offer choices within each menu category. Remember, the ultimate decision is up to the customer. The road to good nutrition is really a chain of events, and the food professional provides a crucial link.

In helping patrons make healthful choices, it is important to recognize what they are looking for in terms of both offering and selling healthful menu options. It is too costly to develop these items and too difficult in terms of freshness of the item to prep for only one or perhaps no orders. In addition, menu language and wait-staff training are crucial factors in selling these alternatives.

Healthful menu alternatives should be virtually indistinguishable from regular menu items in quality, taste, appearance, and price. For example, if the majority of patrons come to eat beef, offer a healthful beef alternative. There may be a chicken or fish item on the menu for those who prefer these meats to beef that might also serve as a healthful alternative. However, if beef is what customers are coming in for, it is in the restaurant's interest from a marketing standpoint to offer a beef dish lower in fat and sodium than regular menu items. This may be achieved by changing the cut of meat, portion size, preparation, or perhaps all three. Whether a restaurant is classical French, Tex-Mex, or regional American, options should be in step with the rest of the menu. Basic concepts should not be changed for healthful items. A spartan piece of dry-broiled fish with paprika and a lemon slice on top, for example, will not be appealing to someone who came for tacos or bistro fare or beef fillet in red wine sauce. Healthful menu items should closely resemble richer items visually and, especially, in taste quality.

Taste is as important as appearance, and, for most people, it is more important than nutritional qualities. A study of a family-style restaurant used three sets of menu language to describe a daily special. One time the special was described in terms of how healthful it was. Another time the description emphasized ingredients and preparation, thus indicating how it might taste (preparation also alluded to healthfulness). A third description stated only that the dish was the daily special. Results of the study indicated that patrons selected the healthful special only when menu language emphasized flavor. For these customers, taste came first (American Journal of Preventive Medicine, 1987).

All this does not mean that unless food in restaurants is labeled as healthy, it is not nutritious. Many restaurants serve many items that meet criteria for being healthful. To do so may not involve a conscious effort but reliance on fresh, simple food. Even more elaborate dishes can be healthful. Sometimes it is what the customer adds that makes a dish less than desirable healthwise. Some menu items are not healthful, are not meant to be, and are enjoyed for what they are—a treat. This is fine, too.

It therefore pays to be attentive to general trends in terms of consumer preference and, importantly, to the needs and food choice patterns of particular customers. Patrons should be informed about specific healthful qualities of menu alternatives (this will be discussed in more detail under menu planning), and wait-staff should be instructed to communicate interest in the well-being of clientele. Personalization of a product is an important marketing tool—if it is promoted and carried out in terms of menu planning, freshness of product, careful attention to preparation, and balance and attractiveness of presentation.

To facilitate customer acceptance and sales of healthful menu options, remember the following suggestions:

1. Healthful menu alternatives should not be perceived as different in any way from popular, regular menu items—in taste, presentation, or cost.
2. Know customer preferences and tailor menu options to your specific target market.
3. Do not offer items requiring a separate mise en place—use ingredients prepped for regular items.
4. Try the marketing approach of repositioning two or three regular, popular items using healthful cooking techniques.
5. Wait-staff training and menu copy are important merchandising factors.

The bottom line is that no one approach works for all restaurants—concept, style, food, clientele and location influence the manner in which nutrition is introduced to the operation. For patrons, healthful menu options can remove the burden of decision when ordering; remove the stigma of eating something healthful but "different"; and, for frequent customers, certainly influence the quality of that person's diet over a period of time.

REFERENCES

American Journal of Preventive Medicine, 1987. Promoting the selection of healthy food through menu item description in a family-style restaurant. *American Journal of Preventive Medicine 3* (3), 171–177.

Bunch, K., and Hall, L. 1983. *Factors Affecting Nutrient Composition.* Ithaca, N.Y.: Cornell University.

Fisher, M. F. K. 1971. *The Physiology of Taste.* New York: Alfred A. Knopf. (Translation of Brillat-Savarin's *Physiologie du Gout.*)

Food Marketing Institute Conference. 1986. *Promoting Health in Today's Food Marketplace.* Washington, D.C.: FMI, March 17–18.

National Restaurant Association. 1982. *Consumer Attitude and Behavior Study: How Consumers Make the Decision to Eat Out.* Washington, D.C.: NRA.

National Restaurant Association. 1983. *Changes in Consumer Eating Habits.* The Gallup Organization, Washington, D.C.: NRA.

National Restaurant Association. 1984. *Food Service Industry Pocket Factbook.* Washington, D.C.: NRA.

National Restaurant Association. 1986. Nutrition continues to affect restaurant choices. *NRA News.* June/July, pp. 35–38.

National Restaurant Association. 1986. Remarks presented at research conference, Chicago, Ill.

Public Voice for Food and Health Policy. 1983. *Nutrition and the American Restaurant.* Washington, D.C.: Public Voice.

Stratton, B., and Schlossberg, H. 1986. Color us nutritional. (Fast Food) *Restaurants and Institutions Magazine 96* (19), 151–154.

Chapter 7

DEVELOPING HEALTHFUL
MENU ALTERNATIVES

At a food conference, a speaker chose Nutrition for the Upscale Restaurant as a topic. The program description promised a how-to formula for an exciting menu that was nutritionally balanced. At first glance, it sounded great. But in reality, it was like promising a quick and easy way to lose weight. Unfortunately, there is no single sure-fire formula for creating a successful (in terms of sales percentages), nutritionally balanced alternative menu for all operations.

As discussed in Chapter 6, a menu is dictated by many factors, including concept, clientele, budget, personnel capabilities, equipment, and season. The important thing to remember is to use selected nutrition guidelines that meet the perceived needs of customers and can be realistically implemented within the scope of the operation.

The most difficult aspects of initiating healthy menu alternatives are: (1) defining a nutritional philosophy (will the menu reflect a general healthful/ fresh approach; or will it follow specific guidelines such as those of the American Heart Association; or will the approach be targeted, such as low calorie); (2) developing or obtaining a set of nutritional guidelines that reflect the philosophy; (3) developing recipes that meet the guidelines; (4) training kitchen and dining room staff; and (5) communicating the message to the public. When challenged with developing recipes that meet nutritional guidelines, cooks usually enjoy the creativity involved in substituting ingredients or devising preparation techniques to reduce fat, sodium, and so on. The key is to have a set of nutritional guidelines and motivate staff to follow them accurately for designated menu items.

Motivation comes from understanding the relationship between diet and health, realizing that healthful cooking need not be restrictive (classically trained chefs traditionally use many ingredients reduced or omitted in healthy menu items), and taking pride and pleasure in presenting attractive, good-tasting, yet healthful food. Implementation requires in-house training and follow-up.

Restaurateurs often seek help in choosing appropriate nutritional guidelines and evaluating products to see if they conform to those guidelines. Guidelines range from general ones, such as following the Dietary Guidelines with a statement to that effect on the menu, to specific ones, such as nutrient calculations for specific dishes or a computerized nutrient printout for the entire menu. Or they can fall somewhere in between, such as offering a fixed price menu of 500 calories in which fat accounts for no more than 20 percent or stating that foods are cooked in vegetable oil without added salt. The options are vast. This is why it is important to work within the framework of the existing operation, if successful, and needs of the clientele as revealed through formal or informal in-house market research.

A safe way to start is to choose existing dishes that are low in sodium, fat, and cholesterol, and identify them on the menu. Then, choose a few other dishes that are familiar to your patrons and modify them slightly. Next, develop new dishes, and so forth. It has become chic to offer an alternative cuisine. But remember, not everyone eating out is going to be health conscious or diet restricted. Choice is the key. And the more closely the healthful items resemble the regular menu, the greater their acceptance will be.

Menu Terminology

At this point, a word about menu terminology is needed. Currently, healthful menus or menu item alternatives may be described as "lite," "alternative," "fit 'n healthy," "spa" (Spa Cuisine™ is a trademark of The Four

Seasons restaurant in New York), and the like. What do these descriptions really tell the customer? Because the term "lite" has customer appeal, many restaurants are adding "lite fare" to their menus. These items, however, may not meet health-related criteria in terms of low fat, low calorie, low sodium, and so on. When some "lite" menu items, such as three-egg omelettes, overstuffed deli meat sandwiches with potato chips, and quiche, cost the same as regular items such as baked scrod with vegetables, it is tempting to ask, what is "lite?"

Contradictions abound. Ideally, all food should be carefully prepared, using fresh ingredients when possible. But it is not. There are, however, appropriate ways to designate menu items that meet nutritional criteria. Dishes can be flagged and a brief, descriptive statement can be inserted at the bottom of the menu. Or a flier or separate menu can be used. Perhaps menu copy for the dishes can suffice as the clue that the item is low-fat or otherwise healthful. Descriptive terminology would then become an important consideration in menu planning, with use of terms such as poached, or finished with wine, stock reduction, and herbs, or whatever statement best describes ingredients and preparation.

Ways to express nutrient values with menu mock-ups using symbols, statements, and nutrient breakdown are illustrated in Figures 7.1 through 7.4 on the following pages.

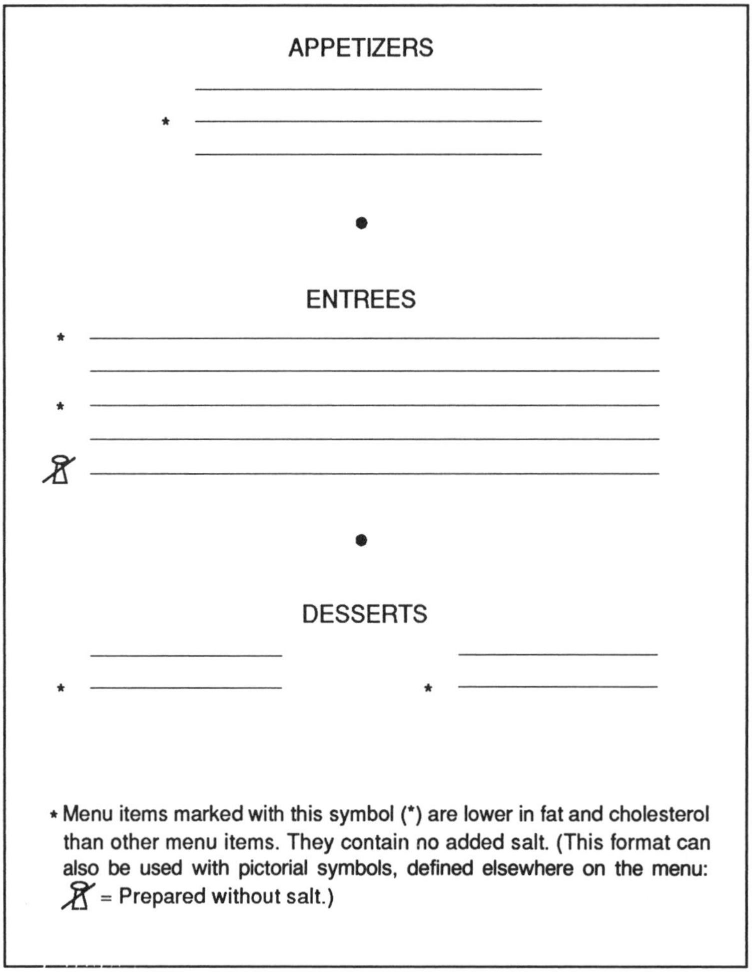

APPETIZERS

ENTREES

DESSERTS

* Menu items marked with this symbol (*) are lower in fat and cholesterol than other menu items. They contain no added salt. (This format can also be used with pictorial symbols, defined elsewhere on the menu: = Prepared without salt.)

NOTE: This format could also be used if participating in a program by replacing the * or with the program logo and replacing the general statement with program guidelines.

FIGURE 7.1 Alternative menu items indicated with symbol plus statement.

DINNER
Tuesday

_____
_____
_____

•

_____
_____

•

_____
_____

This menu offers selections which have been prepared to reduce fat, cholesterol, sodium, and calorie content. ① Choice of an appetizer, main course and dessert total 600 calories or less.②

NOTE: This menu statement could be worded to: omit the calorie information (②); or to omit the general statement (①) and include more detailed nutrient information.

FIGURE 7.2 Separate alternative menu with statement.

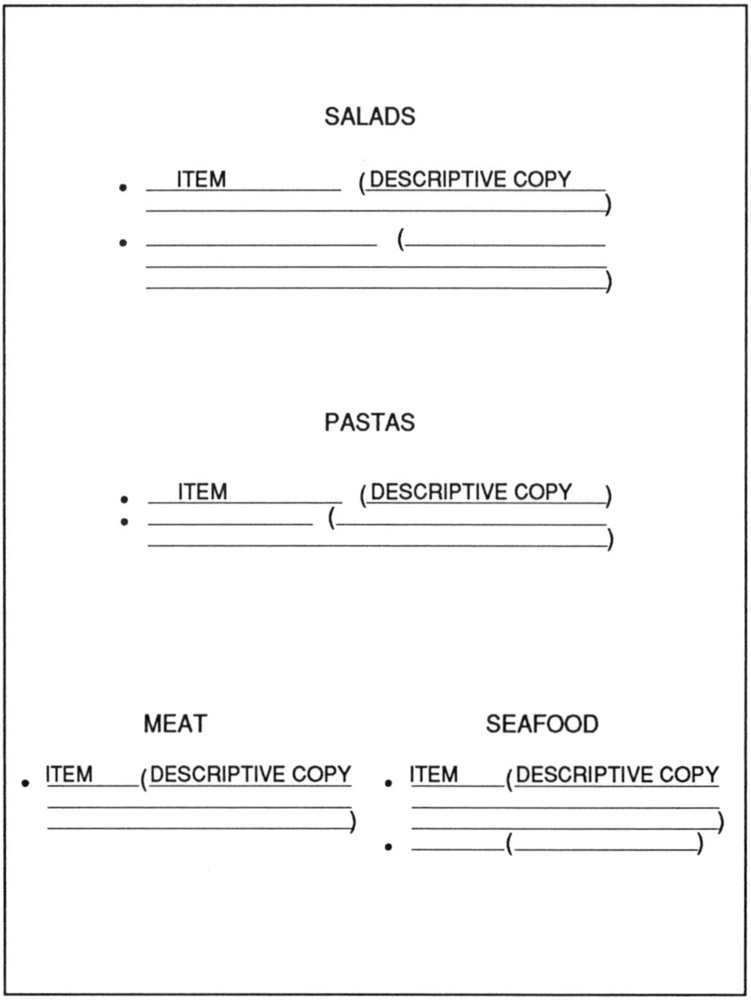

SALADS

- ITEM (DESCRIPTIVE COPY)
- ( )

PASTAS

- ITEM (DESCRIPTIVE COPY)
- ( )

MEAT

- ITEM (DESCRIPTIVE COPY)

SEAFOOD

- ITEM (DESCRIPTIVE COPY)
- ( )

FIGURE 7.3 Healthfulness of menu items implied in menu copy.

(1) _____
     _____
     ____ Calories   ____ % Fat

                      OR

(2) _____
     _____
     _____
     ____ gm fat; ____mg cholesterol; ____mg sodium

                      OR

(3) * _____

        * Nutrient information available upon request

NOTE: The above illustrates 3 methods of providing
detailed nutrient information:
   (1) expressed as numbers and/or percents
   (2) expressed as weights
   (3) nutrient information available as separate printout

FIGURE 7.4 Alternative menu items with nutrient information provided.

Coping with the Nutrition Issue

In addition to terminology, there are other areas that need to be addressed as more restaurants look to nutrition as an important operational component. Seventy-eight percent of all foodservice professionals surveyed by the trade publication *Food Management* listed nutrition among their top four concerns. It followed quality, cost containment, and sanitation, respectively—all crucial links in the chain of operational components. Of these priorities, nutrition seems to be the most difficult to deal with from a management standpoint (Schuster, 1985). Is healthful eating presented in a manner that benefits the customer healthwise and is profitable (or worthwhile) to the restaurateur? The following factors affect the foodservice professional's ability to cope with the nutrition issue, as well as the customer's perception of healthful items as presented on the menu and the plate.

Nutrition Education

To date, most restaurateurs, executive chefs, and cooks have had very little nutrition training. The result of this is frustration in terms of knowing what to do and how to do it and the necessity of relying on outside assistance or just winging it with a generalistic approach that may or may not meet nutritional criteria. This situation is changing, however. Culinary schools are including nutrition courses in their curriculums and nutrition activities in food labs, and student-run restaurants are featuring healthful menu items. Also, as a result of nutrition requirements for certification developed by the American Culinary Federation and proposals for similar requirements by other professional culinary organizations, there are now professional studies and continuing education courses in nutrition. The American Heart Association offers nutrition education for restaurateurs participating in AHA programs. This new educational emphasis on nutrition in restaurants and in culinary schools probably will ease the burden for many managers and chefs who are planning and developing menu items to meet selected nutritional criteria.

Even with nutrition education, though, it is important for those chefs in the field to keep abreast of changes in food-related nutrition issues through professional associations and publications. Trends may develop slowly, but nutrition recommendations can seemingly crop up overnight. Food professionals must keep pace with a rapidly growing and changing body of information on topics such as cruciferous vegetables, fiber, calcium, omega-3 fish oils, monounsaturated fats and so forth. Fortunately, restaurant trade journals have beefed up coverage of nutrition issues.

Menu Alternatives

Another consideration is how much time should be devoted to developing menu alternatives and how should they be represented on the menu. Many restaurant menus meet all criteria for healthy eating through simplicity—the use of absolutely fresh ingredients and uncomplicated preparations. In such cases, nutritional information may not need to be offered because the quality and healthfulness of the food can be seen on the plate. Ambitious nutritional aspirations and complex food, however, can present a real challenge.

First of all, it is difficult for a chef to work within the confines of a menu that tells customers they are getting x number of calories, y grams of fat, and so on. Cooks learn to taste and adjust seasonings and correct items that are not quite right. Techniques other than swirling butter into a sauce to finish it or adding salt or cream to achieve balance have to be developed. It may become necessary to rethink preparation techniques, flavoring sources, and ingredient compositions. The nouvelle movement produced some spectacular creations, as well as some bizarre combinations. The same could occur when developing an alternative cuisine. Fortunately, with a new emphasis on simple cooking and less fussed-over food, the new alternative cooking may escape this pitfall. Of the three major elements of a cuisine—ingredients, technique, and flavor—the last seems to be the most elusive when developing tasteworthy, healthful dishes.

Accurate Representation of Dishes

A potential area for concern is the temptation to cheat. There are "lite" menus that are not really light. A low-calorie dish does not necessarily mean it is also low in sodium or cholesterol. That healthful dish may actually contain ersatz ingredients. It is important to think through nutritional goals in terms of menu language carefully. If a restaurant offers a printout of many nutrients, the meal or dish must match it. If the menu states that a dish has x number of calories or y percent fat, then so it must.

Become aware of federal and local laws related to documentation for nutrition claims. Many local jurisdictions have written truth-in-menu clauses into local health codes. Nutritional breakdowns on menus should cite the source of information. Never make a menu statement that is not accurately represented in the food it describes.

How is nutritional information presented in terms of menu design? First, goals must be chosen in terms of clientele, staff abilities, and so forth. When these are established, the menu must present them in a straightforward, accurate manner. The approaches vary. Some restaurants focus on the calorie content of the food, for example, a restaurant with a spa-type cuisine that lists a half-dozen spa entrees and makes a statement that spa-type cuisine is 400 calories or less. Other menus might inform customers that food is prepared with little fat, no salt, and fresh ingredients. Hilton Hotels developed a Fitness First menu to go with their fitness program for traveling executives. The menu emphasizes calories but uses the word "about" to allow for flexibility in terms of ingredient changes and substitutions; a menu item would read "about x calories." Other restaurants give complete descriptions of each dish, detailing ingredients and preparation methods which allude to its healthfulness.

Many restaurants focus on food items that are classified as light or "lite"; nevertheless, their menus might indicate that the customer talk to wait-staff regarding items that *are* actually low in fat, sodium, and so on. Depending on a customer's specific needs, this may lead to adaptation of the light food item or even the use of an entirely different dish. The point to be made is that words such as light can be meaningless in terms of giving customers a clue as to nutritional content. Perhaps the term is used to signify smaller portions or simple preparation. It also can be misleading because customers equate light with certain nutritional characteristics in terms of calories or fat, for example. A seemingly light dish made with high-fat ingredients, such as a mousse or a butter-finished sauce, would not necessarily be light in terms of calories or fat. Light is ambiguous. Be straightforward with menu statements.

Some restaurants affiliate with diet or health and fitness programs, thereby agreeing to conform to their guidelines and, in some cases, stipulation of ingredients or substitutions. Negative feedback from the kitchen can result from narrow ingredient restrictions. Allowing flexibility in terms of foods and ingredients seems to be a more successful approach. Menu items that conform to program guidelines are usually flagged, and a statement identifying the program and its guidelines appears on the menu. Most program guidelines, like those of the American Heart Association, focus on decreasing fat, saturated fat, cholesterol, and sodium.

Many alternative menus, menu items, nutritional criteria, and statements are general or focus on what might be called the major components of food as they relate to cooking—amount of saturated fat and cholesterol in food and added during preparation, or salt added, for example. Others go into more detail, citing additional information on vitamins and minerals. It can involve considerable work on the part of a restaurant to determine which macro- and micronutrients are important to emphasize on the menu in the context of the type of food offered, to develop and calculate recipes, and to reproduce these exact calculations accurately in terms of food preparation methods, variability of ingredients, staff monitoring, and so forth.

Some restaurants analyze all menu nutrients, A to Zinc, and offer a printout of the information. This is a commendable effort, but one might question its feasibility in most restaurant settings, its necessity healthwise, and its usefulness to customers. It leaves no room for flexibility in terms of substituting green beans for broccoli that did not look good or in a preparation technique. Some preparations are variable: the amount of flour varies when making pasta, for example, due to humidity and other factors.

Culinary students learn the importance of weighing ingredients. Calculating nutrients can be excellent training also. They develop a feel for preparing nutritionally balanced meals and an eye for ingredient selection in terms of weights, sizes, and proportions. But do these calculations please patrons?

The National Restaurant Association has concluded that customers are not looking for this type of information. People looking for healthy food do not necessarily want to see numbers (Gindin 1984). They do, however, want to feel that the restaurant cares about the healthful qualities of the foods. This seems to indicate that a general statement about the ingredients is beneficial and practical for both the restaurateur and the customer. A general statement or a percentage can be more easily visualized. A statement that a menu item "Contains less than 30 percent of total calories as fat, in accordance with American Heart Association recommendations," for example, is more meaningful than "contains *x* grams of fat." One would need to know total calories in the item as well as the number of calories per gram of fat to determine the proportion of fat in that item. Most people will not be up to that mental arithmetic.

When designating calorie content of an alternative menu, keep in mind that the 600-calorie meal may be fine for one diner and may even approximate a third of their daily intake. For the person's companion across the table, however, this number may be way over or under, depending on what they ate before, plan to eat later on, and of course, individual requirements. It may be best to offer a calorie range for items in each menu category and then let customers tally their own. Also, remember that many patrons will order the low-calorie meal and then have a rich dessert.

Nutritional status is determined by the nutritional quality of the diet over a period of time. This is best addressed by an overall focus on a variety of foods, consumed in moderation. Normal, healthy individuals who follow the general advice in the Dietary Guidelines and choose foods from all of the food groups should not have to analyze in detail the nutrient content of every meal they consume to remain healthy. Nor should restaurants have to do this.

Restaurants should follow current, scientific guidelines in terms of reducing the amount of fat, saturated fat, cholesterol, and sodium in the foods they serve, then look to the four food groups to give patrons a balance of micronutrients and fiber. If all away-from-home food were prepared according to these principles, using fresh, minimally processed ingredients, the health of the eating-out public would improve immensely.

If, in the competitive race for the healthy food dollar, nutrient printouts for menu items become a marketing tool, they will detract from the emphasis on healthy dining and may even temporarily dampen the food-as-health trend. It is important for food professionals to be aware of diet-related health issues and to know which groups of foods are good sources of major nutrients and which food components should be used sparingly. This knowledge should be built into a balanced menu mix that offers patrons a choice. Then it is up to customers to select foods from that menu to fulfill their personal dietary needs.

A possible problem area lies within nutritional analysis itself, however simple it may be. Many of today's trendy or regional ingredients have not made it into computer software or printed nutrient data sources. Further, these resources do not reflect diverse preparation methods and variable recipes. Therefore, any analysis is an approximation. If, for example, a person watching sodium intake ate a dish containing prepacked sun-dried tomatoes and the sodium content of the dish was calculated without the tomatoes because they were not in the database, the analysis (or a guess) would not reflect the true sodium content of the recipe.

Regional Preferences and Availability

Other concerns for large operations or chains doing a specific alternative menu is regional food preferences and availability of ingredients. It may be better to develop individual site, rather than corporate, healthful menus, using products available in each location that reflect regional food preferences.

In summary, most restaurants would be better off developing a generalized set of guidelines that reflect current health concerns and looking at the large picture rather than focusing on details such as multiple vitamin and mineral analysis. One does not need to obtain 100 percent of the RDA for every nutrient every day, let alone in one meal. Several national health groups have issued guidelines on optimum amounts of fat and sodium in the diet. This advice is easy to apply in the kitchen by changing cooking oils, reducing the amount of cooking fat used in preparation or accompanying sauces, removing skin from chicken, substituting herbs for salt, and so forth. A statement that marked menu items conforming to specific established guidelines would suffice. Think of nutrition guidelines in terms of product selection, cooking techniques, and menu balance. Positive statements such as "Contains less than 700 calories and is prepared with fresh local ingredients using a minimum of fat, no saturated fat, and no added salt" would satisfy most patrons that the food was prepared with their welfare in mind.

Providing Nutritionally Balanced Meals

Food service personnel are not responsible for patrons' selections in terms of a balanced diet. But it is their responsibility to offer a choice of items that make it possible for customers to eat a healthful meal. As commercial foodservice provides for a greater percentage of the public's nutritional needs, the professional's responsibility with respect to the menu increases. This is at the root of the current issues concerning nutrition in restaurants —with more people consuming more foods prepared outside of the home, foodservice operators are placing more importance on the nutritional considerations of menu planning and recipe development. This is particularly evident in the fast-food industry, where in the past it has been difficult to select a meal that meets the Dietary Guidelines. With more individuals relying on fast food and its inroad into college, school, and highway food operations, however, it is encouraging to see some companies including more healthful menu items. Foodservice operations that provide individuals with most of their food, such as in nursing homes, hospitals, prisons, and schools, have an increased responsibility to provide nutritionally balanced meals.

Menus and Marketing

A restaurant's menu is its primary merchandising medium. It reflects both food philosophies and policies, and it is through the menu that customers' images of the operation are formed. This is why restaurant nutritional guidelines should be carefully thought through and accurately represented both on the menu and in the food.

Menu composition, however, has changed. The traditional French-inspired order of appetizer, soup, entree with vegetables, salad, dessert, and coffee is on the wane. Both the number of courses and selections within courses have decreased on most menus. And there is the trend toward customer "grazing" through a menu, choosing items randomly in a sequence that suits an individual's whim. This makes the nutritional aspects of balancing and coordinating selections within each course trickier. Do nutrition-conscious patrons want a fixed menu with choices and nutrient description? Or do they want to pick and choose and deal with the nutrient composition themselves? There is an increase in short, two- to three-item, single-choice menus and menus that list items by the type of food rather than course, that is, pizzas, pastas, fish, meat, grilled items and so forth.

When thinking about incorporating nutrition in the menu, a market analysis is essential. How nutrition oriented is the clientele? What is the present style? How can specific menu items be adapted within the limits of the production capacity of the kitchen? If patrons rely on the restaurant frequently, then healthful alternative(s) should be changed daily. Popular items can draw patrons back; perhaps one or two standard alternative items would appeal to transient and repeat customers alike.

From a sales perspective, it is best to keep the number of alternative items in proper proportion to the rest of the menu items. If the menu features six entrees, begin with two alternatives. Some customers will not switch to the alternatives right away, even though they indicated an interest. Many restaurants have spent time and money developing healthful alternatives only to find they do not sell, perhaps because of lack of patron interest, taste, or attractiveness of the foods. Remember, alternatives should closely resemble other menu items and should taste good. Steamed halibut wrapped in lettuce leaves may not sell in a steak house, but a grilled petite tenderloin and vegetable kabobs combo with baked potato chips probably will. The bottom line is that the nutritious alternative menu or menu items respect the preferences of customers and at the same time reflect current trends in the market.

Statistics on portions sold will disclose patron preferences, but in the case of alternative items, they will not indicate whether the items were or were not popular because of interest in health, taste, appearance, or all three. Where nutrition is concerned, it is important to distinguish between interest in nutrition and healthful eating and appeal in terms of taste and appearance (*American Journal of Preventive Medicine* 1987).

Other factors that might influence the sales of healthful offerings are season and time of day. People living in a changing climate tend to choose differently in the summer than in winter. Customers on the go, such as at noontime and before and after the theater, may tend to order less food than those who have settled in for the evening. Pricing is important, too. People tend to pay more for something that is tailored to their needs. They will not pay for a dish that is perceived to be of less value in terms of quantity or quality. Freshness, flavor, and presentation are of utmost importance. Menu accuracy is a must. If an item is described as cholesterol-free, a person under such dietary restrictions must trust that statement. If someone in the kitchen uses butter instead of margarine, the menu has become misleading and inaccurate. The Environmental Health Administration in Washington, D.C., has developed Accuracy in Menu Language Guidelines for the Food-service Industry. Where nutrition is concerned, inaccurate representation could, over the long run, adversely affect someone's health.

REFERENCES

American Journal of Preventive Medicine. 1987. Promoting the selection of healthy food through menu item description in a family-style restaurant. *American Journal of Preventive Medicine 3* (3), 171–177.

Erdman, J. W. 1979. Effect of preparation and service of food on nutritional value. *Food Technology 33* (2) 38–74.

Gindin, R. 1984. Menus for the active generation. *Restaurant Business* May, 166.

Green, E. F., Galen, G., and Drake, F. 1978. *Profitable Food and Beverage Management: Operations.* Rochelle Park, N.J.: Hayden.

Kotschevar, L. 1975. *Management by Menu.* Chicago, Ill.: National Institute for the Food Service Industry.

Livingston, G. E., and Chang, C. M. 1979. Food service operation, design for nutrient retention in foods. *Food Technology 33* (3) 32.

Miller, J. 1980. *Menu Pricing and Strategy.* New York: Van Nostrand Reinhold.

Schuster, K. 1985. You, the foodservice professional. *Food Management* December, 51–57.

Chapter 8

NUTRITIONAL ASPECTS OF
RECIPE DEVELOPMENT

Purchasing, Storing, and Preparing Foods

The nutritional quality of the food that ends up on the consumer's plate is affected by every stage at which it is handled, from farm/producer to kitchen. If a food product is not fresh when it is purchased or deteriorates as a result of storage and handling procedures, its nutritional quality will be poor. Nutritional quality is only as good as the quality of the food product.

Sometimes less than optimal quality products do go into food preparation. Reasons given are that it does not matter if it is going to be cooked, or nutrients will be lost in the kitchen anyway, so why buy peak products. High nutrient quality foods, however, can and should be a goal in the kitchen. That is the subject of this section. Nutrition aside, the current emphasis on simple cooking techniques and food close to its natural state will make it difficult to mask less than optimum quality food products.

Storage and cooking procedures affect the nutrient content of foods. Farmers produce and send food to the market, and the rate at which distributors move the foods through the marketplace affects the nutrient content. By the time foods reach the kitchen, some nutrients have been lost. This applies to both processed and fresh foods. More nutrients may be lost when the food is stored, prepared, and served. Physical loss occurs when parts of foods are removed, such as in trimming vegetables. Chemical loss comes from changes in structure of plant or animal tissue due to storage time, temperature, light, humidity, and exposure to temperature and water in preparation. The significance of nutrient loss depends on the extent of the loss and the importance of the food as a source of a particular nutrient(s).

The length of time raw vegetables are stored, as well as the temperature and humidity of the storage area, affect nutrient retention. Freshly harvested vegetables have more vitamins than stored ones. Fruits and vegetables require high humidity and low temperatures. If canned fruits and vegetables are used, the longer the storage period and the higher the storage temperature, the greater the nutrient loss. Drained solids in canned vegetables contain about two-thirds of the soluble nutrients and the liquid contains the other one-third. If storage means freezing, remember that quality and nutrient content will deteriorate at temperatures higher than $-18°C$ ($0°F$). Even at $0°F$, losses occur over time. Thawing and refreezing not only adversely affect nutrient content, but increase risk of spoilage. Temperature also affects fresh and dried eggs. When refrigerated, they retain nutrients well. At room temperature, however, nutrient loss occurs, particularly for dried eggs, which can lose up to one-third their vitamin A in 6 months. Higher temperatures accelerate losses (USDA 1983). Light affects many foods. It speeds rancidity in fats and oils and can reduce thiamin and riboflavin content of foods containing these nutrients if the food is not properly packaged.

During preparation, trimming can affect the nutrient content of vegetables. Leaves, for example, are rich in many nutrients. These nutrient losses can be recovered to some extent by putting trimmings into a vegetable stock or soup base. Also, cutting exposes surface areas, and both air and heat hasten the destruction of vitamin C. Therefore, prepare vegetables as close to cooking and service as possible; the more intact the produce, the greater the nutrient retention. See how larger pieces fit into the presentation. Use sharp knives—bruising fruits and vegetables hastens loss of vitamins A and C. When preparing vegetables, wash them quickly and thoroughly to remove pesticide residue. The longer food is soaked in water, the greater the nutrient loss. (Trimming fat from meats, on the other hand, is recommended to reduce the amount of saturated fat.)

The amount of nutrients in cereal products depends on what is left after milling, what nutrients are added, and how the product is cooked. The process of using large quantities of water, draining off the water and rinsing wastes nutrients. Most packaged grains are clean; however, some imported packaged grains as well as bulk grains should be washed to remove dirt and impurities. Washing rice before cooking can cause a 25 percent loss of thiamin in regular rice and 10 percent in brown rice. This loss is unfortunate for persons for whom rice is a dietary staple. Cooking causes little nutrient loss from ready-to-cook breakfast cereals. Thiamin content can be preserved by not overbaking grains and limiting the area exposed to heat (USDA 1983).

Cooking losses in meats are primarily in the form of water, which evaporates or goes into the drippings. Protein losses are minimal. Some thiamin and vitamin B_6 are lost — the more meat is cooked, the greater the loss. This is not an indication to eat very rare or raw meat, however; that entails its own risks.

A general rule is the lower the temperature and the shorter the cooking period, the less nutrient loss. This is reflected in the low nutrient losses when cooking eggs, which require these conditions.

Three major factors in preserving nutrients when cooking vegetables include little surface area (cut surfaces), short time period, and as little water as necessary. The smaller the amount of water, the more B vitamins and vitamin C are retained. Stir-frying and steaming (if the time is short) are good methods to preserve these nutrients. Also, baking root vegetables in their skins results in significant increase in vitamin retention over peeling, cutting, or boiling. Remember, holding and reheating cooked foods, particularly vegetables, causes additional nutrient loss, particularly vitamin C.

Vegetables are most vulnerable to nutrient loss and changes during cooking. Factors to consider include utensils and color changes. Deeply scratched copper utensils can result in loss of some nutrients, including vitamin C. Cast iron, on the other hand, can add beneficial amounts of iron. Loss of color in green vegetables results in olive drab. When vegetables are overcooked, the cells burst, releasing acid that reacts with the magnesium in the chlorophyll (the green coloring). The result is pheophytate, a substance that absorbs light differently and gives the characteristic olive color, which is very unappealing. Yellow and orange pigments are carotenoids. They are soluble in water but do not change color in an acid or alkaline medium. Red and blue colors are from anthocyanin pigments, which are soluble in water and become bright red in an acid medium and blue-gray in an alkaline environment. Witness how wine or vinegar, for example, keeps red cabbage attractive. White vegetables contain anthoxanins, which change to yellow in alkaline environments. Therefore, vegetables, one of the most important sources of a variety of nutrients, are fragile in terms of appearance and nutrient retention in cooking and handling. Brightly colored, crunchy vegetables have taste, texture, and appeal. They also give patrons a bonus nutrition-wise. Become aware of timing when cooking vegetables so they are crunchy but not raw.

Because of the similarity of many food products, substitutions are often made. These substitutions may be due to nondelivery, availability, merchandising considerations, or price. When such substitutions are effected, be certain these changes are reflected on the menu. Common substitutions that affect nutrition content of the foods include ice cream/ice milk, powdered/fresh eggs, milk/skim milk, whipped topping/whipped cream, tropical oil/corn or safflower oil, cream/half and half, margarine/butter, nondairy creamers/cream or milk, ground beef/ground sirloin, capon/chicken, standard/premium ice cream, noodles/egg noodles, cheese/processed cheese food, cream sauce/nondairy cream sauce, stock from scratch/commercial base, seafood analogs (surimi)/fresh seafood, salad dressing/mayonnaise, sour cream/yogurt (Massachusetts Restaurant Association 1978).

Modifying Recipes

Volumes can be written about the various ways to develop or modify recipes to reduce fat, saturated fat, cholesterol, sodium, sugar, calories, or whatever other food components warrant adjusting. Some books contain pages of suggestions for changing cooking techniques, substituting ingredients, and enhancing flavors when salt is omitted. Some even designate specific herbs and spices for certain foods, as if the only herb that can be used with tomatoes is basil! It is fine to share recipes, flavorings, and techniques that have produced good results. But since the possibilities are vast and trends keep techniques and food/flavor combinations in constant flux, this section will offer general suggestions or guidelines that have dietary significance for particular food products and techniques as used in the kitchen which are applicable to all items, whether a sandwich or an upscale entree.

For instance, fat and sodium may be simple issues to deal with in stocks and soups, but when those stocks are used in sauces, reducing fat content becomes more complex. Sometimes change is not the major factor, portion control is. And sometimes additional food items may be used to enhance simply cooked foods such as vegetable jams, inventive chutneys, salsa or vegetable purees in sauces. This involves change only by addition, such as poached tuna with a red bell pepper, onion, and garlic jam. For cooks, developing and modifying recipes beyond classical boundaries to create healthful concepts can be an exciting challenge. For example, replacing heavy cream with low fat ricotta and egg whites in a seafood terrine may not produce an acceptable product the first time, nor the second. But that is how the process of developing recipes works. It is an ongoing process of adjusting, tasting, and learning. This is true for any style of cooking, whether it is classical French, Chinese, American, Tex-Mex, or "spa." Many of the new alternative menus have borrowed from ethnic and regional cuisines such as the American South, Southwest, and West Coast. French, Italian, and Oriental techniques and seasonings have had a large influence. Techniques, ingredients, and flavorings are combined in a crossover to produce a new cuisine that is actually the sum of many long-established elements.

Anatomy of a Healthful Recipe

The benchmark of nutritious alternatives is the healthful changing of a dish (often referred to as "lightening") by reducing ingredients, substituting alternative ingredients, and adapting or changing cooking techniques. Sometimes simplicity, that is, using absolutely fresh products and uncomplicated, straightforward preparations, is the method. Many restaurants, in fact, have long been preparing food this way, whether or not they make a nutritional statement. Grilling, for example, seems to be synonymous with healthful cooking and good, simple food.

If health is seen as a major marketing tool, "spa" will become trendy

before its basic premises become ingrained in all cooking—using a minimum of fat, emphasizing mono- and polyunsaturated oils, reducing added
salt, seeing smaller portions of individual foods as good rather than as not
giving enough for the money, and reemphasizing foods that have been in
the back seat, so to speak, such as different grains and plebeian vegetables. A
firm training in culinary techniques or a good deal of cooking experience is
a must for experimenting with healthful food alternatives. Many culinary
schools, including the Culinary Institute of America, are providing specialized training in healthful alternative cooking along with classical training.

As with nouvelle, a cooking health trend could result in some bizarre
food combinations. In experimenting with techniques, liberties are being
taken with cooking terminology. Dry sautéing and sautéing in a nonstick
pan or a pan barely brushed with oil are popular techniques. When the term
sauté is used to describe food that is literally boiled in a small amount of
stock, wine, water, and so on, however, it is misleading, particularly on
menus. The difference between the classical method of searing food in a
small amount of hot fat and boiling it in a liquid (no matter how quickly) is
apparent in the taste, texture, and appearance of the finished product.
"Wet" sautéing, or whatever it should be called, is not even a braise or a
poach. Be very careful in recipe and menu terminology, lest people think
they are getting something they are not. It is better to use the words "thinly
sliced breast of chicken quickly cooked in wine and stock reduction" rather
than sauté. Perhaps the chicken could be poached and sliced, then placed in
the pan at the end of the reduction to achieve color and a syrupy glaze.
These are the details to learn through hands-on experimentation.

Nouvelle cuisine introduced portion control in terms of plate design. This
was a significant emphasis, though, because one of the key elements in
healthful dining is portion control. Now, the health-conscious patron does
not balk at smaller portions of meat, if there is ample food on the plate.
And, thanks to the California influences, people like vegetables and starches
more. Food that looks natural is returning—food that is attractive and
stunning in presentation, but not handled and pushed and arranged. Sauces
are becoming uncomplicated, such as reduced pan juices, for example. In
many cases they have been replaced by accompaniments such as relishes,
dipping sauces, and glazes baked or grilled on the food.

Achieving Taste Some cooks have become so preoccupied with health that
they forget taste. Seppi Renggli of The Four Seasons restaurant says in his

book *The Four Seasons Spa Cuisine* (Renggli 1986) that he has relied heavily on the use of sweet and hot peppers to give zip to his Spa Cuisine dishes. Another chef says he sneaks bitters into sauces. And everyone knows about the flavor-enhancing qualities of lemon, vinegar, and herbs. The point is to add taste. A thin slice of chicken wrapped around green beans and carrots, poached in chicken stock, then placed in the poaching liquid is not going to wow them in the dining room. (Just mentally taste test it.) But it will if the stock is flavored, the chicken breast is coated with mustard and herbs, the poaching liquid is reduced, and a dollop of vegetable puree is added.

The majority of patrons will opt for taste and order a regular dish that is full of flavor, such as grilled lamb sausage with a garlicky cheese and potato gratin over a healthful but tasteless, diminutive alternative. Flesh out plates with a variety of vegetables, not just one. Six wafer-thin slices of potato fanned around one grilled lamb noisette will probably not satisfy many people. They want to see some food on the plate. In addition to the six slices of thin potato, also tuck in two or three other vegetables in a complementary manner such as roasted peppers, leeks and garlic; then the alternative lamb dish becomes as tasty and appealing as the regular lamb sausage entree. Remember, variety is important for optimum nutrient intake as well as interest. Nothing is as discouraging as a meal in which the meat or seafood item is the only one on the plate, garnished with a few julienned vegetables, two or three baby vegetable items, or two small boiled potatoes. Make ample portions of vegetables an integral part of the presentation!

Using Optional Ingredients and Techniques

The rest of this section will discuss general principles for modifying food components in recipes so menu items are healthful, tasty, and attractive. Take fat, for example. Think about which foods contain the most fat. Obviously, many meats fall into this category. Rather than serve only chicken breasts, reduce portions and use leaner cuts. (Cutting saturated fat by these methods will automatically reduce cholesterol as well as calories.) So, these methods achieve four objectives—reducing fat, saturated fat, cholesterol, and calories. To serve a larger portion of meat, use white meat skinless chicken (or fish) instead. Dairy products are also high in fat, but there are low-fat alternatives. Here again, quantities can be cut—use a small amount so that it is negligible on a per-person basis. Remember trade-offs. Vegetables and grains contain no saturated fat (except for palm, palm kernel and coconut oil) or cholesterol and are low in calories in moderate portions. The appearance of plenty can be achieved by using a variety of foods instead of the old meat-with-a-dab-of-vegetable routine.

Bases, including stocks, soups, and sauces, in which fat and sodium content can be problematic, can be made more healthful. To begin, a stock should not be salted in the making; however, flavors can be intensified in brown stocks by caramelizing, adding tomato puree, and roasting the bones and vegetables until deep brown. Vary the vegetables, add herbs, then reduce the finished product to intensify flavors. The more flavorful the base, the easier it is to develop acceptable salt-free sauces. Many chefs balk at omitting salt altogether. If the amount added to the sauce or soup results in an acceptable per-person sodium content for one dish, it would be acceptable. Remember to represent menu statements regarding sodium, fat, and any other ingredient about which a nutritional claim is made accurately. And keep in mind commonly used ingredients that will add sodium to foods, such as soy sauce, bouillon cubes, most sauce bases, canned broths, and powdered seasoning mixes.

Fat can be easily removed from stocks and soups in a number of ways, the best being to chill and remove the solidified chunk of fat from the top. In sauce making, however, fat is used as a liaison as well as for taste and glossy appearance. These, in fact, are the major functions of fat in a sauce. In reducing the amount of fat, keep in mind techniques that compensate for its reduction or elimination that achieve similar, acceptable results. Butter, various oils, cream, and egg yolk are the major sources of fat in sauces. It is easier to deal with the taste and appearance issues than the liaison functions. For sauces low in fat thicken with arrowroot, potato, or cornstarch, being careful to use only the amount necessary to tighten the sauce to coating consistency. Too much will result in a viscous, unattractive product. Other methods include reduction of the sauce, sometimes in conjunction with the use of arrowroot and the like, or a bit of butter added for gloss and taste. If the amount of butter or any fat needed to make or finish a sauce is so small that the per-person amount does not raise the total fat, saturated fat, or cholesterol amounts above recommended amounts for a dish or a meal, this is acceptable. The bottom line is to keep total fat low. Compromising by using some butter in a sauce and then eliminating some fat from elsewhere, for example, also achieves the broad concept of balance.

Still other techniques include using vegetable purees, low-fat "creams" consisting of yogurt and ricotta or cottage cheese blends, gelatin, and so forth. Some thickening methods lend themselves to heartier dishes, such as using starchy vegetables, bread crumbs, pasta, and cooked pureed rice and lentils. A strong foundation in the concepts of nutrition, a knowledge of food composition and strong cooking skills make it easier to devise methods for reducing the amounts of less healthful ingredients and increasing the overall nutritional quality of meals served in the restaurant.

Modifying Meat and Seafood Recipes

When working with meats and seafood, trim all visible fat from the product before cooking. This generally includes chicken skin, although there may be times when the skin is necessary to keep the meat moist. In that case remove it after cooking, although the meat will be somewhat higher in fat than if the skin were removed in the beginning. The trend toward cleaner cooking methods, such as broiling, grilling, roasting, baking, poaching, or steaming over water or in papillote, plastic film, lettuce, or other vegetable leaves or husks, can be done with little or no cooking fat. Stir-frying is also a popular low fat way to cook. If the fat is hot when the food is added, less will be absorbed. Dry sautéing and cooking meats quickly in a small amount of liquid are other techniques. Use the latter method with care, choosing a type of meat in a portion size that will cook before it toughens.

Use of nonstick pans has increased, as has the use of unsaturated fats in spray form. Another way to achieve lower fat content is to lightly paint pans, racks, grills, or the meat or fish itself with a small amount of oil, butter, or moisture agent.

Modifying with Vegetables and Fruits

As with meats, vegetables can be grilled, steamed, stir-fried, and cooked in numerous ways without fat. To make them glossy, lightly touch the tops with an oil-seasoned pastry brush. Vegetables, as well as fruits, can be caramelized to intensify their color and flavor. Fruits also respond well to baking and poaching with low-fat ingredients.

Salads need not have a heavy coating of fat-based dressing to be flavorful;

such dressings actually detract from the interest and quality of the salad ingredients themselves. There are many flavorful vegetable, nut-based, and olive oils that enhance taste when used with a light hand. Cream and egg yolk–based dressings add fat and calories, but they can be diluted to some extent with broth or skim milk. Broth alone is a good base for salad dressings, as are pureed fruits and vegetables and fruit and vegetable juices.

Modifying with Pasta and Grains

Pasta and grains can be cooked in broth and accented with herbs, a grating of pepper, nutmeg, or hard flavorful cheese. They also can be mixed and matched, such as using a bland rice with a more forceful-tasting kasha. Many types of rice as well as other grains are nutty and flavorful on their own. An example is basmati rice; the brown basmati resembles popcorn in aroma when cooking.

Offer a selection of whole grain as well as white bakery products in the breadbasket. Provide both butter and margarine, thereby giving the customer the choice. The choice can be on the table or mentioned on the menu. But keep in mind that the role of the restaurateur is to provide options, not decide for customers.

Popular items such as crepes, egg rolls, pizzas, calzones, pasta dishes, burritos, tacos, and tostadas can be easily adapted to meet most dietary guidelines and can include a variety of nutritious ingredients.

Modifying Desserts

Desserts are probably the most difficult area in which to keep fat, saturated fat, cholesterol, and calories at bay. But it is not impossible. Yolkless soufflés with a thick puree of fruit as the base can be very successful. This same concept can be applied to a first course or entree soufflé made with a thick puree of vegetables or fish, for example. Much can be done with fruit, sherbet, ice milk, compotes, crustless tarts and cakes. Some places are even doing small dessert "pizzas." Evaporated skim milk and thickeners such as cornstarch can aid in sauce making.

Artificial sweeteners, nondairy products (many of which contain palm or

coconut oils), and even egg substitutes are not good alternatives. The value
—nutrition, taste, texture, and appearance—of fresh, real food products
cannot be emphasized too strongly. Portion control is the key to lowering
totals of offending ingredients in desserts. Fat is more difficult to work
around than is sugar, but it can be done. A wonderful gingerbread, for
example, can be made with dark beer and crystallized ginger. Although its
total sugar and fat content is low, it is delicious served in small pieces on a
slightly lemony sauce based on evaporated skim milk. It has deep flavor and
substance and is made with real foods. Cutting the servings into large but
thin rounds gives the appearance of a larger serving.

This section has provided nutritional ways to tailor alternative menu
selections. It did not suggest that whole egg soufflés, pastries, and Roquefort
dressing disappear from menus. Nutritional status is not determined by one
meal, or even two or three. It is determined by the overall balance of one's
diet over a period of time. Many of the techniques have therefore focused
on how to eliminate excessive amounts of sodium, fat, saturated fat, and
cholesterol from all dishes on the menu (see Figures 7.1 to 7.4). Some day
more healthful, lighter menu items will, it is hoped, become an integral part
of all menus. Then instead of flagging and counting numbers, these items
would be self-evident. It is also hoped that a new awareness of the direct
relationship between diet and disease will be reflected in the selection and
careful preparation of all foods—not in terms of elimination but in quality
of ingredients, moderation in use of some ingredients and increase in use of
others as suggested in the dietary guidelines, sensible portions, variety of
items, and attention to freshness of flavor and attractiveness of presentation. From there on it is up to every individual to select the foods that best
fit his or her needs. As a guide, refer to Table 8-1, which lists nutrition-
related terminology for food service managers and cooks.

Health Tips for Food Purchasing and Cooking

A problem confronting many chefs is how to translate recommendations
for a healthy diet into menu planning, food purchasing, and preparation
activities in the restaurant. In general, it means placing more emphasis on
grains; vegetables and fruits; lean meat, poultry, and fish; and vegetable oils.
In addition, food product manufacturers are developing an increasing num-

TABLE 8.1   Dietary Terminology for Managers and Cooks

Triglycerides	Major fat found in foods from plant and animal sources. Also manufactured by the body from all foods and beverages and deposited as fatty tissue. Fat circulates in the body mainly as triglycerides.
Cholesterol	Waxy substance used in many of the body's biochemical processes. A high level of blood cholesterol increases the risk of developing cardiovascular disease. Blood cholesterol comes from two sources: It is manufactured in the body, and it is obtained when foods of animal origin are consumed.
Saturated fats	Usually solid at room temperature and found mostly in animal foods such as lard, butter, cheese and some vegetable oils such as coconut, palm kernel and palm oils, and cocoa butter. They raise blood levels of cholesterol significantly and should be consumed in moderation.
Monounsaturated fats	Liquid or semisolid; found mostly in foods of plant origin such as olives, olive oil, avocadoes and nuts. They lower blood cholesterol levels.
Polyunsaturated fats	Usually liquid oils of plant origin such as safflower, sunflower, corn, sesame and soybean. They lower blood cholesterol levels.
Note	All foods are combinations of saturated, monounsaturated and polyunsaturated fats. For practical purposes, however, fats from animal sources are mostly saturated and fats from vegetable sources are mostly unsaturated. Notable exceptions: Coconut, palm kernel and palm oils, and cocoa butter which, even though of plant origin, are highly saturated; and fish oils, which even though of animal origin, are primarily unsaturated. Polyunsaturated oils in fish, which differ in chemical composition from those found in most vegetable oils, are beneficial in lowering blood cholesterol levels. They tend to make blood platelets less sticky and less likely to clump together in an artery, to form a potentially harmful clot.
Hydrogenation	Chemical process that increases the saturation of vegetable oils to make them semisolid or solid at room temperatures. The hydrogenated vegetable oil then resembles a saturated fat.

TABLE 8.1 Dietary Terminology for Managers and Cooks *(continued)*

Dietary fat	Food sources of fat include meat, poultry, fish, eggs, dairy products, nuts, seeds, and cooking fats and oils. Menu items prepared with these ingredients reflect their fat content unless the type and quantity of the ingredients or preparation methods for dishes containing them are adjusted accordingly.
Dietary cholesterol	Cholesterol is found exclusively in foods of animal origin—meats, seafood, eggs, dairy products, and cooking fats such as butter or lard. There is no cholesterol in vegetables, fruits, grains, nuts, or seeds. In animal foods, cholesterol is present in lean tissue, which explains why some low-fat foods such as shrimp can be relatively high in cholesterol. Foods high in cholesterol should be consumed infrequently or in moderation. Cholesterol can be reduced in a recipe by changing or eliminating an ingredient or by reducing the amount used in the recipe or portion size of the finished item.
Salt and sodium	Salt is a condiment and flavor enhancer. It is also a major source of sodium, which may contribute to high blood pressure. It may be added to foods during processing, preparation or at the table. Sodium in prepared foods can be reduced by reducing or eliminating salt in a recipe or substituting another flavor-enhancing ingredient. It is recommended that sodium intake be between 1 and 3 grams per day. Since salt is 40 percent sodium, 1 teaspoon of salt contains approximately 2 grams of sodium (5 grams of salt).
Calorie	Unit for measuring the heat- or energy-producing value of food when burned by the body. The energy supplied by fat is 9 calories per gram; protein and carbohydrates contribute 4 calories, and alcohol, 7 calories per gram.

SOURCE: Adapted from *Restaurant Heart Health Education Program Chef/Manager Workshop Manual,* Carol Hodges, American Heart Association, Massachusetts Affiliate, Needham, Mass. 1988.

ber of healthful low-sodium and low-fat foods. The following are some food purchasing suggestions.

1. Margarine manufacturers are now packaging polyunsaturated margarines in individual pats for quantity users. Ask the manufacturer for the specification sheet and check the list of ingredients. If it has liquid safflower, corn, sunflower, or soybean oil as the first ingredient, followed by one or more partially hydrogenated vegetable oils, the margarine is recommended. For cooking, select solid margarine with the ingredient label as described above, or use liquid unsaturated oils—safflower, corn, grape seed, sunflower, soybean, sesame, peanut, canola, or olive. These oils should also be used to make salad dressing. *Note:* Canola oil (also called rapeseed oil) has a higher proportion of monounsaturates than any other oil except olive oil. Recently approved by the FDA, canola oil is a light, nearly flavorless oil, suitable for all cooking purposes. The smoke point is 455°F.

2. When possible, select nonfat or low fat dairy products. Skim or partially skim milk cheeses or processed and modified-fat cheeses are recommended. Some, however, may not be acceptable tastewise.

3. Avoid packaged or convenience foods that list animal fat or coconut, palm kernel, and palm oil among the ingredients. These oils are frequently found in nondairy creamers, dairy substitutes, cake mixes, pie fillings, commercially prepared cakes and cookies, cereals, and bars. If using soup and sauce bases, choose ones that are sodium free. Many canned and packaged foods are now available in low or sodium-free versions.

4. When purchasing meat, keep in mind the leaner the cut the better. Trimming and preparation techniques can also alter the fat content of the finished product (American Heart Association 1986).

Tips for Cooking

1. Sautéing and browning: Use a nonstick pan, or coat the surface of the pan with cooking oil using a pastry brush. Use nut oils, olive, or sesame for flavor, but remember the pan must be filmed with oil only. This means that when it is turned upside down, no oil drains out. Many meat items can be dry sautéd, and foods can be cooked in a small amount of stock, water, wine, and so on, browning them as the liquid evaporates. Stir frying is an acceptable alternative if oil is used only to film the pan.

2. Broil/grill (with food suspended so fat can drain off), steam, poach, or roast (suspending food so fat drains) instead of frying. Eliminate the browning of meat and vegetables in a braise, and chill cooking liquids to remove fat before using in a sauce.

3. Purchase choice or, preferably, select grades of meat when possible. Organ meats such as liver, brains, kidney, and sweetbreads are high in cholesterol. Trim meats of all visible fat. Paint meats with oil using a pastry brush, baste them with stock to prevent the surface from drying, cover them with vegetable leaves, or bake them in parchment or foil.

4. Use stock reductions in sauces, with a small amount of corn or potato starch for liaison if necessary. Limit the use of roux, beurre manié, butter, cream, and egg yolks. Use natural pan juices or liquid left from deglazing, with fat skimmed from the top.

5. Chill stocks and soups to remove all traces of fat from the top.

6. Use flavorful nut oils and olive oil for flavor in salad dressing. Dilute cream-based dressings with broth, juice, or skim milk. Use fruit, vegetable juices, or purees as a base instead of cream, sour cream, egg yolk, or mayonnaise.

7. Choose margarine carefully when substituting for butter. The first ingredient on the label should be liquid vegetable oil — safflower, sunflower, and corn oils are the best.

8. Substitute sandwich meats such as fresh roasted turkey, beef, chicken, or ham in place of high-fat cold cuts, pâté, and the like.

9. Read labels on nondairy substitutes to make sure they do not contain highly saturated coconut, palm kernel, or palm oils.

10. Substitute low-fat dairy products such as low fat, skim, and

evaporated skim milk and yogurt for cream and sour cream, or use a reduced-fat version of sour cream. Experiment with blends of cottage cheese and yogurt, adding corn starch if the mixture is to be heated. Use cheese in moderation — all cheese is relatively high in fat, and low-fat versions may be inferior in taste.

11. Read labels for terms that reveal the presence of cholesterol or saturated fats in packaged products: eggs and yolk solids; palm, palm kernel and coconut oils; imitation or milk chocolate, shortening, partially hydrogenated oils, lard, butter, chocolate, cocoa butter, and suet.

12. When baking, reduce cholesterol by using only egg whites or discarding every other yolk and substituting a teaspoon of polyunsaturated oil for each discarded yolk.

13. Reduce the amount of fat in recipes by a third to a half. For commercial mixes to which fat or oil is added, use an unsaturated oil, reduce the amount by a third, and increase the water.

14. Develop an egg substitute that contains only the whites and polyunsaturated oil. Make yolkless soufflés using vegetable, meat, or fruit purees; make béchamel with an unsaturated fat.

15. Substitutes for salt include herbs and spices, lemon juice, peppers and chilies, concentrated stocks, pan juices, wine, vinegar, bitters, or other cooking liquids.

16. Keep in mind that most processed packaged foods, unless otherwise stated on the label, are high in sodium and may be high in saturated fat.

17. When looking at an entire recipe, remember that if all fat is kept to an absolute minimum and poly- and monounsaturated fats are emphasized, the dietary cholesterol will probably fall within recommended amounts. (See item 3 for foods particularly high in cholesterol.)

18. If it is necessary to add salt, sprinkle the amount of salt to be used on a sheet of deli wrap. Then measure it into a teaspoon. Remember, a teaspoon is a day's allotment! Try adding only a pinch of this.

Nutritional Calculation of Recipes

If a menu gives specific nutritional data for items, a nutritional analysis of the recipes should be done to make sure they conform to claims for number of calories, percentage of fat, milligrams of sodium and cholesterol, and so on. Backing a nutritional statement with facts need not be a hassle with the resources available.

There are several ways to substantiate nutritional claims. With time, patience, and a calculator, it can be done by an individual. But since it is very time-consuming, a nutrition consultant can be hired or assistance from the nutrition department of a local university or the dietary department of a local hospital can be sought. Another route is to join a program such as the one offered by the American Heart Association through its affiliate chapters across the United States. (Appendix E lists sources of nutrition information, including print references, groups, and agencies.)

Three references are widely used to calculate calories or nutrients in recipes: (1) *Agriculture Handbooks No. 8-1 to 8-16* (USDA 1977–1986); (2) *Food Values of Portions Commonly Used* (Pennington and Church 1985); and (3) *Nutrients in Foods* (Leveille, Zabik, and Morgan 1983). The first two are standard references for nutrient composition. At least one is a must for the office of every kitchen, or at workstations for taking notes on nutrient calculations for new ingredients or changes in recommendations. It should become a recipe workbook. Also, use this text as an overall reference for developing nutritional philosophy and guidelines for menu planning.

A good adjunct to nutrient-composition books is a computerized kitchen scale. Scales, which give nutrient information based on the type of food and its weight, are suitable for small-scale operations since they are limited in the number of items that can be weighed. The quickest, most efficient way to do nutrient analysis is by computer, using software specifically developed for that purpose.

Limitations of Nutrient Data

It is important to realize some limitations of nutrient data. A major one is primary nutrient assay. Since methods for assessing nutrients in food are still being refined, data on some nutrients are inconclusive.

Another limitation is the variability in nutrient content of foods due to growing conditions, degree of ripeness, and handling procedures. The latter, which includes changes that result from food preparation, is an important consideration in recipe analysis in terms of whether the computer program accounts for nutrient retention after preparation procedures. Since nutrient retention data are incomplete in many instances, it is difficult to estimate nutrient values from a recipe. Changes in processing techniques, new foods, and changes in enrichment and fortification affect nutrient content and, in the case of new products, introduce new data (Hoover and Pelican 1984). This is an important consideration when working in product development.

Another major limitation is in nutrient printout interpretation. One cannot judge the effect of the nutritional adequacy of any one meal on the health status of any one person, even if the person is a repeat customer. Nutritional status is determined by the nutritional quality of all foods consumed over a period of time. Total nutritional balance need not be the goal for one dish or one meal. However, computerized data indicating percent fat, saturated fat, etc., are useful indicators that current dietary recommendations are being met. Cooks prepare food based on what is available in the marketplace. Variety of foods and current dietary guidelines should be key factors when bidding, buying or cooking, not computer-generated data for specific nutrients.

It is important to choose software that is compatible with the operation's nutritional guidelines and menu statements. If a menu gives only general information, such as "fat content of these dishes is under 30 percent in conformance with the dietary guidelines," most programs provide such information. If detailed information is needed, however, choose one with a large food/nutrient database. In this case, if a complete nutritional analysis of recipes is being done, keep in mind that the larger the database, the less need to make ingredient substitutions and the less chance for inaccuracy. (Of course, very trendy items probably will not appear on any database.) Some program features to look for are ability to calculate portion size, storage capability for analyzed recipes, and ways to account for nutrient losses (JNE 1984).

Based on a study of clients' comprehension of computerized nutrient analysis, researchers at Pennsylvania State University concluded that misconceptions based on generalizations from dietary information (computerized nutrient analysis) may lead to undue concern. The most problematic aspect of nutrition education by computer is the inability to correctly interpret data without assistance of a health professional (such as a registered dietitian) (Smicklas-Wright et al. 1984; Sorenson et al. 1983).

The approach to offering customer nutrition information should be determined by established guidelines as reflected in in-house capabilities, menu language, and cost–benefit analysis. If computer assistance is not feasible, it will be necessary to generate data used for menu statements by hand.

For a general statement regarding total percentage of fat in a dish, use the following calculations: Calculate the total calories in the dish. Then calculate the total grams of fat [Convert ounces (oz) to grams (g) if necessary; 1 oz = 28 g]. Multiply the number of grams by 9 to get calories (1 g of fat contains 9 calories). Divide the total number of calories of the dish into the number of fat calories to get percentage of fat.

Here are some additional suggestions for menu evaluation:

1. Assuming that 2000 milligrams (mg) (about 1 teaspoon) of sodium per day is acceptable, 500–600 mg ($\frac{1}{4}$ teaspoon) per meal is a good guideline.
2. Current recommendations for cholesterol are 300 mg or less per day. Therefore, try to keep the total for a meal under one-third that amount. (See the role of dietary cholesterol in cardiovascular disease in Chapter 3).
3. Fat intake is suggested to be less than 30 percent of total calories, or less than 60 g per day. Either calculate percentage of fat per dish or meal, or give absolute grams of fat. The total should be less than 20 g per meal.
4. Carbohydrate and protein are best viewed in terms of the percentages discussed in Chapter 3 for the dietary pie. Try to keep within 55 to 60 percent carbohydrate (with emphasis on complex carbohydrates and naturally occurring sugars such as in fruits and vegetables), less than 30 percent fat (with emphasis on poly- and monounsaturates over saturated fats), and the remainder, usually 12 to 15 percent, protein. The average adult needs 50 to 60 g of protein per day, but this amount is frequently exceeded.
5. Calories should be considered as providing a third of the daily

requirement. Therefore, 500 to 700 calories per meal is a good guideline; however, a 500-calorie meal might be fine for one person, but not another. It depends on the meal, what the person ate before, and what he or she will eat later on.

To get a quick idea of the amount of fat and calories (as well as carbohydrate and protein to balance a dietary pie), refer to Figure 8.1, which shows computation bases for food exchanges. They do not account for sodium and cholesterol or differentiate between saturated and mono- and polyunsaturated fats; however, they are a useful tool for restaurateurs who wish to make a general statement and it can help determine the overall balance of a menu or a course in terms of the dietary pie.

Figure 8.1 shows an easy way to set up the computations. There are six major groups: meat, fat, milk, bread, vegetables, and fruit.

Be sure to separate ingredients into appropriate categories (see Appendix B for a complete listing). For example, the meat group also includes most cheeses and peanut butter in the high fat category and eggs in the medium fat category. One exchange is 1 oz for meats and cheeses, one egg, or one tablespoon of peanut butter. The fat exchanges include butter, margarine, oils, cream, sour cream, cream cheese, mayonnaise and salad dressings, bacon, olives, and avocadoes. One exchange is one teaspoon for most oils and spreads, one strip of bacon, one-eighth of an avocado, two tablespoons for light creams, and one tablespoon for heavy cream and cream cheese. The milk group includes yogurt (one cup); the exchange size varies with butterfat content. The bread group includes cereals, grains, pasta, dried beans and lentils, and starchy vegetables such as corn, lima beans, peas, potatoes, and winter squash. An exchange ranges from one slice of bread or one-half muffin or bagel to one-third cup of rice and dried beans and one-half cup of most starchy vegetables and pasta. The vegetable group contains all nonstarchy vegetables, from asparagus to zucchini, including the cabbage family, greens, eggplant, and mushrooms. An exchange is one-half cup, but vegetables are usually not counted in tallies because they contain insignificant amounts of components of concern. The fruit group includes all fruits; exchange sizes range from one apple to twelve cherries to one-third cantaloupe to one-half banana.

Figure 8-2 shows a sample format for calculating a recipe using food exchanges.

	1oz. Meat or Equivalent	1 Teaspoon Butter or Equivalent Fat Exchange	1 Cup Milk	1 Piece Bread or 1/2 Cup Grain or Starchy Vegetable Equivalent	1/2 Cup Cooked Vegetable or 1 Cup Raw	1/2 Cup Fresh Fruit
CALORIES	FAT 100 MED. 75 LEAN 55	45	WHOLE 150 LOW FAT 120 SKIM 90	80	25	60
CARBOHYDRATE (grams)	——	——	12	15	5	15
FAT (grams)	FAT 8 MED. 5 LEAN 3	5	WHOLE 8 LOW FAT 5 SKIM trace	——	——	——
PROTEIN (grams)	7	——	8	3	2	——

ADAPTED FROM EXCHANGE LISTS FOR MEAL PLANNING, AMERICAN DIABETES ASSOCIATION AND AMERICAN DIETETIC ASSOCIATION 1986

FIGURE 8.1 Computation base for food exchanges. (Adapted from *Exchange Lists for Meal Planning*, American Diabetes Association and American Dietetic Association, 1986.) *Note:* The complete food exchange lists appear in Appendix B.

The abbreviated computation chart can be useful in menu planning only if kitchen staff members are familiar with exchange equivalents in terms of amount of foods and proper categories for foods. Once they are at ease with thinking of foods in terms of the exchange list, calories and total fat content (and fat as a percentage of calories) can be quickly estimated.

Another general method of getting an idea of what a menu looks like in terms of the dietary pie, four food groups, variety of nutrients, and amount of animal (saturated) fat is the menu gaming exercise described in Chapter 9; it is also useful for staff training.

The resources are out there, including nutrition education for chefs, consultants, software and printed materials. The best place to start is to

SAMPLE MENU

Poached Salmon with Lime Butter*
Rice Salad Mold   Green Beans

INGREDIENTS

5 oz. salmon
1 tablespoon butter
1/2 cup rice
1/4 cup chopped red pepper and scallions
1 tablespoon walnut oil
1/2 cup green beans

FORMAT FOR CALCULATION

FOOD ITEM	CALORIES	CHO (gm)	FAT (gm)	PROTEIN (gm)
SALMON	275	——	15	35
FAT/OIL (Butter and Walnut Oil)	270	——	30	——
RICE	80	15	——	3
VEGETABLES (Pepper, Scallion, Green Beans)	38	8	——	3
TOTAL	663	23	45	41

*NOTE: Lime zest not included in calculations

FIGURE 8.2 Sample format for calculating a recipe using the food exchange format. *Note:* The complete food exchange lists appear in Appendix B.

determine the nutritional philosophy with regard to clientele and type of food. Next, formulate guidelines based on internal capabilities. Then, further refine the guidelines in terms of specific nutritional objectives during menu planning and when developing methods (such as adapting cooking techniques) with which to achieve the objectives. Determine how much to say about nutrition on the menu. Will the nutritious qualities be self-evident from menu item descriptions and the food presentations themselves? If so, a general statement, or no statement, may be appropriate. In that case, wait-staff training becomes important, so that any nutritional concerns of customers can be addressed personally. This entire approach can range from general to specific (i.e., specific nutrient information). Whatever it is, though, keep in mind style of operation, clientele, staff capabilities, and budget.

Menu Disclaimer   This is a good place to discuss menu disclaimers, which many restaurants are including, regarding possible misinterpretation of generalized nutrition information in terms of therapeutic diets. Patrons on medically restricted diets are aware of their requirements. If they choose to cheat, that is their responsibility. Many restaurants, however, feel compelled to protect themselves with a statement such as, "The menu selections and/or nutritional information offered here do not necessarily meet the requirements of individual medically prescribed diets."

REFERENCES

Adams, C. 1975. Nutritive value of American foods in common units. *Agriculture Handbook* No. 456. Washington, D.C.: USDA Agricultural Research Service.

Adams, C., and Richardson, M. 1981. Nutritive value of foods. *Home and Garden Bulletin* No. 72. Washington, D.C.: USDA.

American Dietetic Association and American Diabetes Association. 1986. *Exchange Lists for Meal Planning*. Chicago, Ill.

Brody, J. 1985. *Jane Brody's Good Food Book*. New York: W. W. Norton.

Franey, Pierre. 1984. *Pierre Franey's Low Calorie Gourmet*. New York: Times Books.

Giobbi, E., and Wolff, R. 1985. *Eat Right, Eat Well the Italian Way.* New York: Alfred A. Knopf.

Guerard, M. 1976. *Cuisine Minceur.* New York: William Morrow and Company.

Hoover, L. W., and Pelican, S. 1984. Nutrient data bases—Considerations for educators. *Journal of Nutrition Education 16* (2), 58–59.

JNE. 1984. Computers in nutrition education. *Journal of Nutrition Education 16* (2), 63.

Leveille, G. A., Zabik, M. E., and Morgan, K. J. 1983. *Nutrients in Foods. The Nutrition Guild.* Cambridge, Mass.: Nutrition Guild.

Massachusetts Restaurant Association. 1978. *Accuracy in Menus.* Wakefield, Mass., pp. 1–9.

Mosimann, Anton. 1985. *Cuisine Naturelle.* New York: Atheneum.

National Restaurant Association. 1984. *Food Service Industry Pocket Factbook.* Washington, D.C.: NRA.

Pennington, J. A. T., and Church, H. N. 1985. *Food Values of Portions Commonly Used.* New York: Harper and Row.

Renggli, S. 1986. *The Four Seasons Spa Cuisine.* New York: Simon and Shuster.

Smicklas-Wright, H., Pelican, S., Byrd-Bredbenner, C. and Shannon, B. 1984. Client's comprehension of a computer-analyzed dietary intake printout. *Journal of Nutrition Education 16* (2), 69.

Sorenson, A., Seltser, R. and Wyse, B. 1983. Personal computers for health. *The Professional Nutritionist 15,* 1–3, 6.

Underwood, G. 1985. *Gourmet Light.* Chester, Conn.: Globe Pequot Press.

U.S. Department of Agriculture. 1976–1983. *Composition of Foods—Raw, Processed, Prepared.* Agriculture Handbook No. 8 (10-part series). Washington, D.C.: USDA.

U.S. Department of Agriculture. 1983. Conserving the nutritive value of foods. *Home and Garden Bulletin* Number 90. Washington, D.C.: Human Nutrition Information Service.

Winston, M., and Eshleman, R., Eds. 1985. *The American Heart Association Cookbook.* New York: Ballantine Books.

Chapter 9

STAFF TRAINING

Nutrition in the restaurant requires a total staff commitment. With high turnover prevalent in many foodservice operations, staff training is an important aspect in achieving nutritional objectives in the kitchen and communicating them in the front of the house. In addition to the basics of healthful eating, it is important for foodservice staff to be aware of the psychological aspects of customer food choices. These result from life-style changes, including the fitness craze of the eighties and an increased interest in diet and health. It also helps if staff members understand that the nutritional aspects of food service in commercial operations (i.e., the healthy eating trends) did not just pop up to annoy and frustrate them. Certain aspects of the current trend have been a part of the history of food in the United States since the early 1900s. The waves of interest rise and recede, but they do not disappear. It is also important for staff to realize that interest in nutrition as it relates to health is high for some patrons, and if it recedes it will not be because of declining interest but because consumer needs are being met in the marketplace. In other words, if healthful alternatives become the norm, there will be less need to focus attention on requesting/recommending them.

Influence of Nutrition on Food and Cooking Trends

In early Europe, diet-consciousness was seen as the cuisine of health spas, which date back to the early Romans and Greeks. In the nineteenth century, spas were part and parcel of the grand hotels of Europe. People, attributing their body afflictions to gustatory indiscretion, took the cure at these resorts. A luxury cuisine was also available for guests with no health complaints. This choice of grand or sparse cuisine is seen in many contemporary European spas such as Michele Guerard's Les Pres d'Eugenie in southwest France, home of Cuisine Minceur. This choice also prevails in many contemporary American health resorts and spas. Perhaps this is why so many alternative menus in restaurants include the word spa. It has been synonymous with health for centuries.

In the United States, an interest in vegetarianism led to the development of many spas in the late 1800s and early 1900s. During that period, the health doctrines of the Seventh Day Adventists, headquartered (as was Kellogg's) in Battle Creek, Michigan, contributed much to the interest in the food–health relationship. Carson, in his book, *The Cornflake Crusade,* describes the contribution of the early health philosophies to the history of healthy eating. He lists three major areas: the elevation of the stature of grains, a widening of nutrition knowledge, and an interest in a lighter and more varied diet—all the things recommended today. In fact, the diet at Kellogg's Battle Creek Sanatorium was lacto-ovo vegetarian, although here again, there was the choice between meat or no meat (Carson 1976). And it is interesting to note that early spa-goers were served a concoction called granula, to later be called granola by Kellogg's in 1875! (Carson 1976).

Health-consciousness in the 1800s and early 1900s evolved in much the same way as the health-consciousness of the 1960s, in which people sought pure food. But what happened between the early 1900s and the renewed interest in food and health that began to spread across the country in the sixties, primarily as the "health food movement"? World War II intervened, causing nutrition to take a backslide as food technology after the war encouraged reliance on processed and packaged foods. That was also a time when meat began to take center place on the dining table (Carson 1976).

About the time the sixties' back-to-the-land approach to eating gained momentum, medical researchers and public health officials began to draw attention to the negative health implications of rich, high fat, overly sweet, and salty diets of the American public. As a result of media coverage of dietary recommendations and health agency guidelines linking diet to disease, consumers showed increasing interest in food and its relationship to health and fitness.

Thus, new knowledge about what one can do to have a healthier diet and life plus the fitness enthusiasm of the last decade has produced a new breed of consumer. The new consumer is more sophisticated and knowledgeable about food from a cooking and eating, as well as health and nutrition, perspective. And these people are not meek. They are making their interests known in the marketplace and are getting response. Consumers are increasingly interested in healthy dining and good eating. Tastes have been broadened by travel, and palates are more sophisticated. All of this has created a marketing tool for restaurants and other food-related businesses.

Health-related nutrition trends have influenced cooking trends. Although Guerard's Cuisine Minceur never took off in this country, nouvelle cuisine did. It introduced portion control in terms of plate design and "lighter" sauces based on stock reductions and butter rather than flour and roux. Vegetables were there, but as accents and garnishes to meat-with-sauce presentations—a diamond of zucchini here, a baton of carrot there. Admiring customers paid for quality rather than quantity. On the heels of nouvelle, there was an interest in American regional cuisine and fresh, locally produced products that are simply prepared and presented, and a simultaneous movement to reinterpret classical regional dishes to "lighten" them without sacrificing integrity.

The postnouvelle new American cuisine traveled from California (where it began as many trends do) across the country, bringing with it Cajun, Tex-Mex, southern, southwestern, and New England classics with local regional products and finesse. Accompanying the regional movement has been an emphasis on simple but good food, reflected in cooking techniques such as grilling. In fact, grilling seems to be de rigueur across the country. And bistro and country French cooking are increasing in popularity. There is a trend to casualness, open kitchens, and fresh, unadorned food. These examples of recent trends are reflections of the new health-conscious approach to food. Very often the freshness and goodness of the food, whether it is a salad, meat or seafood dish, or dessert, bespeaks health to consumers, whether or not any nutritional claims are made.

Influences on Food Choices

As emphasized throughout this book, it is important to give customers choices—such as fruit or sherbet as alternatives to pastries, for example. The factors governing what people choose are complex, however, ranging from psychological, physiological and socioeconomic factors to time of meal, anticipated size of meal, and perceived food palatability.

When foods are familiar, one's preconceptions of how something will taste create expectations that may affect where to eat, what to eat, and how much to eat. Verbal or written descriptions of foods can also create expectations, particularly if they mention a specific treatment of a familiar food. For example, swordfish may be a familiar food, but a restaurant review of a specially prepared swordfish dish will stimulate mental tasting and result in a preconception of what the dish should taste like. Whether or not to try it will then depend on the appeal of that specific preparation. Often, in fact, a preconception will override a signal that food might be inappropriate, such as buying an ice cream cone on the way home from a restaurant even though feeling full (Booth 1983).

For unfamiliar foods that allow no preconceptions as to whether they might be pleasing or not, visual appearances create perceptions as to how pleasant or unpleasant they might be. This is why presentation is so important. How many times has the sight of a neighbor's entree influenced a choice in a restaurant? Sometimes a negative perception will persist despite the pleasantness of food combinations or preparation methods. For example, someone might order an artichoke (which he or she does not like much) stuffed with lobster because of its attractive appearance and presence of a favorite food (lobster). Dislike of artichokes will continue, however, even though temporarily tolerated in combination with the lobster (Booth 1983).

Food Habits

Preconceptions as to like or dislike of a food and expectations about what it will taste like combine to establish food habits that continue through life. Some preconceptions and expectations are based on food memories. Since it seems that people remember food tastes early in life, exposure to different flavors during infancy and childhood may determine flavor preferences and food selection in adult life. The extent to which flavor information can get from short-term memory (precise recollection of flavors in a memorable dinner the evening before) to long-term memory (retasting that dinner 20 years later) depends on distinctiveness of flavors, duration of contact, and postingestive consequences (Barker 1983).

A particular treatment of a food or a food with a distinctive flavor will be remembered long after bland, uninteresting foods are forgotten. This does not mean the food has to make a loud statement; indeed, the flavor can be subtly distinctive. The point is people remember the taste as significant and unusual. In addition, the longer the time a distinctive food is savored, the better the chances of it being remembered. If food is hurriedly gulped, memory of its distinctive flavor would probably be relatively short. A good or bad experience directly associated with a food will also influence memory of it. Similarly, repeatedly eating a food that was distinctively flavored will most likely place it into long-term memory (Barker 1983). These concepts are important to the food professional, particularly when trying to develop healthful menu alternatives that will sell consistently, not just occasionally.

Availability of Food

The availability of foods also affects selection. At a buffet where a large variety of foods is presented, for example, are small amounts of many foods eaten, or just the one or two dishes liked best? Most people would take a variety, but a few will eat only familiar and favorite foods. On return trips to the buffet, do those who concentrate on two or three items initially choose the same amounts of the same foods, or do they take smaller helpings, or try different foods? Most probably they eat the same foods but take smaller helpings on successive trips.

Rolls et al. (1983), in a study of variety in food choices, found that before a meal there is anticipation and interest in the food(s) to be eaten. After eating, however, there is a decrease in the perceived pleasantness of the food in terms of eating more. Therefore, when one returns to a buffet table, less of the same foods would be taken. However, if those foods were replaced on the buffet with different ones, the size of the servings of the new food items would be the same as for the first foods, presumably because anticipation was high.

Overeating may, therefore, occur when there is a wide variety of foods and many are chosen. This may be why some fad diets are designed to be monotonous. Of course, what happens is that when food is too boring, people lose interest altogether. Human beings appear to have a built-in mechanism that helps ensure they eat a variety of foods if available. As a particular food is eaten, its taste is liked less but the taste of other foods is unchanged (Rolls et al. 1983). This may also explain the popularity of the tasting menu and the trend toward grazing—eating two appetizers, a salad, and a dessert, for example, rather than an entree and a salad.

These concepts underscore the importance of choice in terms of variety of menu items. This does not mean a long menu. The trend is toward short menus and frequent change. What is important is variety within a limited menu to make it possible for customers with different interests and dietary needs to select accordingly. Also important is variety within any one item. Salad vegetable combinations, for example, are endless: Offer a variety. Likewise, two or three vegetable and grain accompaniments to a meat or seafood entree not only add more interest but are more in keeping with healthy eating guidelines and the tendency of many patrons to prefer smaller portions of a variety of foods rather than larger portions of one or two items.

The nutritional and health status of a population is largely determined by the availability of food and factors influencing food choices in the marketplace. The availability of food, of course, depends on environmental factors and agricultural food production. But social factors, economics, marketing, consumer knowledge, and even things such as storage facilities and food preparation skills play an important role in food availability and selection (Krondl and Lau 1983).

Social Factors

Social factors affecting food selection help explain why prestige or trendy foods may be popular in one type of food operation, whereas hearty standard fare may be popular in another. Consider advertising and marketing, which create images of foods that influence food selection. For some markets, food products are endorsed by a personality to reflect a sought-after image. For other markets, the nutritional qualities of food are used to create images.

According to researchers Krondl and Lau, health attributes of foods and flavor exert more influence on food choices than social determinants such as price, convenience, and prestige. This is consistent with National Restaurant Association survey results, which indicate that decisions to eat out were based on variety of menu items, nutritiousness of food, and availability of special menu items. The same study indicated that many patrons try to go to establishments that offer food perceived as a balanced meal. And the higher the price, the higher the expectations in terms of freshness of food, taste, and the like. An example was cited for tablecloth restaurants, where patrons felt that special meals should be served, wait-staff should be knowledgeable, kitchens should be flexible on special requests, and high-quality, fresh ingredients should be used (National Restaurant Association 1982).

Life-style

Life-style also influences food choices, both in terms of where to eat and what to eat. Today, work schedules often emphasize convenience foods, whether prepared at home or purchased away from home, speed of eating, and informality of eating and types of foods eaten. Many people live by the clock, which can lead to doing several things at once — grabbing fast food on the way to a meeting or eating a frozen dinner while watching a football game and paying bills. Meals seem to be more casually structured; the family sit-down meal is giving way in many instances to separate meals for each family member, at different times and with the help of a microwave. People are eating out more, too. And foods that used to be thought appropriate for dinner only are now finding their way onto the breakfast table and into the lunchbox.

All of these life-style trends have produced a market for new food products and new concepts in food service. For example, many institutional food services, such as hospital and corporate operations, offer catering services. Another new trend is to provide foods that employees can pick up after work, take home, heat, and eat.

Advertising and marketing of new food products and services, such as home delivery, personalize them. In so doing, three areas of influence on food choice have to be considered: life-style changes, social concepts, such as health and nutrition consciousness, and personal expectations based on memories or preconceptions and expectations of foods to be eaten.

Staff Training

Changes in trends occur slowly. Likewise, changes in food service operations to meet customer demands occur slowly. This is as it should be, because with any change in concept, staff training is the key to success or failure. In the kitchen, it may be necessary not only to educate staff in the principles of healthy cooking but to ask them to change or adapt a lifetime of learned kitchen techniques. This is particularly true for the European or classically trained chef. Cooking schools are now beginning to include practical experience in healthful cooking techniques. Some, like the Culinary Institute of America, are putting this training to use in a campus restaurant that features healthful menu items. In the dining room, wait-staff need training to communicate with customers in a knowledgeable manner, whether it is to explain the preparation of a low-fat menu item or to respond to a special request.

In the kitchen, any approach to healthful menu alternatives, after nutritional philosophy and guidelines, if any, are determined, will start with menu planning. Most restaurants try to make it possible for customers who order healthy dishes to select combinations from at least first and second courses that meet nutritional criteria established in the menu statement, whether the dishes are listed in the à la carte menu or as a separate fixed-price menu.

Menu Game

A particularly helpful tool in the brainstorming stage of what to feature is the menu game (see Figures 9.1 and 9.2). It can give a reliable ballpark estimate of the nutritional balance of a menu. There are two stipulations for its use: Those using the game must be knowledgeable about food composition in terms of major food nutrients and they must recognize that it cannot be used as a substitute for nutritional analysis of the menu that may be required by any nutrition-related statements. The game is useful only to predict the general healthfulness of a proposed menu in terms of macronutrient information, variety of micronutrients as represented by food groups, and added salt. Specific amounts of ingredients are not used; analysis is by unit or predominant ingredient only. The game can, however, be surprisingly on target in terms of assessing compliance with current dietary guidelines. It is most useful in initial stages of menu planning and recipe development as a quick check for dietary pie balance and variety of micronutrients represented by the four food groups when a computer is not available. Using the game, time is not spent on items that do not meet established nutritional criteria, and it gives the "big picture" in terms of what types of ingredients are causing unbalances and what to delete, reduce or introduce.

To use the game, paint it on a chalkboard or similar surface in the kitchen so ingredient marks can be erased after each evaluation. Then simply write down or call out all of the ingredients in each dish (as staff become at ease with using it, ingredients can be chalked up from memory). Then place marks on the game chart under appropriate headings that describe the ingredient. For example, whole milk would be marked under simple (natural) CHO, saturated fat, animal protein, and milk group, the predominating nutritional factors. A sample menu is marked on the menu game in Figure 9.2, with corresponding notations under each ingredient.

Herbs, spices, and minute quantities of ingredients are not listed. For example, one tablespoon of cream in a recipe for eight would be insignificant in terms of a per-person amount for normal healthy persons. In terms of type of fat, only the predominating fat is listed (e.g., in beef it is saturated). Vegetables, when used as a flavoring agent in a liquid, might contribute small amounts of micronutrients but not fiber. A list of reminders such as these posted next to the game clears up most uncertainties.

The game reinforces nutrition education in terms of food nutrient composition. Two of its most helpful aspects are pinpointing "hot spots" in terms of excess of an undesirable food component and visualizing gaps in balance. For example, if there is a predominance of marks on the game chart under saturated fat, ingredient substitutions should be considered, such as vegetable oil for butter.

More elaborate forms of the game include small diagrams of the dietary pie, four food groups affixed to the game chart, and a brief list of specifications, such as one whole egg per recipe allowed for each four persons. A sample of this format appears in Figure 9.3.

Gaming is a useful tool to evaluate recipes and whole menus, as well as to acquaint staff with the nutritional aspects of ingredients used in recipes. When used daily during staff meetings, it is surprising how quickly everyone becomes attuned to various ways to mark a healthy menu game chart.

CREAM OF CARROT SOUP

CHICKEN STOCK
Animal Protein

LEEKS
Fiber
Fruit/Vegetable Group

CARROTS
Natural Sugar
Fiber
Fruit/Vegetable Group

CREAM
Saturated Fat

COLD POACHED TROUT WITH MUSTARD MAYONNAISE

WATER, CARROTS, ONIONS, HERBS
Flavor Only

TROUT
Animal Protein
Polyunsaturated Fat
Meat Group

EGG YOLKS
Insignificant
Amt./Person

OLIVE OIL
Monounsat. Fat

MUSTARD AND LEMON SAUCE
Insignificant Amt.

STIR-FRY BROCCOLI

SAFFLOWER, SESAME OILS
Polyunsat. Fat

BROCCOLI
Fiber
Fruit/Vegetable
Group

SOY SAUCE
Added Salt

SESAME SEEDS
Vegetable Protein
Polyunsat. Fat
Fiber

WHOLE WHEAT ROLLS,
UNSALTED BUTTER

WHOLE WHEAT FLOUR
Complex Carbohydrate
(Starch)
Fiber
Vegetable Protein
Grain Group

BUTTER
Sat. Fat

STRAWBERRY MOUSSE

STRAWBERRIES
Simple Carb.
(Natural)
Fiber
Fruit/Veg. Group

EGG WHITES
Animal Protein
Meat/Egg Group

HEAVY CREAM
Sat. Fat

SUGAR
Simple
Carb. (Refined)

GELATIN
Insignif. Amt.

FIGURE 9.1 Sample menu (ingredients are "scored" on the menu game chart in Figure 9.2).

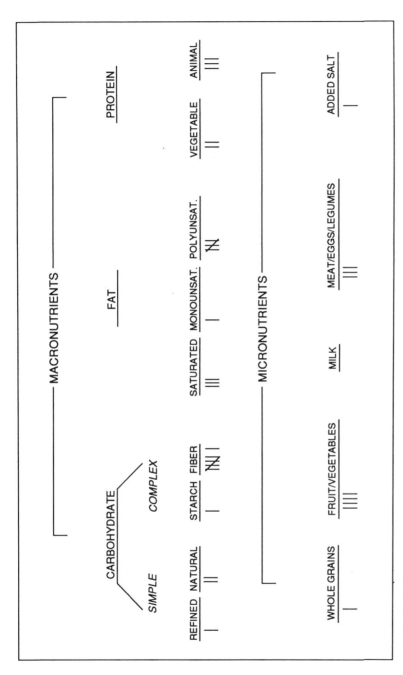

FIGURE 9.2 Menu game chart. This sample chart has been marked using the menu in Figure 9.1 as an example.

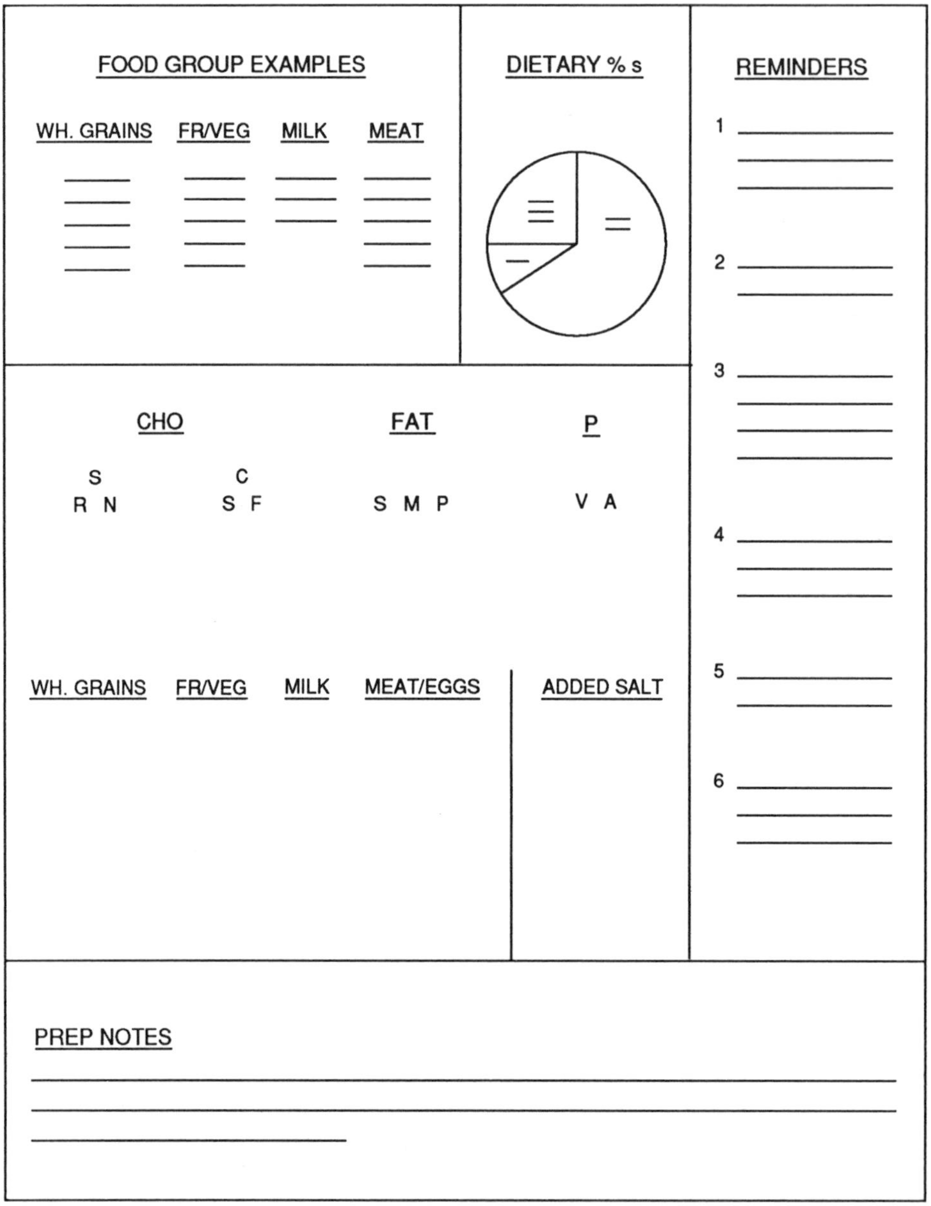

FOOD GROUP EXAMPLES

WH. GRAINS   FR/VEG   MILK   MEAT

DIETARY % s

REMINDERS

1 _____
_____
_____

2 _____
_____

3 _____
_____
_____

CHO   **FAT**   **P**

S   C
R   N   S   F   S   M   P   V   A

4 _____
_____
_____

WH. GRAINS   FR/VEG   MILK   MEAT/EGGS   ADDED SALT

5 _____
_____

6 _____
_____
_____

PREP NOTES
_____
_____
_____

FIGURE 9.3 Sample menu game chart with reminders for menu evaluation and prep notes.

When healthful menu alternatives have been developed, the game chart can also be helpful in wait-staff training.

Merchandising Healthful Menu Items

Once nutritional guidelines for appropriate menu items have been set and kitchen staff have been trained to think nutrition, a good deal of the success of items in terms of sales depends on the ability of wait-staff to talk nutrition. This means describing the items in an accurate but appealing manner and answering customers' questions regarding nutritional qualities of menu items or responding to special requests. The kitchen may be responsible for developing and carrying out nutritional philosophy of the food operation, but it is the wait-staff who will become the "nutrition advisors" and as such provide important feedback to the kitchen regarding patrons' health concerns, likes, and dislikes.

Wait-staff thus have special demands requiring at least a rudimentary knowledge of nutrition as it relates to current health concerns. They must be able to recommend dishes that meet customers' dietary needs and interests. If the menu gives some nutrient breakdown, wait-staff need to translate the detail into general nutritional descriptions. On the other hand, if the menu features simply prepared, fresh food and no nutrition information, wait-staff will have to know about ingredients and preparation method of each dish and which dishes fall into categories of nutritional concern to customers. Despite menu copy, questions will be asked.

Methods for helping wait-staff range from information sheets on the bulletin board in the kitchen to structured training programs complete with manuals, descriptions of dietary guidelines, and role-playing sessions. (The menu game has proved useful in role playing; wait-staff call out menu items, and kitchen staff score them on the chart. Then, based on the nutritional information provided on the chart, wait-staff and—depending on time constraints and structure of training sessions—kitchen staff take turns ordering, questioning, describing, and discussing the menu items.)

Many operations find lack of time and high staff turnover major constraints in implementing and communicating menu objectives. One way to attack this problem is to hand out take-home materials with general nutritional information, then test knowledge when specific menu items are discussed at staff meetings. A nutrition information component can be added to managers' handbooks, perhaps with frequently asked nutrition-related questions and their answers.

It is important not to overwhelm patrons with detailed descriptions of ingredients and cooking methods. Let the customer guide wait-staff with questions. Accurate and concise answers are best — do not recite, but be prepared to answer if asked. If patrons want information, they *will* ask. Answers should be kept in the affirmative. For example, instead of telling a person on a low-fat diet that the meat entree he has ordered is full of saturated fat or, worse yet, is an "artery clogger," suggest a more appropriate dish. If that same person later orders a high-fat pastry item for dessert, service personnel should not comment. The professional obligation ends with providing a choice.

There is some debate as to how far wait-staff should go in talking nutrition. On one side are those who predict that all nutrition and health language will disappear from menus; on the other are those who feel that customers welcome the information. In any case, it is safe to say that not everyone who enters a restaurant is on a self- or medically restricted diet. In the absence of specific questions, a dish could be described both on the menu and by the wait-person in such a way that its healthfulness is evident without resorting to terms such as low sodium or low fat. For example, instead of saying, "Our low-fat chicken entree," begin with, "Tonight we have a poached chicken breast with fresh artichoke," thus including health clues in the dialogue. If the menu states the preparation method (such as poached, grilled, etc.), the server could add, "We serve it with a simple reduction of the wine and stock-based poaching liquid." Thus, the healthfulness of that item, at least in terms of fat, is indicated on the menu and reinforced by the server without undue repetition or lengthy detailed descriptions.

It is also important for service personnel to know what foods taste like. A customer may ask how spicy a dish is, or which flavors predominate, or if a fish is strong in taste. Wait-staff should be objective in answering questions. Even if the staff member does not like mackerel, for example, he or she should describe it positively, such as having a distinctive flavor rather than a "strong" or "fishy" flavor. Wait-staff are sales staff, and the ability to sell food is influenced by their knowledge of the products. This is especially important with healthful menu alternatives, which some people perceive as being healthy but uninteresting and bland.

In summary, established nutritional guidelines for a food operation will be successful on the plate only with support and total commitment to the philosophies by all staff, both in the kitchen and in the dining room.

REFERENCES

Barker, L. M. 1982. *The Psychobiology of Human Food Selection.* Westport, Conn.: AVI Publishing Co.

Barker, L. M. 1983. Building memories for foods. In *The Psychobiology of Human Food Selection.* L. M. Barker (Ed.). Westport, Conn.: AVI Publishing Co.

Booth, D. A. 1983. How nutritional effects of foods can influence people's dietary choices. In *The Psychobiology of Human Food Selection.* L. M. Barker (Ed.). Westport, Conn.: AVI Publishing Co.

Carson, G. 1976. (Reprint of 1957 edition.) *The Cornflake Crusade.* Salem, N.H.: Ayer Co.

Dahmer, S. J., and Kahl, K. W. 1982. *The Waiter and Waitress Training Manual.* New York: CBI Van Nostrand Reinhold Co.

Kelly, P. B. 1984. Training your staff to talk nutrition. *NRA News* January, 25–27.

Kotschevar, L. H. 1975. *Management by Menu.* Chicago, Ill.: National Institute for the Foodservice Industry.

Krondl, M., and Lau, D. 1983. Social determinants in human food selection. In *The Psychobiology of Human Food Selection.* L. M. Barker (Ed.). Westport, Conn.: AVI Publishing Co.

Miller, J. 1980. *Menu Pricing and Strategy.* New York: CBI Van Nostrand Reinhold Co.

National Restaurant Association. 1982. *Consumer Attitude and Behavior Study: How Consumers Make the Decision to Eat Out.* Washington, D.C.: NRA.

Rolls, B. J., Rolls, E. T., and Rowe, E. A. 1983. The influence of variety on human food selection and intake. In *The Psychobiology of Human Food Selection.* L. M. Barker (Ed.). Westport, Conn.: AVI Publishing Co.

Wyrwicka, W. 1981. *The Development of Food Preferences.* Springfield, Ill.: Charles C. Thomas.

Chapter 10

PHYSIOLOGICAL STRESS AT THE WORKSITE: NUTRITION AND FITNESS RECOMMENDATIONS FOR FOOD PREPARATION WORKERS

The importance of diet and fitness to health and general well-being is becoming firmly established in personal life-style and, to an increasing degree, at the worksite. One of the most recent and influential areas of business to promote the diet–fitness–health relationship has been the restaurant industry. Healthful menu options are becoming as widespread as personal fitness programs. But, unlike other corporate businesses, which are rapidly inaugurating health and fitness programs for their employees, restaurants are developing healthy eating opportunities for their customers. While chefs and other foodservice personnel are creating nutritious meals to reflect patrons' changing life-styles, they may be receiving little benefit in terms of personal health and fitness.

The job of preparing meals in any foodservice operation is both physically and emotionally demanding. Problem areas include psychological stress, fatigue, dehydration, heat exhaustion, vascular problems, poor nutrition, weight gain or loss, and muscular strain. Thus, the need to know about nutritional and physical fitness is just as important for culinary personnel as it is for the customers. But studies indicate that up to 70 percent of employees at a worksite can be overweight and practice poor nutrition habits (Murphy 1983). Nutrition and fitness education should therefore be integrated into professional education seminars, which frequently address topics such as stress management, to achieve optimal psychological and physiological performance by employees, in this case, the food and beverage manager or working chef who supervises a full staff of kitchen employees with these same needs.

Fitness and nutrition programs for chefs will help transform negative health practices into positive ones. Chefs and other culinary personnel are frequently subject to the perils of environmental hazards, improper physical conditioning and poor nutrition. Nutritional status provides a base for the general health and well-being of the nonathletic individual as well as for those individuals in which demands are placed on body systems by sports or physically demanding occupations. Physical fitness provides the ability to carry out daily tasks without undue fatigue and with energy left for recreational pursuits and unforeseen stressful situations.

Job-related stress and emotional tensions can create muscular tension, and tense muscles can cause fatigue and susceptibility to illness and injury. This chain of events leads to lowered productivity. Physical activity reduces muscular tension. Many of today's serious illnesses and degenerative conditions tend to be more frequent in sedentary rather than active persons. Much low back pain, a frequent cause of job absenteeism, is due to lack of adequate physical activity. Fitness programs also help combat emotional difficulties, stress, and nonspecific fatigue. Active people are probably not obese and have lower blood pressure and greater strength, flexibility, and breathing capacity (President's Council 1977). All of these factors are important considerations for the culinary professional who may not be physically active outside of work.

Health Problems

Job-related problems affecting the health of the working chef can be categorized into three areas: nutrition, physiology, and environment. Nutrition-related problems, which in turn cause physiological and performance difficulties, include eating on the run, night eating, poor food choices, use of supplements and special diets, low energy reserves, and salt and sweat losses. Physical problems range from limb injuries, burns, and lacerations to muscle strains and cramps. More subtle but just as serious physical conditions include vascular problems, heat exhaustion, dehydration, fatigue, and stress. Environmental conditions that can adversely affect physiological well-being include air pollution, high heat and humidity, hard and/or slippery floor surfaces, uncomfortable equipment and work surface heights, and heavy or potentially dangerous equipment. The food industry is competitive, and psychological concerns regarding success can become physical problems when long hours of hard work become a way of life in which nutrition and physical fitness take a back seat.

Eating on the run, night eating, and poor food choices are, ironically, commonplace for the culinary worker. Fast-paced production schedules often dictate grabbing a bite here or there. Food choices are seldom balanced and may be limited to tastings or leftovers. Staff meals, if any, are usually more reflective of budget and time constraints than nutrition. Skipping meals and eating on the run causes one to overeat at the end of the day. If one sleeps on a full stomach, these food calories are more easily converted to fat by the body, adding pounds.

These eating habits can cause fatigue and then a search for quick energy. Candy bars or soda can lead to a fast rise and quick drop in blood glucose levels, making the situation worse (Clark 1983). Work production suffers, and the vicious cycle begins again. Fatigue in the restaurant kitchen is a commonplace problem fueled by poor eating habits; chronic fatigue impairs one's ability to deal with job demands.

Environmental Problems

A chef works daily in a hot environment. Hours of strenuous activity in a hot kitchen can dehydrate the body through loss of water from blood plasma. When this happens, the body's ability to transport nutrients, remove wastes, and regulate temperature is compromised. Dehydration is one of the major occupational hazards of the professional chef.

As kitchen temperature rises in relation to body temperature, body heat loss is slowed and perspiration begins. If fluid intake is insufficient, physiological changes resulting from dehydration will affect performance rapidly. Contrary to popular belief, there also seems to be an increase in energy requirement when working in a hot environment. Continuous exposure to heat increases some body physiological activities, such as those that permit sweating. In addition, higher body temperature increases metabolic rate and, therefore, calories burned. After long-term exposure to a hot environment, however, people become acclimatized and heat is better tolerated because of increased perspiration (resulting in lower skin and body temperature) and lower heart rate and sodium loss (Astrand and Rodahl 1977).

The following factors should be taken into consideration when determining the effects of heat in the kitchen: air temperature, air motion, relative humidity, radiant temperature, body heat, and clothing. Specialized equipment, including wet and dry bulb thermometers, is necessary for obtaining the index used to determine risk from heat in kitchens.

Heat is not uncomfortable until the skin becomes 60 percent wet from sweat. Clothing permeability is a factor here. When the ability to perspire fails to cool the body sufficiently, heart rate increases until collapse occurs. High humidity in the commercial kitchen hinders sweating capabilities. Heat stress also impairs blood flow to the brain, resulting in loss of judgment and hostile mannerisms (R. Goldman, personal communication 1985). Here it might be appropriate to note that the chef's uniform with its long-sleeved tunic, neckerchief, and long apron securely tied around the waist does not permit much air flow around the skin.

Physical Problems

Physiological problems resulting from the biomechanical aspects of the process of food preparation fall into the category of musculoskeletal disorders. Studies have indicated that frequent or sustained exertions, particularly when performed in awkward body positions, contribute to these problems. When muscles hurt, they are also developing fatigue. Mechanical damage due to tissue fatigue can affect tendons and joints. Thus, if the injurious activity is frequently repeated over a period of time, chronic pain and tissue damage can develop (Chaffin and Anderson 1984).

When the work surface is too low, a prolonged, forward-stooping posture is necessary for chefs working in a standing position. Back muscle endurance decreases in stooped postures that are beyond the range of muscles' ability to support the body in this posture. Thus, rounded shoulders usually accompany a stooped posture, resulting in fatigue and pain. When the surface is too high, it will cause arm and shoulder pain. Figure 10.1 illustrates the pathways to muscle dysfunction that result from frequent and prolonged activities. Improper work heights accelerate the process (Chaffin and Anderson 1984).

Fitness and Nutrition Needs

During the past few years, corporate health care centers have been emerging to help individuals prepare themselves for physiological stress stemming from the worksite. Some individuals may need to protect their bodies from the adverse effects of a sedentary job, whereas others, like chefs, need to condition themselves to prevent injury from physically demanding jobs. Many of the physical problems just described, however, are related to adverse environmental conditions. Since in most cases it is not feasible to change the physical plant (i.e., the kitchen) and therefore mitigate many of the environmental dangers, these factors are best dealt with by preparing individuals to withstand these hazards of the trade.

This need creates another problem, as many culinary training curricula do not emphasize nutrition or physical fitness for the chef, and facilities planning courses do not address the science of ergonomics, that is, improving worker safety and performance through the study of the interactions between humans and the working environment (Chaffin and Anderson 1984). The goal, therefore, is a personal fitness and nutrition program unique to the needs of food preparation workers. Such a program will help increase staff productivity and decrease absenteeism due to stress, illness, and injury.

Occasionally, chefs have a role in determining the design of the equipment for a commercial kitchen. By and large, though, they find themselves in a preexisting environment that may or may not be an optimum worksite in which to spend 8 to 16 hours per shift. Therefore, if a foodservice operation is in the process of designing or redesigning facilities, environ-

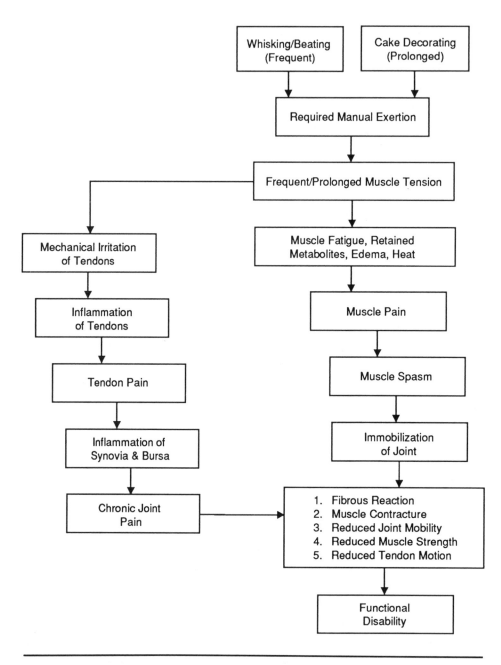

FIGURE 10.1 Pathways to musculoskeletal dysfunction during food preparation activities. (Adapted with permission from Chaffin, A., and Anderson, G., *Occupational Biomechanics,* John Wiley & Sons: New York, 1984.)

mental factors should direct this effort. If redesign to correct inherent environmental problems in an existing facility is not feasible, it would be advantageous in terms of productivity to use in-house or local safety, hygiene, and medical/public health agencies or a private consultant to remedy any major problems.

Many food service workers change jobs frequently. Most commercial kitchens present a variety of environmental hazards. Therefore, a personal program of physical fitness and proper nutrition is the individual's best approach in tackling stresses inherent in this particular type of work.

Fitness and Diet Recommendations

A main goal in terms of job-related physical conditioning is to develop strength, endurance, and flexibility for the type of work done. This entails training of sufficient intensity, duration, and frequency to produce measurable improvement in functions for which the person is training. To achieve this goal, physiological stress greater than what is regularly encountered on the job is necessary. An exercise physiologist is the best person to assess one's needs and provide an individualized program. It is important for an individual to meet his or her needs, which may be different from those of coworkers.

Many chefs and other food service personnel claim that they are fit because they are so physically active on the job. It is important to recognize that physical activity per se is not synonymous with physical conditioning. The activity has to be maintained at a certain level of intensity, duration, and frequency in order to result in a training effect. To prepare for the physical challenges of the job, seek out appropriate professionals to determine present level of fitness. Then, a personalized program should develop cardiovascular capacity, increase strength in specific muscle groups, and increase joint range of motion and flexibility. To obtain an effective program and prevent injury, it is important to seek the advice of a professional with training in exercise physiology. Also consult a physician before embarking on any strenuous physical conditioning program. Persons with possible symptoms of cardiovascular disease or with risk factors including

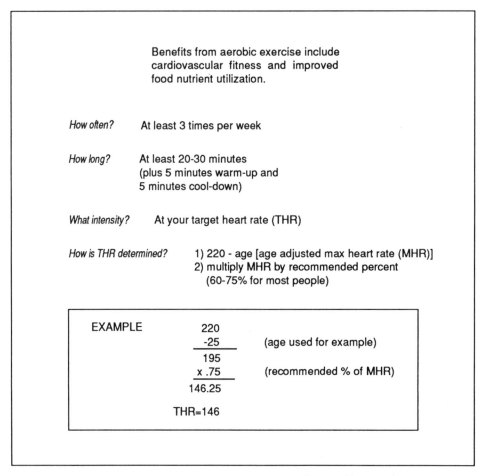

FIGURE 10.2 Determining target heart rate for aerobic exercise.

age, should have a (moving) stress EKG performed before starting a physical fitness program. Once a level of conditioning is reached, a regular program must be followed in order to maintain the desired effects (see Figure 10.2).

Strength training for the chef will help prevent injuries, especially those caused by frequent lifting of heavy objects such as stock pots. A combination of specific muscle strength and joint flexibility exercises will facilitate bending to remove heavy items from the oven or whisking and beating for an extended period of time. General aerobic and cardiovascular conditioning will help to improve overall fitness, control weight, reduce stress and fatigue, prevent lower limb vascular problems, and combat air pollution, heat, and other problematic environmental conditions.

Once normal body composition and desirable weight have been determined, activity levels must be assessed to determine energy requirements. The body weight will remain stable only when caloric intake equals expenditure. Just 3500 calories more or less equals one pound of added or lost body fat.

Maintaining Body Energy Balance

Energy demands are greatest during physical activity, and the body obtains energy from food. Many chefs, however, are unable to maintain a body energy balance, and either gain or lose weight. Causes for gain usually include overconsumption of food and a lack of appropriate exercise. Weight loss may be related to underconsumption and/or dehydration. Of course, there may be other physiological factors involved, but inability to maintain a desirable body weight is usually attributable to an energy imbalance.

Aside from internal cues that signal real hunger, there are environmental cues that send signals to eat. Chefs are constantly exposed to the latter—the constant sight, feel, taste, and smell of food, its display, and food-related activities such as menu planning. Often foods eaten are inappropriate in terms of nutrition and/or quantity to maintain good nutritional status and provide proper fuel for optimum work performance.

In this mechanized age, daily workload will seldom stress the body in terms of training effect. Therefore, energy stores are used primarily for routine changes of pace that occur during the day, and are more than sufficient to accommodate a day of intermittent hard work, descriptive of most foodservice positions. Physical aerobic conditioning enhances enzyme activity necessary for the release of energy for muscular work. Therefore, an exercise program is important for the efficient use of food fuel taken in during the day.

Many worksite as well as sports activities demand bursts of heavy exercise. Metabolic "reflexes" provide energy as ATP to cover these short bursts of exercise even if they are repeated at frequent intervals. A person at rest usually uses a ratio of two-thirds fat and one-third carbohydrate for fuel. Short-term strenuous exercise uses mostly carbohydrate. Long-term endurance exercise uses mostly fat, as carbohydrate stores diminish. Carbohydrate predominates during a burst of intensive work until a steady state resumes (Katch and McArdle 1983).

It is evident from this discussion and that in previous chapters that carbohydrates are the most important and most readily available source of energy. The level of glycogen stores in muscles is modified by diet. Trained, fit persons can store more glycogen in their muscles than a casual exerciser and the latter more than a relatively inactive person. As the body becomes more fit, one will have more energy and control of body weight, and will be more productive in work and recreational exercise.

Many chefs feel that vitamin and mineral supplements and extra protein are necessary to meet physical demands of the job. With a balanced diet of wholesome foods and an exercise program, supplements are not necessary. In fact, as more energy is expended, caloric requirements will increase. Additional food, in turn, will provide more vitamins and minerals if chosen wisely. Vitamins and minerals do not themselves provide energy, but they are necessary for the body to extract it from foods eaten. Nonendurance physical activity such as food service activities does not increase need for protein.

As a rule, chefs eat most of their calories in the evening. Calories, however, are burned more efficiently when someone is awake rather than asleep. Foods consumed at night, perhaps when hunger signals are strong, tend to be consumed in larger quantities. Snacking all day, tasting this and that, can lead to a voracious appetite later on. It is better to eat at regular intervals during the day to maintain a desired weight.

Kitchens are hot, and cooks perspire in an attempt to maintain normal body temperature. In only a few hours, performance will deteriorate if water intake is inadequate. With continuous high heat, thirst may fail to signal an adequate fluid intake, so drink cool water, juice, club soda, and so on, at frequent intervals throughout a shift. Drinking beer, wine, or other alcoholic beverages will not substitute for water, juice, or the like, to replace fluid loss via sweat. They will not provide energy for muscles and will inhibit release of antidiuretic hormone, which helps keep fluid in the body. Drinking alcoholic beverages while working in a hot kitchen will only result in increased dehydration.

When fatigued, many persons grab a candy bar for quick energy. Chefs heading for the pastries can actually exacerbate the problem. The sweets will enter the bloodstream quickly, stimulating insulin production and glucose uptake by tissues. A rapid decrease in blood glucose levels can then create a feeling of weakness again. Concentrated sugars also promote dehydration. Snacking on nutritious foods throughout the day will maintain energy levels without ups and downs.

In summary, an exercise program coupled with a healthful diet as described throughout this book will improve energy levels, concentration, and work productivity, as well as help one withstand work-related physiological stresses.

REFERENCES

Astrand, P., and Rodahl, K. 1977. *Textbook of Work Physiology.* New York: McGraw-Hill.

Chaffin, A., and Anderson, G. 1984. *Occupational Biomechanics.* New York: John Wiley and Sons.

Clark, N. 1983. *The Athlete's Kitchen.* Boston, Mass.: CBI Publishing Co.

Katch, F., and McArdle, W. 1983. *Nutrition, Weight Control and Exercise.* Philadelphia: Lea & Febiger.

Murphy, C. 1983. Nutrition education at the worksite. *Nutrition News 46* (4) 13–16.

President's Council on Physical Fitness and Sports. 1977. Scientific proof of exercise benefits. *Physical Fitness Research Digest 7, 2.*

APPENDICES

Appendix A

SODIUM CONTENT OF FOODS

Salt and Sodium Conversions

Grams to milligrams	Multiply weight in grams by 1,000
Sodium into salt (NaCl) equivalent	Milligrams of sodium content + .40 = milligrams of salt
Salt into sodium	Milligrams of salt × .40 = milligrams of sodium
Sodium in milligrams to sodium in milliequivalents[1]	Milligrams of sodium +23 (atomic weight of sodium) = milliequivalents of sodium
Milliequivalents of sodium to milligrams of sodium	Milliequivalents of sodium ×23 = milligrams of sodium

[1]Medical prescriptions are often given as milliequivalents (mEq).

Beverages and Fruit Juices	Portion	Weight (grams)	Sodium (milligrams)
Alcoholic:			
Beer	12 fl oz	360	25
Gin, rum, whisky	2 fl oz	60	1
Wine:			
Red:			
Domestic	4 fl oz	120	12
Imported	4 fl oz	120	6
Sherry	4 fl oz	120	14
White:			
Domestic	4 fl oz	120	19
Imported	4 fl oz	120	2
Breakfast drink, instant:			
Grape	8 fl oz	240	0
Citrus fruits	8 fl oz	240	14
Carbonated:			
Club soda	8 fl oz	240	39
Cola:			
Regular	8 fl oz	240	16
Low calorie	8 fl oz	240	21
Fruit flavored:			
Regular	8 fl oz	240	34
Low calorie	8 fl oz	240	46
Ginger ale	8 fl oz	240	13
Root beer	8 fl oz	240	24
Cocoa mix, water added	8 fl oz	240	232
Coffee:			
Brewed	8 fl oz	240	2
Instant:			
Regular	8 fl oz	240	1
Decaffeinated	8 fl oz	240	1
With chicory	8 fl oz	240	7
With flavorings	8 fl oz	240	124
Substitute	8 fl oz	240	3
Fruit drinks, canned:			
Apple	8 fl oz	240	16
Cranberry juice cocktail	8 fl oz	240	4
Grape	8 fl oz	240	1

Lemonade	8 fl oz	240	60
Orange	8 fl oz	240	77
Pineapple-grapefruit	8 fl oz	240	80
Fruit drinks, dehydrated, reconstituted:			
Sweetened:			
Lemonade	8 fl oz	240	50
Orange	8 fl oz	240	35
Other fruit	8 fl oz	240	0
Unsweetened, all flavors	8 fl oz	240	0
Fruit juices:			
Apple cider or juice	1 cup	248	5
Apricot nectar	1 cup	251	9
Citrus:			
Grapefruit juice:			
Canned	1 cup	250	4
Frozen, diluted	1 cup	247	5
Lemon or lime juice:			
Canned	1 cup	244	2
Frozen, diluted	1 cup	248	4
Orange juice:			
Canned	1 cup	249	5
Frozen, diluted	1 cup	249	5
Tangerine juice	1 cup	249	2
Grape juice, bottled	1 cup	253	8
Peach nectar	1 cup	249	10
Pear nectar	1 cup	250	8
Pineapple juice	1 cup	250	5
Prune juice	1 cup	256	5
Mineral water:			
Perrier	8 fl oz	240	4
Poland Spring	8 fl oz	240	1
Vichy Celestins	8 fl oz	240	284
Tea:			
Hot:			
Brewed	8 fl oz	240	1
Instant	8 fl oz	240	2
Iced:			
Canned	8 fl oz	240	9
Powdered, lemon flavored:			
Sugar sweetened	8 fl oz	240	1
Low calorie	8 fl oz	240	15
Thirst quencher	8 fl oz	240	140

Dairy Products	Portion	Weight (grams)	Sodium (milligrams)
Cheese:			
Natural			
Blue	1 oz	28	396
Brick	1 oz	28	159
Brie	1 oz	28	178
Camembert	1 oz	28	239
Cheddar:			
Regular	1 oz	28	176
Low sodium	1 oz	28	6
Colby	1 oz	28	171
Cottage:			
Regular and low fat	4 oz	113	457
Dry curd, unsalted	4 oz	113	14
Cream	1 oz	28	84
Edam	1 oz	28	274
Feta	1 oz	28	316
Gouda	1 oz	28	232
Gruyère	1 oz	28	95
Limburger	1 oz	28	227
Monterey	1 oz	28	152
Mozzarella, from:			
Whole milk	1 oz	28	106
Part skim milk	1 oz	28	132
Muenster	1 oz	28	178
Neufchâtel	1 oz	28	113
Parmesan:			
Grated	1 oz	28	528
Hard	1 oz	28	454
Provolone	1 oz	28	248
Ricotta, made with:			
Whole milk	½ cup	124	104
Part skim milk	½ cup	124	155
Roquefort	1 oz	28	513
Swiss	1 oz	28	74
Tilsit	1 oz	28	213
Pasteurized processed cheese:			
American	1 oz	28	406
Low sodium	1 oz	28	2
Swiss	1 oz	28	388

Cheese food:			
American	1 oz	28	337
Swiss	1 oz	28	440
Cheese spread:			
American	1 oz	28	381
Cream, sweet:			
Fluid, all types	1 tbsp	15	6
Whipped	1 tbsp	3	4
Cream, sour, cultured	1 tbsp	12	6
Cream products, imitation:			
Sweet:			
Coffee whitener:			
Liquid	1 tbsp	15	12
Powdered	1 tbsp	6	12
Whipped topping	1 tbsp	4	2
Sour, cultured	1 oz	28	29
Milk:			
Fluid:			
Whole and low fat	1 cup	244	122
Whole, low sodium	1 cup	244	6
Buttermilk, cultured:			
Salted	1 cup	245	257
Unsalted	1 cup	245	122
Canned:			
Evaporated:			
Whole	1 cup	252	266
Skim	1 cup	255	294
Sweetened, condensed	1 cup	306	389
Dry:			
Nonfat:			
Regular	½ cup	60	322
Instantized	1 cup	68	373
Buttermilk	½ cup	60	310
Milk beverages:			
Chocolate	1 cup	250	149
Cocoa, hot	1 cup	250	123
Eggnog	1 cup	254	138
Malted:			
Natural flavor	1 cup	265	215
Chocolate flavor	1 cup	265	168
Shakes, thick:			
Chocolate or vanilla	1 shake	306	317

Dairy Products	*Portion*	*Weight (grams)*	*Sodium (milligrams)*
Milk desserts, frozen			
Ice cream:			
Chocolate	1 cup	133	75
Custard, French	1 cup	133	84
Strawberry	1 cup	133	77
Vanilla:			
French, soft serve	1 cup	173	153
Hardened	1 cup	140	112
Ice milk:			
Vanilla:			
Hardened	1 cup	131	105
Soft serve	1 cup	175	163
Novelty products:			
Bars:			
Fudge	1 bar	73	54
Orange cream	1 bar	66	27
Vanilla, chocolate-coated			
Ice cream	1 bar	47	24
Ice milk	1 bar	50	31
Cones, vanilla, chocolate-coated	1 small	71	64
Sandwich	1 sandwich	62	92
Sherbet, orange	1 cup	193	89
Milk desserts, other:			
Custard, baked	1 cup	265	209
Puddings:			
Butterscotch:			
Regular, whole milk	½ cup	148	245
Instant, whole milk	½ cup	149	445
LoCal, skim milk	½ cup	130	130
Ready-to-serve	1 can	142	290
Chocolate:			
Home recipe	½ cup	130	73
Regular, whole milk	½ cup	148	195
Instant, whole milk	½ cup	149	470
LoCal, skim milk	½ cup	130	80
Ready-to-serve	1 can	142	262
Vanilla:			
Home recipe	½ cup	128	83

Regular, whole milk	½ cup	148	200
Instant, whole milk	½ cup	149	400
LoCal, skim milk	½ cup	130	115
Ready-to-serve	1 can	142	279
Tapioca, cooked	½ cup	145	130
Yogurt:			
Plain:			
Regular	8 oz	227	105
Low fat	8 oz	227	159
Skim milk	8 oz	227	174
With fruit	8 oz	227	133

Eggs, Fish, Shellfish, Meat, Poultry, and Related Products	Portion	Weight (grams)	Sodium (milligrams)
Eggs:			
Whole	1 egg	50	59
White	1 white	33	50
Yolk	1 yolk	17	9
Substitute, frozen	¼ cup	60	120
Fish:			
Bass, black sea, raw	3 oz	85	57
Bluefish:			
Baked with butter	3 oz	85	87
Breaded, fried	3 oz	85	123
Bonito, canned	3 oz	85	437
Catfish, raw	3 oz	85	50
Cod, broiled with butter	3 oz	85	93
Eel, raw	3 oz	85	67
Flounder (includes sole and other flat fish)			
baked with butter	3 oz	85	201
Haddock, breaded, fried	3 oz	85	150
Halibut, broiled			
with butter	3 oz	85	114
Herring, smoked	3 oz	85	5,234
Lingcod, raw	3 oz	85	50
Mackerel, raw	3 oz	85	40
Mullet, breaded, fried	3 oz	85	83
Ocean perch, fried	3 oz	85	128
Pollock, creamed	3 oz	85	94
Pompano, cooked	3 oz	85	48
Rockfish, ovensteamed	3 oz	85	57
Salmon:			
Broiled with butter	3 oz	85	99
Canned:			
Salt added:			
Pink	3 oz	85	443
Red	3 oz	85	329
Silver	3 oz	85	298
Without salt added	3 oz	85	41
Sardines, canned:			
Drained	3 oz	85	552

In tomato sauce	3 oz	85	338
Shad, baked with butter	3 oz	85	66
Snapper, raw	3 oz	85	56
Trout, lake, raw	3 oz	85	67
Tuna, canned:			
Light meat, chunk:			
Oil pack	3 oz	85	303
Water pack	3 oz	85	288
Grated	3 oz	85	246
White meat (Albacore)			
Chunk, low sodium	3 oz	85	34
Solid:			
Oil pack	3 oz	85	384
Water pack	3 oz	85	309
Shellfish:			
Clams, raw:			
Hard	3 oz	85	174
Soft	3 oz	85	30
Crab:			
Canned, drained	3 oz	85	425
Steamed	3 oz	85	314
Lobster, boiled	3 oz	85	212
Mussels, raw	3 oz	85	243
Oysters:			
Raw	3 oz	85	113
Fried	3 oz	85	174
Frozen	3 oz	85	323
Scallops:			
Raw	3 oz	85	217
Steamed	3 oz	85	225
Shrimp:			
Raw	3 oz	85	137
Fried	3 oz	85	159
Canned	3 oz	85	1,955
Squid, dried	1 serving	4	183
Meat:			
Beef:			
Cooked, lean	3 oz	85	55
Corned:			
Cooked	3 oz	85	802
Canned	3 oz	85	893
Dried, chipped	1 oz	28	1,219

Eggs, Fish, Shellfish, Meat, Poultry, and Related Products	Portion	Weight (grams)	Sodium (milligrams)
(Meat, *cont'ed*)			
Lamb, cooked, lean	3 oz	85	58
Pork:			
Cured:			
Bacon:			
Cooked	2 slices	14	274
Canadian	1 slice	28	394
Ham	3 oz	85	1,114
Salt pork, raw	1 oz	28	399
Fresh, cooked, lean	3 oz	85	59
Veal, cooked, lean	3 oz	85	69
Organ meats:			
Brain, raw	1 oz	28	35
Gizzard, poultry, simmered	1 oz	28	17
Heart:			
Beef, braised	1 oz	28	29
Calf, braised	1 oz	28	32
Poultry, simmered	1 oz	28	14
Kidney, beef, braised	1 oz	28	71
Liver:			
Calf, fried	1 oz	28	33
Pork, simmered	1 oz	28	14
Poultry, simmered	1 oz	28	16
Sweetbreads, calf, cooked	1 oz	28	32
Tongue, beef, braised	1 oz	28	17
Tripe:			
Commercial	1 oz	28	13
Poultry and game:			
Chicken, roasted:			
Breast with skin	½ breast	98	69
Drumstick with skin	1 drumstick	52	47
Products:			
Canned	1 5-oz can	142	714
Frankfurter	1 frankfurter	45	617
Duck, roasted, flesh and skin	½ duck	382	227

Goose, roasted, flesh and skin	½ goose	774	543
Rabbit:			
Leg, raw	4 oz	113	40
Flesh, cooked	4 oz	113	70
Turkey, small, roasted:			
Breast with skin	½ breast	344	182
Leg with skin	1 leg	245	195
Sausages, luncheon meats, and			
spreads:			
Beer salami, beef	1 slice	6	56
Bologna:			
Beef	1 slice	22	220
Beef and pork	1 slice	22	224
Bratwurst, cooked	1 oz	28	158
Braunschweiger	1 slice	28	324
Brotwurst	1 oz	28	315
Chicken spread	1 oz	28	115
Frankfurter	1 frankfurter	57	639
Ham:			
And cheese loaf	1 oz	28	381
Chopped	1 slice	21	288
Deviled	1 oz	28	253
Spread	1 oz	28	258
Kielbasa	1 slice	26	280
Knockwurst	1 link	68	687
Lebanon bologna	1 slice	18	228
Liver cheese	1 slice	20	245
Old-fashioned loaf	1 slice	22	275
Olive loaf	1 slice	21	312
Pepperoni	1 slice	6	122
Salami:			
Cooked:			
Beef	1 slice	22	255
Beef and pork	1 slice	22	234
Dry or hard, pork	1 slice	10	226
Sausage:			
Cooked:			
Pork	1 link	13	168
Pork and beef	1 patty	27	217
Smoked	1 link	28	264
Thuringer	1 slice	22	320
Tuna spread	1 oz	28	92

Eggs, Fish, Shellfish, Meat, Poultry, and Related Products	Portion	Weight (grams)	Sodium (milligrams)
(Sausages, luncheon meats, and spreads *cont'ed*)			
Turkey roll	1 oz	28	166
Vienna sausage	1 link	16	152
Prepared main dishes:			
Beef:			
And macaroni:			
Frozen	6 oz	170	673
Canned	1 cup	227	1,185
Cabbage, stuffed, frozen	8 oz	226	63
Chili con carne with beans, canned:			
Regular	1 cup	255	1,194
Low sodium	1 cup	335	100
Dinners, frozen:			
Beef	1 dinner	312	998
Meat loaf	1 dinner	312	1,304
Sirloin, chopped	1 dinner	284	978
Swiss steak	1 dinner	284	682
Enchiladas	1 pkg	207	725
Goulash, canned	8 oz	227	1,032
Hash, corned beef, canned	1 cup	220	1,520
Meatballs, Swedish	8 oz	227	1,880
Peppers, stuffed, frozen	8 oz	226	1,001
Pizza, frozen:			
With pepperoni	½ pie	195	813
With sausage	½ pie	189	967
Pot pie:			
Home baked	1 pie	227	644
Frozen	1 pie	227	1,093
Ravioli, canned	7.5 oz	213	1,065
Spaghetti, canned:			
And ground beef	7.5 oz	213	1,054
And meatballs	7.5 oz	213	942
Sauce	4 oz	114	856
Stew, canned	8 oz	227	980
Chicken:			
And dumplings, frozen	12 oz	340	1,506

And noodles, frozen	¾ cup	180	662
Chow mein, home recipe	1 cup	250	718
Dinner, frozen	1 dinner	312	1,153
Pot pie:			
Home recipe	1 pie	232	594
Frozen	1 pie	227	907
Fish and shellfish:			
Fish dinner, frozen	1 dinner	248	1,212
Shrimp:			
Dinner, frozen	1 dinner	223	758
Egg roll, frozen	1 roll	71	648
Tuna, pot pie, frozen	1 pie	227	715
Pork, sweet and sour, canned	1 cup	275	1,968
Turkey:			
Dinner, frozen	1 dinner	333	1,228
Pot pie:			
Home recipe	1 pie	227	620
Frozen	1 pie	233	1,018
Veal Parmigiana	7.5 oz	214	1,825
Without meat:			
Chow mein, vegetable, frozen	1 cup	240	1,273
Pizza, cheese	¼ 12-in pie	90	447
Spanish rice, canned	1 cup	221	1,370
Fast foods:			
Cheeseburger	1 each	111	709
Chicken dinner	1 portion	410	2,243
Fish sandwich	1 sandwich	164	882
French fries	2½ oz	69	146
Hamburger:			
Regular	1 each	92	461
Jumbo	1 each	236	990
Frankfurter	1 frankfurter	93	728
Pizza, cheese	¼ pie	110	599
Shake	1 shake	308	266
Taco	1 taco	75	401

Fruits	*Portion*	*Weight (grams)*	*Sodium (milligrams)*
Apples:			
Raw or baked	1 apple	138	2
Frozen, slices	1 cup	200	28
Frozen, scalloped	8 oz	227	45
Dried, sulfured	8 oz	227	210
Applesauce, canned			
Sweetened	1 cup	250	6
Unsweetened	1 cup	250	5
With added salt	1 cup	250	68
Apricots:			
Raw	3 apricots	114	1
Canned:			
Peeled	1 cup	258	27
Unpeeled	1 cup	258	10
Dried	1 cup	130	12
Avocado, raw	1 avocado	216	22
Banana, raw	1 banana	119	2
Berries:			
Blackberries (Boysenberries):			
Raw	1 cup	144	1
Canned	1 cup	244	3
Blueberries:			
Raw	1 cup	145	1
Canned	1 cup	250	2
Raspberries:			
Raw	1 cup	123	1
Frozen	1 package	284	3
Strawberries:			
Raw	1 cup	149	2
Frozen, sliced	1 cup	255	6
Cherries:			
Raw	1 cup	150	1
Frozen	8 oz	227	3
Canned	1 cup	257	10
Citrus:			
Grapefruit:			
Raw	½ grapefruit	120	1
Frozen, unsweetened	1 cup	244	6
Canned, sweetened	1 cup	254	4

Kumquat	1 kumquat	19	1
Lemon, raw	1 lemon	74	1
Orange, raw	1 orange	131	1
Tangelo	1 tangelo	95	1
Tangerine	1 tangerine	86	1
Cranberries, raw	1 cup	95	1
Cranberry sauce	1 cup	277	75
Currants:			
Raw	1 cup	133	3
Dried	1 cup	140	10
Dates, dried	10 dates	80	1
Figs:			
Raw	1 fig	50	2
Canned	1 cup	248	3
Dried	1 fig	20	2
Fruit cocktail, canned	1 cup	255	15
Grapes, Thompson seedless	10 grapes	50	1
Mangos, raw	1 mango	200	1
Muskmelon:			
Cantaloupe	½ melon	272	24
Casaba	⅕ melon	230	34
Honeydew	⅕ melon	298	28
Nectarines, raw	1 nectarine	138	1
Papaya, raw	1 papaya	303	8
Peaches:			
Raw	1 peach	100	1
Frozen	1 cup	250	10
Canned	1 cup	256	15
Dried, uncooked	1 cup	160	10
Pears:			
Raw	1 pear	168	1
Canned	1 cup	255	15
Dried	1 cup	180	10
Pineapple:			
Raw	1 cup	135	1
Canned	1 cup	255	7
Plums:			
Raw	1 plum	66	1
Canned	1 cup	256	10
Prunes:			
Cooked	1 cup	213	8
Dried	5 large	43	2

Fruits	Portion	Weight (grams)	Sodium (milligrams)
Raisins, seedless	1 cup	145	17
Rhubarb:			
Cooked, sugared	1 cup	270	5
Frozen	1 cup	270	5
Watermelon	1/16 melon	426	8

Grain Products	Portion	Weight (grams)	Sodium (milligrams)
Barley, pearled, cooked	1 cup	200	6
Biscuits, baking powder:			
Regular flour	1 biscuit	28	175
Self-rising flour	1 biscuit	28	185
With milk from mix	1 biscuit	28	272
Low sodium	1 biscuit	28	1
Bread:			
Boston brown	1 slice	45	120
Corn, homemade	1 oz	28	176
Cracked wheat	1 slice	25	148
French	1 slice	23	116
Mixed grain	1 slice	23	138
Pita	1 loaf	64	132
Rye:			
Regular	1 slice	25	139
Pumpernickel	1 slice	32	182
Salt rising	1 slice	26	66
White:			
Regular	1 slice	25	114
Thin	1 slice	16	79
Low sodium	1 slice	23	7
Whole wheat	1 slice	25	132
Breakfast cereals:			
Hot, cooked, in unsalted water:			
Corn (hominy) grits:			
Regular	1 cup	236	1
Instant	¾ cup	177	354
Cream of Wheat:			
Regular	¾ cup	184	2
Instant	¾ cup	184	5
Quick	¾ cup	184	126
Mix 'n eat	¾ cup	184	350
Farina	¾ cup	184	1
Oatmeal:			
Regular or quick	¾ cup	180	1
Instant:			
No sodium added	¾ cup	180	1
Sodium added	¾ cup	180	283
With apples and cinnamon	¾ cup	180	220

Grain Products	*Portion*	*Weight (grams)*	*Sodium (milligrams)*
(Oatmeal, instant, *cont'ed*)			
With maple and brown sugar	¾ cup	180	277
With raisins and spice	¾ cup	180	223
Ready-to-eat:			
Bran cereals:			
All-Bran	⅓ cup	28	160
Bran Chex	⅔ cup	28	262
40% Bran	⅔ cup	28	251
100% Bran	½ cup	28	221
Raisin Bran	½ cup	28	209
Cheerios	1¼ cup	28	304
Corn cereals:			
Corn Chex	1 cup	28	297
Corn flakes:			
Low sodium	1¼ cup	28	10
Regular	1 cup	28	256
Sugar coated	¾ cup	28	274
Sugar Corn Pops	1 cup	28	105
Granola:			
Regular	¼ cup	34	61
No sodium added	¼ cup	34	16
Kix	1½ cup	28	261
Life	⅔ cup	28	146
Product 19	¾ cup	28	175
Rice cereals:			
Low sodium	1 cup	28	10
Puffed rice	2 cups	28	2
Rice Chex	1⅛ cup	28	238
Rice Krispies	1 cup	28	340
Sugar coated	⅞ cup	28	149
Special K	1¼ cup	28	265
Total	1 cup	28	359
Trix	1 cup	28	160
Wheat cereals:			
Puffed wheat	2 cups	28	2
Sugar coated	1 cup	28	46
Shredded wheat	1 biscuit	24	3
Wheat Chex	⅔ cup	28	190

Wheaties	1 cup	28	355
Wheat germ, toasted	¼ cup	28	1
Breakfast sweets:			
Coffee cake:			
Almond	⅛ cake	42	167
Blueberry	⅛ cake	35	135
Honey nut	⅛ cake	55	110
Pecan	⅛ cake	40	172
Danish:			
Apple, frozen	1 roll	72	220
Cheese, frozen	1 roll	72	250
Cinnamon, frozen	1 roll	72	260
Orange, refrigerated			
dough	1 roll	39	329
Doughnut:			
Cake type	1 doughnut	32	160
Yeast leavened	1 doughnut	42	99
Sweet rolls:			
Apple crunch, frozen	1 roll	28	105
Caramel, frozen	1 roll	29	118
Cinnamon, frozen	1 roll	26	110
Honey	1 roll	28	119
Toaster pastry:			
Apple, frosted	1 pastry	52	324
Blueberry, frosted	1 pastry	52	242
Cinnamon, frosted	1 pastry	52	326
Strawberry	1 pastry	52	238
Cakes, from mix:			
Angel food:			
Regular	1/12 cake	56	134
One step	1/12 cake	57	250
Devil's food	1/12 cake	67	402
Pound	1/12 cake	55	171
White	1/12 cake	68	238
Yellow	1/12 cake	69	242
Cookies:			
Brownies, iced	1 brownie	32	69
Chocolate chip	2 cookies	21	69
Fig bars	2 bars	28	96
Ginger snaps	4 cookies	28	161
Macaroons	2 cookies	38	14

Grain Products	*Portion*	*Weight (grams)*	*Sodium (milligrams)*
(Cookies, *cont'ed*)			
Oatmeal:			
Plain	1 cookie	18	77
With chocolate chips	2 cookies	26	54
With raisins	2 cookies	26	55
Sandwich type	2 cookies	20	96
Shortbread	4 cookies	30	116
Sugar	1 cookie	26	108
Sugar wafer	4 cookies	28	43
Vanilla wafer	6 cookies	24	53
Crackers:			
Graham	1 cracker	7	48
Low sodium	1 cracker	4	1
Rye	1 cracker	6	70
Saltine	2 crackers	6	70
Whole wheat	1 cracker	4	30
Macaroni, cooked	1 cup	140	2
Muffin, English	1 medium	57	293
Noodles, cooked	1 cup	140	2
Pancakes, from mix	1 pancake	27	152
Pancake mix	1 cup	141	2,036
Pies, frozen:			
Apple	⅛ of pie	71	208
Banana cream	⅙ of pie	66	90
Bavarian cream:			
Chocolate	⅛ of pie	80	78
Lemon	⅛ of pie	83	71
Blueberry	⅛ of pie	71	163
Cherry	⅛ of pie	71	169
Chocolate cream	⅙ of pie	66	107
Coconut:			
Cream	⅙ of pie	66	104
Custard	⅛ of pie	71	194
Lemon cream	⅙ of pie	66	92
Mince	⅛ of pie	71	258
Peach	⅛ of pie	71	169
Pecan	⅛ of pie	71	241
Pumpkin	⅛ of pie	71	169
Strawberry cream	⅙ of pie	66	101

Rice, cooked:			
Brown	1 cup	195	10
White:			
Regular	1 cup	205	6
Parboiled	1 cup	175	4
Quick	1 cup	165	13
Rolls:			
Brown and serve	1 roll	28	138
Refrigerated dough	1 roll	35	342
Snacks:			
Corn chips	1 oz	28	231
Popcorn:			
Caramel coated	1 cup	35	262
Oil, salt	1 cup	9	175
Plain	1 cup	6	1
Potato chips	10 chips	20	200
Pretzels:			
Regular twist	1 pretzel	6	101
Small stick	3 sticks	1	17
Spaghetti, cooked	1 cup	140	2
Stuffing mix, cooked	1 cup	170	1,131
Waffle, frozen	1 waffle	37	275

Legumes and Nuts	Portion	Weight (grams)	Sodium (milligrams)
Almonds:			
Salted, roasted	1 cup	157	311
Unsalted, slivered	1 cup	115	4
Beans:			
Baked, canned:			
Boston style	1 cup	260	606
With or without pork	1 cup	260	928
Dry, cooked:			
Great Northern	1 cup	179	5
Lima	1 cup	192	4
Kidney	1 cup	182	4
Navy	1 cup	195	3
Pinto	1 cup	207	4
Kidney, canned	1 cup	255	844
Brazil nuts, shelled	1 cup	140	1
Cashews:			
Roasted in oil	1 cup	140	21
Dry roasted, salted	1 cup	140	1,200
Chestnuts	1 cup	160	10
Chickpeas, cooked	1 cup	169	13
Filberts (hazelnuts), chopped	1 cup	115	2
Lentils, cooked	1 cup	188	4
Peanuts:			
Dry roasted, salted	1 cup	144	986
Roasted, salted	1 cup	144	601
Spanish, salted	1 cup	144	823
Unsalted	1 cup	144	8
Peanut butter:			
Smooth or crunchy	1 tbsp	16	81
Low sodium	1 tbsp	16	1
Peas:			
Blackeye, cooked	1 cup	204	12
Split, cooked	1 cup	237	5
Pecans	1 cup	118	1
Pilinuts	4 oz	113	3
Pistachios	1 cup	125	6
Soybeans:			
Cooked	1 cup	180	4
Curd (tofu)	¼ block	130	9

Fermented (miso):			
Red	¼ cup	72	3,708
White	¼ cup	67	2,126
Walnuts, English	1 cup	120	3

Soups	*Portion*	*Weight (grams)*	*Sodium (milligrams)*
Beef broth, cubed	1 cup	241	1,152
Beef noodle:			
Condensed, with water	1 cup	244	952
Dehydrated, with water	1 cup	251	1,041
Chicken noodle:			
Condensed, with water	1 cup	241	1,107
Dehydrated, with water	1 cup	252	1,284
Chicken rice:			
Condensed, with water	1 cup	241	814
Dehydrated, with water	1 cup	253	980
Clam chowder, Manhattan, condensed, with water	1 cup	244	1,029
Clam chowder, New England, condensed:			
With water	1 cup	244	914
With milk	1 cup	248	992
Minestrone, condensed, with water	1 cup	241	911
Mushroom:			
Condensed, with water	1 cup	244	1,031
Condensed, with milk	1 cup	248	1,076
Dehydrated, with water	1 cup	253	1,019
Low sodium	1 cup	244	27
Pea, green:			
Condensed, with water	1 cup	250	987
Dehydrated, with water	1 cup	271	1,220
Tomato:			
Condensed, with water	1 cup	244	872
Condensed, with milk	1 cup	248	932
Dehydrated, with water	1 cup	265	943
Low sodium	1 cup	244	29
Vegetable:			
Condensed, with water	1 cup	241	823
Dehydrated, with water	1 cup	253	1,146
Vegetable beef:			
Condensed, with water	1 cup	244	957
Dehydrated, with water	1 cup	252	1,000
Low sodium	1 cup	244	51

Sugars and Sweets	*Portion*	*Weight (grams)*	*Sodium (milligrams)*
Candy:			
Candy corn	1 oz	28	60
Caramel	1 oz	28	74
Chocolate:			
Bitter	1 oz	28	4
Milk	1 oz	28	28
Fudge, chocolate	1 oz	28	54
Gum drops	1 oz	28	10
Hard	1 oz	28	9
Jelly beans	1 oz	28	3
Licorice	1 oz	28	28
Marshmallows	1 oz	28	11
Mints, uncoated	1 oz	28	56
Peanut brittle	1 oz	28	145
Taffy	1 oz	28	88
Toffee bar, almond	1 oz	28	65
Jams and jellies:			
Jam:			
Regular	1 tbsp	20	2
Low calorie	1 tbsp	20	19
Jelly:			
Regular	1 tbsp	18	3
Low calorie	1 tbsp	18	21
Chocolate flavored:			
Thin	1 tbsp	19	10
Fudge	1 tbsp	19	17
Syrups:			
Corn	1 tbsp	20	14
Maple:			
Regular	1 tbsp	20	1
Imitation	1 tbsp	20	20
Molasses:			
Light	1 tbsp	20	3
Medium	1 tbsp	20	7
Blackstrap	1 tbsp	20	18
Sugar:			
Brown	1 cup	220	66
Granulated	1 cup	200	2
Powdered	1 cup	120	1

Vegetables, Vegetable Juices, and Salads	Portion	Weight (grams)	Sodium (milligrams)
Artichokes:			
Cooked	1 medium	120	36
Hearts, frozen	3 oz	85	40
Asparagus:			
Raw	1 spear	20	1
Frozen	4 spears	60	4
Canned:			
Regular	4 spears	80	298
Low sodium	1 cup	235	7
Beans:			
Italian:			
Frozen	3 oz	85	4
Canned	1 cup	220	913
Lima:			
Cooked	1 cup	170	2
Frozen	1 cup	170	128
Canned	1 cup	170	456
Low sodium	1 cup	170	7
Snap:			
Cooked	1 cup	125	5
Frozen:			
Regular	3 oz	85	3
With almonds	3 oz	85	335
With mushrooms	3 oz	85	145
With onions	3 oz	85	360
Canned:			
Regular	1 cup	130	326
Low sodium	1 cup	135	3
Beansprouts, mung:			
Raw	1 cup	105	5
Canned	1 cup	125	71
Beets:			
Cooked	1 cup	170	73
Canned:			
Sliced	1 cup	170	479
Low sodium	1 cup	170	110
Harvard	1 cup	170	275
Pickled	1 cup	170	330

Beet greens, cooked	1 cup	145	110
Broccoli:			
Raw	1 stalk	151	23
Frozen:			
Cooked	1 cup	188	35
With cheese sauce	3.3 oz	94	440
With hollandaise			
sauce	3.3 oz	94	115
Brussels sprouts:			
Raw	1 medium	18	1
Frozen:			
Cooked	1 cup	150	15
In butter sauce	3.3 oz	94	421
Cabbage:			
Green:			
Raw	1 cup	70	8
Cooked	1 cup	144	16
Red, raw	1 cup	70	18
Carrots:			
Raw	1 carrot	72	34
Frozen:			
Cut or whole	3.3 oz	94	43
In butter sauce	3.3 oz	94	350
With brown sugar			
glaze	3.3 oz	94	500
Canned:			
Regular	1 cup	155	386
Low sodium	1 cup	150	58
Cauliflower:			
Raw	1 cup	115	17
Cooked	1 cup	125	13
Frozen:			
Cooked	1 cup	180	18
With cheese sauce	3 oz	85	325
Celery, raw	1 stalk	20	25
Chard, cooked	1 cup	166	143
Chicory	1 cup	90	6
Collards:			
Cooked	1 cup	190	24
Frozen	3 oz	85	41

Vegetables, Vegetable Juices, and Salads	Portion	Weight (grams)	Sodium (milligrams)
Corn:			
Cooked	1 ear	140	1
Frozen	1 cup	166	7
Canned:			
Cream style:			
Regular	1 cup	256	671
Low sodium	1 cup	256	5
Vacuum pack	1 cup	210	577
Whole kernel:			
Regular	1 cup	165	384
Low sodium	1 cup	166	2
Cucumber	7 slices	28	2
Dandelion greens, cooked	1 cup	105	46
Eggplant, cooked	1 cup	200	2
Endive, raw	1 cup	50	7
Kale:			
Cooked	1 cup	110	47
Frozen	3 oz	85	13
Kohlrabi, cooked	1 cup	165	9
Leek	1 bulb	25	1
Lettuce	1 cup	55	4
Mushrooms:			
Raw	1 cup	70	7
Canned	2 oz	56	242
Mustard greens:			
Raw	1 cup	33	11
Cooked	1 cup	140	25
Frozen	3 oz	85	25
Okra, cooked	10 pods	106	2
Onions:			
Mature, dry	1 medium	100	10
Green	2 medium	30	2
Flaked	1 tbsp	6	31
Parsley, raw	1 tbsp	4	2
Parsnips, cooked	1 cup	155	19
Peas, green:			
Cooked	1 cup	160	2
Frozen:			
Regular	3 oz	85	80

In butter sauce	3.3 oz	94	402
In cream sauce	2.6 oz	74	420
With mushrooms	3.3 oz	94	240
Canned:			
Regular	1 cup	170	493
Low sodium	1 cup	170	8
Peppers:			
Hot, raw	1 pod	28	7
Sweet, raw or cooked	1 pod	74	9
Potatoes:			
Baked or boiled	1 medium	156	5
Frozen:			
French fried	10 strips	50	15
Salted	2.5 oz	71	270
Canned	1 cup	250	753
Instant, reconstituted	1 cup	210	485
Mashed, milk and salt	1 cup	210	632
Au gratin	1 cup	245	1,095
Pumpkin, canned	1 cup	245	12
Radishes	4 small	18	2
Rutabaga, cooked	1 cup	200	8
Sauerkraut, canned	1 cup	235	1,554
Shallot	1 shallot	20	3
Spinach:			
Raw	1 cup	55	49
Cooked	1 cup	180	94
Frozen:			
Regular	3.3 oz	94	65
Creamed	3 oz	85	280
Canned:			
Regular	1 cup	205	910
Low sodium	1 cup	205	148
Squash:			
Summer:			
Cooked	1 cup	210	5
Frozen, with curry	⅓ cup	71	228
Canned	1 cup	210	785
Winter:			
Baked, mashed	1 cup	205	2
Frozen	1 cup	200	4
Sweet potatoes:			
Baked or boiled in skin	1 potato	132	20

Vegetables, Vegetable Juices, and Salads	Portion	Weight (grams)	Sodium (milligrams)
(Sweet potatoes, *cont'ed*)			
Canned:			
Regular	1 potato	100	48
Low sodium	1 serving	113	27
Candied	1 potato	100	42
Yam, white, raw	1 cup	200	28
Tomatoes:			
Raw	1 tomato	123	14
Cooked	1 cup	240	10
Canned:			
Whole	1 cup	240	390
Stewed	1 cup	240	584
Low sodium	1 cup	240	16
Tomato juice:			
Regular	1 cup	243	878
Low sodium	1 cup	243	9
Tomato paste	1 cup	258	77
Tomato sauce	1 cup	248	1,498
Turnip greens, cooked	1 cup	155	17
Vegetables, mixed:			
Frozen	3.3 oz	94	45
Canned	1 cup	170	380
Vegetable juice cocktail	1 cup	243	887
Salads:			
Bean:			
Marinated	½ cup	130	104
Canned	½ cup	130	537
Carrot-raisin	½ cup	63	97
Cole slaw	½ cup	60	68
Macaroni	⅔ cup	127	676
Potato	½ cup	125	625

Condiments, Fats, and Oils	Portion	Weight (grams)	Sodium (milligrams)
Baking powder	1 tsp	3	339
Baking soda	1 tsp	3	821
Catsup:			
Regular	1 tbsp	15	156
Low sodium	1 tbsp	15	3
Chili powder	1 tsp	3	26
Garlic:			
Powder	1 tsp	3	1
Salt	1 tsp	6	1,850
Horseradish, prepared	1 tbsp	18	198
Meat tenderizer:			
Regular	1 tsp	5	1,750
Low sodium	1 tsp	5	1
MSG (monosodium glutamate)	1 tsp	5	492
Mustard, prepared	1 tsp	5	65
Olives:			
Green	4 olives	16	323
Ripe, mission	3 olives	15	96
Onion:			
Powder	1 tsp	2	1
Salt	1 tsp	5	1,620
Parsley, dried	1 tbsp	1	6
Pepper, black	1 tsp	2	1
Pickles:			
Bread and butter	2 slices	15	101
Dill	1 pickle	65	928
Sweet	1 pickle	15	128
Relish, sweet	1 tbsp	15	124
Salt	1 tsp	5	1,938
Sauces:			
A-1	1 tbsp	17	275
Barbecue	1 tbsp	16	130
Chili:			
Regular	1 tbsp	17	227
Low sodium	1 tbsp	15	11
Soy	1 tbsp	18	1,029
Tabasco	1 tsp	5	24
Tartar	1 tbsp	14	182
Teriyaki	1 tbsp	18	690

Condiments, Fats, and Oils	Portion	Weight (grams)	Sodium (milligrams)
(Sauces, *cont'ed*)			
Worchestershire	1 tsp	6	69
Vinegar	½ cup	120	1
Yeast, baker's, dry	1 package	7	1
Fats, oils, and related products:			
Butter:			
Regular	1 tbsp	14	116
Unsalted	1 tbsp	14	2
Whipped	1 tbsp	9	74
Margarine:			
Regular	1 tbsp	14	140
Unsalted	1 tbsp	14	1
Oil, vegetable, (includes corn, olive, and soybean)	1 tbsp	14	0
Salad dressing:			
Blue cheese	1 tbsp	15	153
French:			
Home recipe	1 tbsp	14	92
Bottled	1 tbsp	14	214
Dry mix, prepared	1 tbsp	14	253
Low sodium	1 tbsp	15	3
Italian:			
Bottled	1 tbsp	15	116
Dry mix, prepared	1 tbsp	14	172
Mayonnaise	1 tbsp	15	78
Russian	1 tbsp	15	133
Thousand Island:			
Regular	1 tbsp	16	109
Low cal	1 tbsp	14	153

From USDA Human Nutrition Information Service, *Home and Garden Bulletin*, Number 233.

Appendix B

FOOD EXCHANGE LISTS

Starch/Bread List

Each item in this list contains approximately 15 grams of carbohydrate, 3 grams of protein, a trace of fat, and 80 calories. Whole grain products average about 2 grams of fiber per serving. Some foods are higher in fiber. Those foods that contain 3 or more grams of fiber per serving are identified with the fiber symbol, ✿.

You can choose your starch exchanges from any of the items on this list. If you want to eat a starch food that is not on this list, the general rule is that ½ cup of cereal, grain, or pasta or 1 ounce of a bread product is one serving.

Your dietitian can help you be more exact.

Cereals/Grains/Pasta

Bran cereals, concentrated ✿	⅓ cup	Grits (cooked)	½ cup
Bran cereals, flaked (such as Bran Buds®, All Bran®)	½ cup	Other ready-to-eat unsweetened cereals	¾ cup
		Pasta (cooked)	½ cup
Bulgur (cooked)	½ cup	Puffed cereal	1½ cup
Cooked cereals	½ cup	Rice, white or brown (cooked)	⅓ cup
Cornmeal (dry)	2½ tbsp.	Shredded wheat	½ cup
Grapenuts	3 tbsp.	Wheat germ ✿	3 tbsp.

Dried Beans/Peas/Lentils

Beans and peas (cooked) (such as kidney, white, split, blackeye) 🌾	⅓ cup
Lentils (cooked) 🌾	⅓ cup
Baked beans 🌾	¼ cup

Starchy Vegetables

Corn 🌾	½ cup
Corn on cob, 6 in. long 🌾	1
Lima beans 🌾	½ cup
Peas, green (canned or frozen) 🌾	½ cup
Plantain 🌾	½ cup
Potato, baked	1 small (3 oz.)
Potato, mashed	½ cup
Squash, winter (acorn, butternut)	¾ cup
Yam, sweet potato, plain	⅓ cup

Bread

Bagel	½ (1 oz.)
Bread sticks, crisp, 4 in. long × ½ in.	2 (⅔ oz.)
Croutons, low fat	1 cup
English muffin	½
Frankfurter or hamburger bun	½ (1 oz.)
Pita, 6 in. across	½
Plain roll, small	1 (1 oz.)
Raisin, unfrosted	1 slice (1 oz.)
Rye, pumpernickel 🌾	1 slice (1 oz.)
Tortilla, 6 in. across	1
White (including French, Italian)	1 slice (1 oz.)
Whole wheat	1 slice (1 oz.)

Crackers/Snacks

Animal crackers	8
Graham crackers, 2½ in. square	3
Matzo	¾ oz.
Melba toast	5 slices
Oyster crackers	24
Popcorn (popped, no fat added)	3 cups
Pretzels	¾ oz.
Rye crisp, 2 in. x 3½ in.	4
Saltine-type crackers	6
Whole wheat crackers, no fat added (crisp breads, such as Finn®, Kavli®, Wasa®)	2–4 slices (¾ oz.)

Starch Foods Prepared with Fat

Count as 1 starch/bread serving, plus 1 fat serving.

Biscuit, 2½ in. across	1
Chow mein noodles	½ cup
Corn bread, 2 in. cube	1 (2 oz.)
Cracker, round butter type	6
French fried potatoes, 2 in. to 3½ in. long	10 (1½ oz.)
Muffin, plain, small	1
Pancake, 4 in. across	2
Stuffing, bread (prepared)	¼ cup
Taco shell, 6 in. across	2
Waffle, 4½ in. square	1
Whole wheat crackers, fat added (such as Triscuits®)	4–6 (1 oz.)

🌾 3 grams or more of fiber per serving

Meat List

Each serving of meat and substitutes on this list contains about 7 grams of protein. The amount of fat and number of calories vary, depending on what kind of meat or substitute you choose. The list is divided into three parts based on the amount of fat and calories: lean meat, medium-fat meat, and high-fat meat. One ounce (one meat exchange) of each of these includes:

	Carbohydrate (grams)	*Protein (grams)*	*Fat (grams)*	*Calories*
Lean	0	7	3	55
Medium-Fat	0	7	5	75
High-Fat	0	7	8	100

You are encouraged to use more lean and medium-fat meat, poultry, and fish in your meal plan. This will help decrease your fat intake, which may help decrease your risk for heart disease. The items from the high-fat group are high in saturated fat, cholesterol, and calories. You should limit your choices from the high-fat group to three (3) times per week. Meat and substitutes do not contribute any fiber to your meal plan.

Meats and meat substitutes that have 400 milligrams or more of sodium per exchange are indicated with this symbol:

Tips

1. Bake, roast, broil, grill, or boil these foods rather than frying them with added fat.
2. Use a nonstick pan spray or a nonstick pan to brown or fry these foods.
3. Trim off visible fat before and after cooking.
4. Do not add flour, bread crumbs, coating mixes, or fat to these foods when preparing them.
5. Weigh meat after removing bones and fat, and after cooking. Three ounces of cooked meat is about equal to 4 ounces of raw meat. Some examples of meat portions are:

   2 ounces meat (2 meat exchanges) =
      1 small chicken leg or thigh
      ½ cup cottage cheese or tuna
   3 ounces meat (3 meat exchanges) =
      1 medium pork chop
      1 small hamburger
      ½ of a whole chicken breast

1 unbreaded fish fillet
cooked meat, about the size of a deck of cards

6. Restaurants usually serve prime cuts of meat, which are high in fat and calories.

Lean Meat and Substitutes

One exchange is equal to any one of the following items.

Beef	USDA Select or Choice grades of lean beef, such as round, sirloin, and flank steak; tenderloin; and chipped beef. 🔖	1 oz.
Pork	Lean pork, such as fresh ham; canned, cured or boiled ham 🔖; Canadian bacon 🔖, tenderloin.	1 oz.
Veal	All cuts are lean except for veal cutlets (ground or cubed). Examples of lean veal are chops and roasts.	1 oz.
Poultry	Chicken, turkey, Cornish hen (without skin)	1 oz.
Fish	All fresh and frozen fish	1 oz.
	Crab, lobster, scallops, shrimp, clams (fresh or canned in water) 🔖	2 oz.
	Oysters	6 medium
	Tuna (canned in water) 🔖	¼ cup
	Herring (uncreamed or smoked)	1 oz.
	Sardines (canned)	2 medium
Wild game	Venison, rabbit, squirrel	1 oz.
	Pheasant, duck, goose (without skin)	1 oz.
Cheese	Any cottage cheese	¼ cup
	Grated parmesan	2 tbsp.
	Diet cheeses (with less than 55 calories per ounce) 🔖	1 oz.
Other	95% fat-free luncheon meat	1 oz.
	Egg whites	3 whites
	Egg substitutes with less than 55 calories per ¼ cup	¼ cup

🔖 400 mg or more of sodium per exchange

Medium-Fat Meat and Substitutes

One exchange is equal to any one of the following items.

Beef	Most beef products fall into this category. Examples are all ground beef, roast (rib, chuck, rump), steak (cubed, Porterhouse, T-bone), and meat loaf.	1 oz.

Pork	Most pork products fall into this category. Examples are chops, loin roast, Boston butt, cutlets.	1 oz.
Lamb	Most lamb products fall into this category. Examples are chops, leg, and roast.	1 oz.
Veal	Cutlet (ground or cubed, unbreaded)	1 oz.
Poultry	Chicken (with skin), domestic duck or goose (well-drained of fat), ground turkey	1 oz.
Fish	Tuna (canned in oil and drained) 🖋	¼ cup
	Salmon (canned) 🖋	¼ cup
Cheese	Skim or part-skim milk cheeses, such as	
	Ricotta	¼ cup
	Mozzarella	1 oz.
	Diet cheeses (with 56–80 calories per ounce) 🖋	1 oz.
Other	86% fat-free luncheon meat 🖋	1 oz.
	Egg (high in cholesterol, limit to 3 per week)	1
	Egg substitutes with 56–80 calories per ¼ cup	¼ cup
	Tofu (2½ in. × 2¾ in. × 1 in.)	4 oz.
	Liver, heart, kidney, sweetbreads (high in cholesterol)	1 oz.

🖋 400 mg or more of sodium per exchange

High-Fat Meat and Substitutes

Remember, these items are high in saturated fat, cholesterol, and calories, and should be used only three (3) times per week. One exchange is equal to any one of the following items.

Beef	Most USDA Prime cuts of beef, such as ribs, corned beef 🖋	1 oz.
Pork	Spareribs, ground pork, pork sausage (patty or link) 🖋	1 oz.
Lamb	Patties (ground lamb)	1 oz.
Fish	Any fried fish product	1 oz.
Cheese	All regular cheeses, such as American, Blue, Cheddar, Monterey, Swiss 🖋	1 oz.
Other	Luncheon meat, such as bologna, salami, pimento loaf 🖋	1 oz.
	Sausage, such as Polish, Italian 🖋	1 oz.
	Knockwurst, smoked	1 oz.
	Bratwurst 🖋	1 oz.

Frankfurter (turkey or chicken) 🖋   1 frank (10/lb.)
Peanut butter (contains unsaturated fat)   1 tbsp.

Count as one high-fat meat plus one fat exchange:
Frankfurter (beef, pork, or combination) 🖋   1 frank (10/lb.)

🖋 400 mg or more of sodium per exchange

Vegetable List

Each vegetable serving on this list contains about 5 grams of carbohydrate, 2 grams of protein, and 25 calories. Vegetables contain 2 to 3 grams of dietary fiber. Vegetables which contain 400 mg of sodium per serving are identified with the symbol 🖋.

Vegetables are a good source of vitamins and minerals. Fresh and frozen vegetables have more vitamins and less added salt. Rinsing canned vegetables will remove much of the salt.

Unless otherwise noted, the serving size for vegetables (one vegetable exchange) is ½ cup of cooked vegetables or vegetable juice, or 1 cup of raw vegetables.

Artichoke (½ medium)	Eggplant	Sauerkraut 🖋
Asparagus	Greens (collard,	Spinach, cooked
Beans (green, wax,	mustard, turnip)	Summer squash
Italian)	Kohlrabi	(crookneck)
Bean sprouts	Leeks	Tomato (one large)
Beets	Mushrooms, cooked	Tomato/vegetable juice 🖋
Broccoli	Okra	Turnips
Brussels sprouts	Onions	Water chestnuts
Cabbage, cooked	Pea pods	Zucchini, cooked
Carrots	Peppers (green)	
Cauliflower	Rutabaga	

🖋 400 mg or more of sodium per exchange

Starchy vegetables such as corn, peas, and potatoes are found on the Starch/Bread List.

For free vegetables, see the Free Food List on page 254.

Fruit List

Each item on this list contains about 15 grams of carbohydrate and 60 calories. Fresh, frozen, and dry fruits have about 2 grams of fiber per serving. Fruits that have 3 or more grams of fiber per serving have a ⚜ symbol. Fruit juices contain very little dietary fiber.

The carbohydrate and calorie content for a fruit serving are based on the usual serving of the most commonly eaten fruits. Use fresh fruits or fruits frozen or canned without sugar added. Unless otherwise noted, the serving size for one fruit serving is ½ cup of fresh fruit or fruit juice, or ¼ cup of dried fruit.

Fresh, Frozen, and Unsweetened Canned Fruit

Apple (raw, 2 in. across)	1 apple
Applesauce (unsweetened)	½ cup
Apricots (medium, raw)	4 apricots
Apricots (canned)	½ cup, or 4 halves
Banana (9 in. long)	½ banana
Blackberries (raw) ⚜	¾ cup
Blueberries (raw) ⚜	¾ cup
Cantaloupe:	
5 in. across	⅓ melon
cubes	1 cup
Cherries (large, raw)	12 cherries
Cherries (canned)	½ cup
Figs (raw, 2 in. across)	2 figs
Fruit cocktail (canned)	½ cup
Grapefruit (medium)	½ grapefruit
Grapefruit (segments)	¾ cup
Grapes (small)	15 grapes
Honeydew melon	
medium	⅛ melon
cubes	1 cup
Kiwi (large)	1 kiwi
Mandarin oranges	¾ cup
Mango (small)	½ mango
Nectarine (1½ in. across) ⚜	1 nectarine
Orange (2½ in. across)	1 orange
Papaya	1 cup
Peach (2¾ in. across)	1 peach, or ¾ cup
Peaches (canned)	½ cup, or 2 halves
Pear	½ large, or 1 small
Pears (canned)	½ cup or 2 halves
Persimmon (medium, native)	2 persimmons
Pineapple (raw)	¾ cup
Pineapple (canned)	⅓ cup
Plum (raw, 2 in. across)	2 plums
Pomegranate ⚜	½ pomegranate
Raspberries (raw) ⚜	1 cup
Strawberries (raw, whole) ⚜	1¼ cup
Tangerine (2½ in. across)	2 tangerines
Watermelon (cubes)	1¼ cup

Dried Fruit

Apples ⚜	4 rings
Apricots ⚜	7 halves
Dates	2½ medium
Figs ⚜	1½

Prunes ✿	3 medium	Grapefruit juice	½ cup
Raisins	2 tbsp.	Grape juice	⅓ cup
		Orange juice	½ cup
Fruit Juice		Pineapple juice	½ cup
		Prune juice	⅓ cup
Apple juice/cider	½ cup		
Cranberry juice			
cocktail	⅓ cup		

✿ 3 or more grams of fiber per serving

Milk List

Each serving of milk or milk products on this list contains about 12 grams of carbohydrate and 8 grams of protein. The amount of fat in milk is measured in percent (%) of butterfat. The calories vary, depending on what kind of milk you choose. The list is divided into three parts based on the amount of fat and calories: skim/very lowfat milk, lowfat milk, and whole milk. One serving (one milk exchange) of each of these includes:

	Carbohydrate (grams)	Protein (grams)	Fat (grams)	Calories
Skim/Very Lowfat	12	8	trace	90
Lowfat	12	8	5	120
Whole	12	8	8	150

Milk is the body's main source of calcium, the mineral needed for growth and repair of bones. Yogurt is also a good source of calcium. Yogurt and many dry or powdered milk products have different amounts of fat. If you have questions about a particular item, read the label to find out the fat and calorie content.

Milk is good to drink, but it can also be added to cereal, and to other foods. Many tasty dishes such as sugar-free pudding are made with milk (see the Combination Foods list). Add life to plain yogurt by adding one of your fruit servings to it.

Skim and Very Lowfat Milk

Skim milk	1 cup	Evaporated skim milk	½ cup
½% Milk	1 cup	Dry nonfat milk	⅓ cup
1% Milk	1 cup	Plain nonfat yogurt	8 oz.
Lowfat buttermilk	1 cup		

Lowfat Milk

2% Milk	1 cup fluid
Plain lowfat yogurt (with added nonfat milk solids)	8 oz.

Whole Milk

The whole milk group has much more fat per serving than the skim and lowfat groups. Whole milk has more than 3¼% butterfat.

Whole milk	1 cup	Whole plain yogurt	8 oz.
Evaporated whole milk	½ cup		

Fat List

Each serving on the fat list contains about 5 grams of fat and 45 calories.

The foods on the fat list contain mostly fat, although some items may also contain a small amount of protein. All fats are high in calories and should be carefully measured. Everyone should modify fat intake by eating unsaturated fats instead of saturated fats. The sodium content of these foods varies widely. Check the label for sodium information.

Unsaturated Fats

Avocado	⅛ medium	Pumpkin seeds	2 tsp.
Margarine	1 tsp.	Oil (corn, cottonseed,	
Margarine, diet*	1 tbsp.	safflower, soybean,	
Mayonnaise	1 tsp.	sunflower, olive,	
Mayonnaise,		peanut)	1 tsp.
reduced-calorie*	1 tbsp.	Olives*	10 small or
Nuts and Seeds:			5 large
Almonds, dry		Salad dressing,	
roasted	6 whole	mayonnaise-type	2 tsp.
Cashews, dry roasted	1 tbsp.	Salad dressing,	
Pecans	2 whole	mayonnaise-type,	
Peanuts	20 small or	reduced calorie	1 tbsp.
	10 large	Salad dressing (all	
Walnuts	2 whole	varieties)*	1 tbsp.
Other nuts	1 tbsp.	Salad dressing,	
Seeds, pine nuts,		reduced-calorie	2 tbsp.
sunflower (without		(Two tablespoons of low-calorie salad	
shells)	1 tbsp.	dressing is a free food.)	

Saturated Fats

Butter	1 tsp.	Cream (light, coffee,	
Bacon*	1 slice	table)	2 tbsp.
Chitterlings	½ ounce	Cream, sour	2 tbsp.
Coconut, shredded	2 tbsp.	Cream (heavy, whipping)	1 tbsp.
Coffee whitener, liquid	2 tbsp.	Cream cheese	1 tbsp.
Coffee whitener, powder	4 tsp.	Salt pork*	¼ ounce

*If more than one or two servings are eaten, these foods have 400 mg or more of sodium.
🥢 400 mg or more of sodium per serving

Free Foods

A free food is any food or drink that contains less than 20 calories per serving. You can eat as much as you want of those items that have no serving size specified. You may eat two or three servings per day of those items that have a specific serving size. Be sure to spread them out through the day.

Drinks

Bouillon or broth without fat 🥢
Bouillon, low-sodium
Carbonated drinks, sugar-free
Carbonated water
Club soda
Cocoa powder, unsweetened (1 tbsp.)
Coffee/Tea
Drink mixes, sugar-free
Tonic water, sugar-free

Nonstick pan spray

Fruit

Cranberries, unsweetened (½ cup)
Rhubarb, unsweetened (½ cup)

Vegetables (raw, 1 cup)

Cabbage
Celery
Chinese cabbage 🌿
Cucumber
Green onion
Hot peppers
Mushrooms
Radishes
Zucchini 🌿

Salad greens

Endive
Escarole
Lettuce
Romaine
Spinach

Sweet Substitutes

Candy, hard, sugar-free
Gelatin, sugar-free
Gum, sugar-free

Jam/Jelly, sugar-free (2 tsp.)
Pancake syrup, sugar-free (1 – 2 tbsp.)
Sugar substitutes (saccharin, aspartame)
Whipped topping (2 tbsp.)

Condiments

Catsup (1 tbsp.)

Horseradish
Mustard
Pickles, dill, unsweetened 🥒
Salad dressing, low-calorie (2 tbsp.)
Taco sauce (1 tbsp.)
Vinegar

Seasonings can be very helpful in making food taste better. Be careful of how much sodium you use. Read the label, and choose those seasonings that do not contain sodium or salt.

Basil (fresh)
Celery seeds
Cinnamon
Chili powder
Chives
Curry
Dill
Flavoring extracts (vanilla, almond, walnut, peppermint, butter, lemon, etc.)
Garlic
Garlic powder
Herbs
Hot pepper sauce
Lemon

Lemon juice
Lemon pepper
Lime
Lime juice
Mint
Onion powder
Oregano
Paprika
Pepper
Pimiento
Spices
Soy sauce 🥢
Soy sauce, low sodium ("lite")
Wine, used in cooking (¼ cup)
Worcestershire sauce

🌾 3 grams or more of fiber per serving
🥢 400 mg or more of sodium per serving

Combination Foods

Much of the food we eat is mixed together in various combinations. These combination foods do not fit into only one exchange list. It can be quite hard to tell what is in a certain casserole dish or baked food item. This is a list of average values for some typical combination foods. This list will help you fit these foods into your meal plan. Ask your dietitian for information about any other foods you'd like to eat. The *American Diabetes Association/American Dietetic Association Family Cookbooks* and the *American Diabetes Association Holiday Cookbook* have many

recipes and further information about many foods, including combination foods.
Check your library or local bookstore.

Food	Amount	Exchanges
Casseroles, homemade	1 cup (8 oz.)	2 starch, 2 medium-fat meat, 1 fat
Cheese pizza, thin crust 🖋	¼ of 15 oz. or ¼ of 10″	2 starch, 1 medium-fat meat, 1 fat
Chili with beans, (commercial) 🌾🖋	1 cup (8 oz.)	2 starch, 2 medium-fat meat, 2 fat
Chow mein 🌾(without noodles or rice) 🖋	2 cups (16 oz.)	1 starch, 2 vegetable, 2 lean meat
Macaroni and cheese 🖋	1 cup (8 oz.)	2 starch, 1 medium-fat meat, 2 fat
Soup:		
Bean 🌾🖋	1 cup (8 oz.)	1 starch, 1 vegetable, 1 lean meat
Chunky, all varieties 🖋	10¾ oz. can	1 starch, 1 vegetable, 1 medium-fat meat
Cream (made with water) 🖋	1 cup (8 oz.)	1 starch, 1 fat
Vegetable or broth 🖋	1 cup (8 oz.)	1 starch
Spaghetti and meatballs (canned) 🖋	1 cup (8 oz.)	2 starch, 1 medium-fat meat, 1 fat
Sugar-free pudding (made with skim milk)	½ cup	1 starch
If beans are used as a meat substitute:		
Dried beans, peas, lentils 🌾	1 cup (cooked)	2 starch, 1 lean meat

🌾 3 grams or more of fiber per serving
🖋 400 mg or more of sodium per serving

The Exchange Lists are the basis of a meal planning system designed by a
committee of the American Diabetes Association and the American Dietetic Association. While designed primarily for people with diabetes and others who must
follow special diets, the Exchange Lists are based on principles of good nutrition
that apply to everyone. (Copyright © 1986 by the American Diabetes Association,
Inc., and the American Dietetic Association.)

Appendix C

SUBSTANCES COMMONLY ADDED

TO FOODS

Key Definitions

♦ **Maintain/Improve Nutritional Quality**

Nutrients: enrich (replace vitamins and minerals lost in processing) or fortify (add nutrients that may be lacking in the diet).

● **Maintain Product Quality**

Preservatives (antimicrobials): prevent food spoilage from bacteria, molds, fungi, and yeast; extend shelf life; or protect natural color/flavor.

Antioxidants: delay/prevent rancidity or enzymatic browning.

■ **Aid in Processing or Preparation**

Emulsifiers: help to distribute evenly tiny particles of one liquid into another; improve homogeneity, consistency, stability, texture.

Stabilizers, thickeners, texturizers: impart body, improve consistency or texture; stabilize emulsions; affect "mouthfeel" of food.

Leavening agents: affect cooking results—texture and volume.

pH control agents: change/maintain acidity or alkalinity.

Humectants: cause moisture retention.

Maturing and bleaching agents, dough conditioners: accelerate the aging process; improve baking qualities.

Anti-caking agents: prevent caking, lumping, or clustering of a finely powdered or crystalline substance.

▲ **Affect Appeal Characteristics**

Flavor enhancers: supplement, magnify, or modify the original taste and/or aroma of food without imparting a characteristic flavor of its own.

Flavors: heighten natural flavor; restore flavors lost in processing.

Colors: give desired, appetizing, or characteristic color to food.

Sweeteners: make the aroma or taste of food more agreeable or pleasurable.

Key to Abbreviations

stabil-thick-tex = stabilizers-thickeners-texturizers

leavening = leavening agents

pH control = pH control agents

mat-bleach-condit = maturing and bleaching agents, dough conditioners

anti-caking = anti-caking agents

Acetic acid	■ pH control	Butylparaben	● preservative
Acetone peroxide	■ mat-bleach-condit		
		Calcium alginate	■ stabil-thick-tex
Adipic acid	■ pH control	Calcium bromate	■ mat-bleach-condit
Ammonium alginate	■ stabil-thick-tex		
		Calcium lactate	● preservative
Annatto extract	▲ color	Calcium phosphate	■ leavening
Arabinogalactan	■ stabil-thick-tex		
Ascorbic acid	▲ nutrient	Calcium propionate	● preservative
	● preservative		
	● antioxidant	Calcium silicate	■ anti-caking
Azodicarbonamide	■ mat-bleach-condit	Calcium sorbate	● preservative
		Canthaxanthin	▲ color
		Caramel	▲ color
Benzoic acid	● preservative	Carob bean gum	■ stabil-thick-tex
Benzoyl peroxide	■ mat-bleach-condit	Carrageenan	■ emulsifier
			■ stabil-thick-tex
Beta-apo-8′ carotenal	▲ color	Carrot oil	▲ color
Beta carotene	◆ nutrient	Cellulose	■ stabil-thick-tex
	▲ color	Citric acid	● preservative
BHA (butylated hydroxyanisole)	● antioxidant		● antioxidant
			■ pH control
BHT (butylated hydroxytoluene)	● antioxidant	Citrus Red No. 2	▲ color
		Cochineal extract	▲ color

Corn endosperm	▲	color
Corn syrup	▲	sweetener
Dehydrated beets	▲	color
Dextrose	▲	sweetener
Diglycerides	■	emulsifier
Dioctyl sodium sulfosuccinate	■	emulsifier
Disodium guanylate	▲	flavor enhancer
Disodium inosinate	▲	flavor enhancer
Dried algae meal	▲	color
EDTA (ethylene-diamine-tetraacetic acid)	●	antioxidant
FD&C Colors:		
Blue No. 1	▲	color
Red No. 3	▲	color
Red No. 40	▲	color
Yellow No. 5	▲	color
Fructose	▲	sweetener
Gelatin	■	stabil-thick-tex
Glucose	▲	sweetener
Glycerine	■	humectant
Glycerol monostearate	■	humectant
Grape skin extract	▲	color
Guar gum	■	stabil-thick-tex
Gum arabic	■	stabil-thick-tex
Gum ghatti	■	stabil-thick-tex

Heptylparaben	●	preservative
Hydrogen peroxide	■	mat-bleach-condit
Hydrolyzed vegetable protein	▲	flavor enhancer
Invert sugar	▲	sweetener
Iodine	◆	nutrient
Iron	◆	nutrient
Iron-ammonium citrate	■	anti-caking
Iron oxide	▲	color
Karaya gum	■	stabil-thick-tex
Lactic acid	■	pH control
	●	preservative
Larch gum	■	stabil-thick-tex
Lecithin	■	emulsifier
Locust bean gum	■	stabil-thick-tex
Mannitol	▲	sweetener
	■	anti-caking
	■	stabil-thick-tex
Methylparaben	●	preservative
Modified food starch	■	stabil-thick-tex
Monoglycerides	■	emulsifier
MSG (monosodium glutamate)	▲	flavor enhancer
Niacinamide	◆	nutrient
Paprika (and oleoresin)	▲	flavor
	▲	color

Pectin	■ stabil-thick-tex
Phosphates	■ pH control
Phosphoric acid	■ pH control
Polysorbates	■ emulsifiers
Potassium alginate	■ stabil-thick-tex
Potassium bromate	■ mat-bleach-condit
Potassium iodide	◆ nutrient
Potassium propionate	● preservative
Potassium sorbate	● preservative
Propionic acid	● preservative
Propyl gallate	● antioxidant
Propylene glycol	■ stabil-thick-tex
	■ humectant
Propylparaben	● preservative
Riboflavin	◆ nutrient
	▲ color
Saccharin	▲ sweetener
Saffron	▲ color
Silicon dioxide	■ anti-caking
Sodium acetate	■ pH control
Sodium alginate	■ stabil-thick-tex
Sodium aluminum sulfate	■ leavening
Sodium benzoate	● preservative
Sodium bicarbonate	■ leavening
Sodium calcium alginate	■ stabil-thick-tex
Sodium citrate	■ pH control

Sodium diacetate	● preservative
Sodium erythorbate	■ preservative
Sodium nitrate	● preservative
Sodium nitrite	● preservative
Sodium propionate	● preservative
Sodium sorbate	● preservative
Sodium stearyl fumarate	■ mat-bleach-condit
Sorbic acid	● preservative
Sorbitan monostearate	■ emulsifer
Sorbitol	■ humectant
	▲ sweetener
Spices	▲ flavor
Sucrose (table sugar)	▲ sweetener
Tagetes (Aztec Marigold)	▲ color
Tartaric acid	■ pH control
TBHQ (tertiary butyl hydro-quinone)	● antioxidant
Thiamin	◆ nutrient
Titanium dioxide	▲ color
Toasted, partially defatted cooked cottonseed flour	▲ color
Tocopherols (vitamin E)	◆ nutrient
	● antioxidant
Tragacanth gum	■ stabil-thick-tex
Turmeric (oleoresin)	▲ flavor
	▲ color
Ultramarine blue	▲ color

Vanilla, vanillin	▲ flavor	Vitamin E (tocopherols)	◆ nutrient
Vitamin A	◆ nutrient		
Vitamin C (ascorbic acid)	◆ nutrient	Yeast-malt sprout extract	◆ flavor enhancer
	● preservative		
	● antioxidant	Yellow prussiate of soda	■ anti-caking
Vitamin D (D_2, D_3)	◆ nutrient		

SOURCE: Reprinted from *FDA Consumer*, April 1979. HEW Publication No. (FDA) 79-2115. U.S. Department of Health, Education, and Welfare, Public Health Service, Food and Drug Administration, Office of Public Affairs.

Appendix D

SELECTED RESTAURANT APPROACHES TO HEALTHFUL DINING

Jerome's — A Fresh Food Restaurant (Chicago)

Jerome's has an all-around approach. It is characterized by a variety of the innovative features that earmark healthful dining out: fresh, quality food, regionally procured; new affiliations with growers and suppliers; a strong waiter training program; menu information; expansion into other areas such as catering and bakery sales; all carried through with personal commitment.

Jerome's is a neighborhood restaurant whose appeal reaches beyond its area, Lincoln Park. The restaurant seats 60 indoors and, weather permitting, 80 on its patio. The patrons are in the upper middle income level. They are mostly professional couples, some with children—although Jerome's does not consider itself a family restaurant. There is a lot of repeat business.

. . . Jerome Kliejunas, formerly of Chicago's "Lettuce Entertain You" restaurant chain, turned his ideas about food into his own business [and] developed an approach to food service that has become the restaurant's forte: "fresh food, simply prepared."

"We're in touch with people's dietary needs" . . . and . . . weight loss and fat content (related to cholesterol and high blood pressure) [are] predominant among these concerns. "But for us, not using preservatives is something we do because food *tastes* better without them." In fact, Jerome's menu includes some of the higher-fat beef dishes popular in the Midwest as well as other heartier fare in addition to lighter items.

Jerome's strives for freshness by combining regional ingredients with do-it-yourself ingenuity. The restaurant prepares, on the premises, its own bread, pasta, salad dressings, mayonnaise and other condiments, along with desserts. The cooks use no processed foods, no preservatives and very little salt. Bread, especially its round loaves of whole wheat millet, is the restaurant's "signature" item. It is unsalted. The bread is sold at a small bakery counter in the restaurant.

In addition, Jerome's looks to its region for fresh food, and varies the menu according to its availability. Examples: "Today's Seafood—provided by our friend Jerry Woznyj at Clearwater Fisheries. House Salad: reflects the produce selection from South Water Market."

Jerome's routinely uses "free-ranging" chickens, as opposed to the mass-produced kind that never roam the chicken yard; and locally grown herbs.

Among the other featured regional items are Wisconsin ducklings, Minnesota wild rice, and Lake Superior whitefish. Almost all the produce is locally grown in the summer; the rest of the time it comes mostly from California.

The front of the menu briefly describes Jerome's commitment to these kinds of chemical-free basics. And the restaurant is also considering adding a statement that it is willing to accommodate special dietary needs upon request.

In addition to lunch and dinner, Jerome's recently started serving fresh breakfasts—homemade granola, juices, cheeses and fruits. And its . . . catering business is thriving.

"Party food and catered food have generally been abominable. . . . We have a different kind of food. It's fresh, made from scratch, and competitive price-wise."

The combination of restaurant and catering works especially well. . . . The two services can share food and space resources as well as promote each other.

Jerome's personalized approach to food extends to its management and service as well. A five-manager group divides kitchen and "floor" responsibilities. The latter include supervision of Jerome's "wait staff"—15 men and women who comprise the core staff that works all year and about 15 summer extras.

Jerome's expects a lot from its wait staff—"They are our ambassadors to the customers" . . . and the restaurant gives a lot in exchange. The wait staff is paid well and treated well. Jerome's has an attractive insurance plan for employees . . . and the restaurant recently built a comfortable shower facility and changing room for them. New staff go through a three-day orientation program and all staff receive what amounts to ongoing training in carrying out their tasks.

"It takes more than words. . . . You do things for people and they take an interest in your place. Job motivation is strong here. There is shared involvement in the restaurant."

As its "ambassadors to customers," Jerome's expects the wait staff to apply menu options to patrons' food preferences.

We want the wait staff "to pick up on special dietary needs." . . . That is how Jerome's conveys information about the healthfulness of its offerings. . . .

"If a customer says, 'Do you have any vegetarian entrees?' the waiter can respond, 'Yes, we make our own pasta, and we can do this without that sauce,' etc. One question can lead to another."

Jerome's prepares its staff for these kinds of exchanges daily. Before each shift, the waiters and waitresses gather to study and taste from the day's menu. The chef explains the preparation and ingredients of the new dishes. The wine is described. The staff dines and discusses. "They have to know everything." . . .

Planning daily fresh food needs is always a problem. "Sometimes you just run out of things. . . . It's hard to plan so you're not left with leftovers." So sometimes patrons don't get the special of their choice.

Not surprisingly, [the] first piece of advice for other restaurants interested in Jerome's concept is: train your staff thoroughly. Next [is] the importance of the visual appearance of the food and room. . . .

"You must appeal to all the senses . . . and you do that by paying attention to detail and serving tasty food." These tactics helped Jerome's turn around initial neighborhood impressions that it was a "health food" restaurant — not a popular idea in the area. . . .

Jerome's uses a "do-it-yourself" approach with food purveyors too. "We inspect fisheries, examine meat plants and work with local butchers." . . . "Local growing and distribution is the healthiest thing."

Nora (Washington, D.C.)

. . . Nora has become something of a Washington institution among health-conscious diners who are interested in fresh, additive-free and sometimes unusual dishes.

The 90-seat restaurant (with enclosed patio) serves about 250 meals a day, twice as many dinners as lunches. . . . Nora attracts a lot of professional people, many of them women, and — at dinner — couples. There is a lot of repeat business.

Nora Pouillon and her two partners shared an initial goal: they wanted to create a restaurant that would promote healthful, tasty, organic food. And they believed they could do it "without making it vegetarian and sacrificing meat." . . .

From the beginning, their focus was . . . organic, especially meat. They thought people's dietary concerns should not stop at fat and salt, but include — perhaps center on—chemicals. And they recognized that while fish and poultry were "lighter" foods, they were not chemical-free any more than meat.

The result of those objectives is Nora's eclectic menu that changes with the season and the availability of additive-free ingredients. It is sophisticated cuisine, but not "health food." . . . It is organic as much as possible, which is about one-third of the ingredients. Pouillon calls it "nouvelle American—not the 'Old American' way of cooking, but a melting pot of dishes adapted from different cultures. You find tofu, ginger and chiles side by side in the supermarket. Why not in a restaurant?"

Nora's focus on additive-free meats (the restaurant cites its supplier on the back of the menu, along with sources for organic dairy products, herbs, produce and cheddar) requires a lot of originality in the kitchen. Nora's beef, veal, lamb and pork come as whole animals—including stew meats and ground meats as well as steaks and chops. It is the chef's challenge to turn the available meat—100 percent organic—into interesting and tasty dishes.

In addition to all organic meat, some of Nora's produce is organic (about 40 percent in season: "In winter we can only get spinach and carrots," she says). The restaurant goes to a small grower for its poultry and local fishermen for fish, but the owners are not assured their purchases are largely organic. Nora grows herbs in a small garden in front of the restaurant and also buys from a local grower. The restaurant uses no sausage, prosciutto or bacon, not even nitrite-free items, "because the base is not organic," says Pouillon.

Despite their organic meats, Nora's owners figure they are not even at the half-way mark in their use of additive-free ingredients. "We're aiming for '10' but we try to be satisfied with '3'." . . .

But it's getting a little easier. The owners find there is an increasing number of "good specialty organic growers" in the area. About five years ago, there were none. In fact, Nora's business supports some of these distributors, the owners say.

Nora takes as much care preparing the food as it does selecting it. Cooking is simple: no deep-fat frying, no breading, no roux. . . . Salt, and then only sea salt, is used sparingly. Vegetables are mostly steamed and seasoned with herbs. Nora makes all its own pastries, sorbets, ice creams and some condiments.

Pouillon herself doesn't let the customers get too attached to specialty dishes. Turkish chicken and Chinese pork chops were popular, but the kitchen moved on; it had to—the meat supplies required it.

Likewise, the meat supply surprises. Beef kabobs received complaints for their toughness; in fact, the beef was too lean for the dish. "If it's melting in your mouth, it was from a fat, lazy animal that never walked around much. . . . One of the features of this restaurant is that you have to use your teeth."

The changing menu is what keeps chef Pouillon charged up. "The format here is creative, so I am not burned out," she says.

Nora's staff is as carefully orchestrated as its ingredients. The restaurant hires people "without lots of experience. . . . They are people who have other interests

—artists, musicians, and so on. They are people who generally never wait tables again."

Then Nora tries them out. The wait staff—nine in all, five for each shift—essentially role-plays its job at the beginning of the evening shift. Waiters and waitresses take turns serving one another the evening meal, suggesting wines, discussing the food. . . . The staff criticizes each other's presentations. Not incidentally, they eat.

When they are finished they know facts like which three or four sauces do not have garlic.

"It's good business to treat your sales staff well. . . . They *are* your sales people." . . .

The owners' overall management style is based on personal values and "a lot of personal energy." . . .

Doing additive-free and health food needs lots of energy, . . . but "what makes a restaurant good for a longer period of time is not overworking the staff. . . . People burn out." . . .

Observations

Nora's approach to nutrition has created a special brand of challenges for the restaurant. First, and foremost, is access to organic food. . . .

Clearly, one of the problems is making sure the item is truly organic. "Even wholesalers don't know where the fish come from." . . . Small growers are more reliable, but—since there are no controls—you still often have to take their word that their products are organically grown, Pouillon points out. . . .

With produce, fresh does not always serve. "You can get fresh vegetables that are full of junk. . . . We choose fresh over frozen or flash frozen, but we choose carefully."

Transportation creates another access problem. Good sources outside the region usually mean difficulties in shipping and getting the desired quantity. Wheat flour from Minnesota might be an example.

Organic meat, delivered to Nora by the carcass, creates other challenges, some already indicated. Pouillon must find uses for the whole animal. "I get tons of ground meat and stew meat to two filets," she says. It's a particular challenge to use these products and cook "light" at the same time. Thus, testicles may find their way onto the menu; but fatty sauces don't. And Nora has to explain why it no longer offers a popular dish for which the meat is, perhaps, not available.

Clearly, the kitchen must work hard to meet these challenges. And the owners cite the additional expenses of buying organic; not least is the labor of a full-time butcher in the kitchen. The restaurant tries to keep its prices down, says Pouillon, despite the additional expenses and the extra work involved.

Pouillon's number-one piece of advice to other restaurateurs is: "find great sources." The ingredients are the basis of an additive-free restaurant. Nora has had better luck with small growers, but they have problems too. Which brings . . . [us] to the next piece of advice: "Never say 'never'. You can't say it's completely organic when you can't be sure."

Spago (Los Angeles)

Spago is an example of a healthful food approach that works in an upscale setting. It demonstrates the chef's personalized philosophy of food as well as fine dining.

Spago, a trendy bistro located on a Hollywood hillside, is a household word among chic diners-out in the Los Angeles area. It is the first restaurant opened by chef Wolfgang Puck, formerly of L.A.'s Ma Maison. . . . The restaurant's specialty is new-style pizzas (topped with duck sausage, mussels or artichokes and goat cheese; not pepperoni).

Spago feeds celebrities and other "locals" on a regular basis; it is so popular that reservations for dinner can require four weeks' notice. His patrons want healthful, tasty, *good quality* food, Puck emphasizes.

"Many people come here three times a week to eat. Repeat customers want to eat healthfully—they can't eat rich food routinely," he says. (Although he notes some of his customers "save up" calories and splurge on desserts.)

His patrons' tastes also differ by age, Puck says. Younger people don't want heavy food, for example. They go out after dinner and they are more health-conscious than the older patrons, who like more traditional dishes. But almost all of his customers come to Spago for the "whole package," says Puck. That includes the ambience as well as the quality and taste of the cuisine. And by focusing on the health aspects of quality and taste, Spago is "one step ahead of other restaurants," says Puck.

Spago's food reflects Puck's personal approach to nutrition combined with lifestyle. . . . In general, Puck thinks people care more about cholesterol and fat than salt: "they want their food flavored." (He will cook without salt on request.) So he serves mostly low-fat meals, emphasizing natural, regional ingredients. There is no beef or veal on the menu. (Beef is too high in fat and veal has too many chemicals, says Puck.) The food is cooked simply. "It is left as close to its natural state as possible," Puck says. "I think the simpler the better."

Thus Spago will grill vegetables and cook the fish whole. It prepares fewer—or lighter—sauces, or serves them on the side. Puck likes mixtures of soy or olive oil, fresh herbs and ginger, for example. For his innovative pizzas, Puck makes his own dough and uses fresh tomatoes instead of tomato sauce. He [also] uses fresh goat cheese. . . .

Spago does not serve something like fish mousse. "It's half cream and half fish—you get as much fat as fish," explains Puck.

In terms of style, "our cooking is geared to the part of the country where we live," he says. Sauces are too heavy and too hot. This is a lifestyle where people watch their weight. "Twenty pounds can look like 40 on the TV or film screen."

In addition to the kinds of ingredients and the style of cooking, Puck focuses on the *quality* of selections. He often chooses the ingredients at market himself, going to specialty growers for some things such as pigeon and lamb. It is the quality of the food that sells his creative dishes, Puck believes. It is quality that "makes it really easy for people to come here to get good fish."

Like most other upscale restaurants, Spago offers no direct nutrition information about its offerings. Puck feels strongly about this.

"A painter doesn't provide you with information about what he's painted—it's there to see," he says. At Spago the menu—and the food—are there to see.

"Our responsibility as a restaurant is to cook healthy food," says Puck. He thinks it is the job of the press to spread the word.

"I make a statement with this restaurant," says Puck. "I offer fresh, quality food at much lower prices. I show that 'nutritious' doesn't have to be boring." In the end, he believes, the customer is going to tell the restaurateur what he or she wants. "If something is bad, people will stop coming." . . .

Puck has two simple rules for duplicating Spago's approach:

1. Use the freshest, best quality food. Don't import it from long distances, or you may be tempted to cover up less-than-fresh fish with sauces. If in Iowa, use trout, he advises as an example.
2. Get very qualified people in the kitchen. "They must do much more than the 'old style' of cooking," says Puck.

Alice Waters' Chez Panisse

In 1972, there was nothing like Chez Panisse, says [former Panisse] chef Jeremiah Tower [now chef-owner of the highly acclaimed Stars in San Francisco].

"There was no goat cheese. No wild mushrooms. No hazelnut oil. No wilted salads."

That is to say there was no inventive restaurant that took sometimes bare, almost always regionally grown ingredients like these and, through simple cooking techniques, turned them into imaginative dishes. Now nationally known for this approach, Chez Panisse has inspired chefs across the country, and many of its former cooks now direct the kitchens of innovative restaurants up and down the West Coast.

What Chez Panisse initiated has been called the "New American Cooking," the "New Cuisine" and the "new food movement." Its wide acceptance has given new credibility to cuisine whose freshness and simply cooked style represent more nutritious restaurant fare. In fact, Chez Panisse epitomizes the major trends found among restaurants that have developed more nutritious dishes for their customers.

These trends include:

- using the freshest ingredients, usually locally grown. The strict requirements of the restaurant's kitchen have resulted in the development of a new, responsive network of food growers and distributors.
- using a simple, natural approach to cooking, with more emphasis on fresh herbal flavorings and less emphasis on sauces, which are always light.
- developing innovative dishes, a challenge enjoyed by chefs who are trying to cook "lighter" and use foods that are in season.
- training chefs to implement all these new ideas, a critical factor in expanding to other restaurants Chez Panisse's special approach to food.

Chef Alice Waters created Chez Panisse. For years, Tower worked with her to develop and carry out the restaurant's unique approach. . . . Tower helped interpret and respond to the interests of Chez Panisse's growing clientele, in part by managing the growing resources of local gardeners and food distributors. . . .

The restaurant's patrons were "looking for something new," says Tower. "They were looking for the best taste; the freshest ingredients."

At the same time, "people were coming to the kitchen with things from their gardens." Tower began to develop recipes to use these "things," and he began to look for other new sources of fresh food as well. He started buying fish from deckhands on charter boats. And he started doing something else he describes as untraditional among chefs—sending back to distributors meat and produce he considered unacceptable.

Local food distributors began to respond, influenced by Panisse patrons who sought the restaurant's ingredients at local groceries, as well as by the growing needs of the restaurant kitchen. . . .

While Tower the chef . . . look[s] ahead to new trends in cooking, his food-philosopher self never loses sight of . . . source[s].

The newest trend, he says, is back to heartier food: "Grandmother's cooking, but modernized. We take traditional dishes and 'clean them up' using newer, simpler cooking techniques," which, he admits, aren't very new.

The key is to use what's regional, whatever your region, and treat it well.

The American Cafe (Washington, D.C.)

The American Cafe is unique in a variety of ways. A specially designed central kitchen serves the multiple, fresh-food needs of . . . restaurants [with] adjoining markets as well as a catering service. The Cafe also has encouraged and carefully used consumer opinion in its menu-planning.

The American Cafe has turned fresh, imaginatively prepared, "casual" food into a diversified and thriving business. . . .

The Cafe's . . . restaurants . . . all feature a creative menu of soups, salads, sandwiches, desserts and "Regional American Entrees." . . .

At the heart of the whole American Cafe enterprise are the food service concepts developed in the first American Cafe. . . .

Then the three co-owners sought to turn their popular Georgetown sandwich shop into a high-quality, reasonably priced, casual yet sophisticated, fresh food restaurant. Such a restaurant, they perceived, would respond to an emerging consciousness among the American public that fresh, healthy food was important.

But the American Cafe did not rest on its perceptions. The co-owners enlisted expert culinary and restaurant design help. They did their own traveling and tasting at other restaurants. They tested their concepts, and their new dishes, on the public. . . .

Clearly, the American Cafe's approach addressed a key food trend. The Cafe has continued to respond to such trends with its markets and catering service, which also service the convenience needs of urban professionals, especially working women.

Identifying the coming food trends, and addressing them through their diversified marketing, distinguishes the American Cafe enterprise. In large part, this rapid expansion and diversification has been made possible by another Cafe innovation —a central commissary that prepares all the skilled or cooked items, which are shipped fresh to the restaurants. The work is done by assembly line. The dishes comprise fresh foods that are suited to central preparation. This means no grilling or frying—in the central kitchen or at the restaurants. (The sites do roast their meats on the premises.) . . .

While freshness is the Cafe's nutrition stock in trade, it follows a variety of "healthful" rules in food preparation as well. The Cafe's smoked products have no chemicals [or] preservatives. . . . Nor does the central kitchen use preservatives in cooking. Herbs are often chosen as major flavorings. . . . Basically . . . the Cafe focuses on "healthy food rather than health food."

The American Cafe focuses less on consumer information about health food. The menu tells customers that "the emphasis is on fresh, natural ingredients presented with imagination and style." And most dishes include careful explanations of how they have been prepared. Waiters also are available to answer some health questions about the food. But the company believes in restaurants as "entertainment centers." . . . "Americans are still eating as many desserts as ever. They do like fresher, more wholesome desserts. But they don't want to be reminded their carrot cake contains 450 calories. . . .

What is their job . . . is to "make sure the carrots and every other ingredient in the cake is as fresh and wholesome as possible."

The American Cafe does solicit information [from] their customers, however. Patrons may be asked to complete surveys on new menu items, or to give comments on items being considered. The restaurant also tracks the sales of items through its register system. . . .

Observations

Keeping ahead of the trends and tracking customer reaction have been special strengths of the American Cafe. . . . Two specific trends that have served as focal points for the Cafe since the beginning: consumer interest in fresh (often regional), healthful food; and the growing importance of food in satisfying social values. These kinds of interests in good food have created a need for a "quality alternative" to casual restaurants and carry-out delicatessens. . . .

As the American Cafe has expanded to take advantage of the new marketing opportunities, it has met its major challenge [of] . . . maintaining quality; "keeping the freshness." . . .

Jonathan's (Chicago)

Jonathan's flexible approach to meeting consumer needs allows it to serve a special clientele, the elderly. The restaurant also handles a specialty food, seafood.

Jonathan's elderly clientele dictates in large part how the food is prepared. These patrons prefer the restaurant's grilling, poaching and broiling methods that are increasingly popular in fresh seafood eateries. But Jonathan's goes farther for its elderly clients.

"The key here is accommodating special requests." . . . That often means cooking plain and serving entrees and side dishes such as baked potatoes and other vegetables without salt, seasonings, butter or other sauces. It can mean boning the chicken or cutting up the meat.

Jonathan's charges nothing extra for these preparations, although they become difficult to carry out on busy nights. To cope, the restaurant asks patrons with special orders to call in advance. On weekends, they are encouraged to dine early, from 5–7 P.M. . . . .

"The this-is-what-we-have-and-you-better-like-it days are over. . . . What brings customers back is personalized service—knowing they can get what they want."

Personalized service means additional work for restaurant staff, in the kitchen and the dining room. [There is] a daily meeting with Jonathan's staff to discuss possible dish substitutions (a frequent request) and other accommodations that can be made. Waiters are instructed to channel questions on food ingredients to the manager himself. This rule grows out of the . . . sulfite controversy; and [Jonathan's] wants to ensure that patrons get the specific information. . . .

Observations

While Jonathan's seeks to expand its clientele to include younger patrons, the restaurant features food and cooking styles that accommodate its large elderly patronage. . . . Key challenges are maintaining the flexibility and staff resources necessary to serve the special needs of patrons. . . .

Greens (San Francisco)

Its waterfront setting and view of the Golden Gate Bridge already distinguish Greens in San Francisco. In addition to its location, however, Greens has gained a reputation as the foremost "vegetarian gourmet" restaurant on the West Coast, perhaps in the country. . . .

Greens attracts a varied clientele, local professionals and other San Franciscans at lunch; more tourists at dinner. While its out-of-the-way location can require special transportation, Greens is always crowded. . . .

The vegetarian community saw a new challenge as restaurateurs: how to make vegetarianism "credible to a lot of people." . . . This has been Greens' primary goal. It serves . . . "wholesome, local, fresh foods prepared simply and with imagination and care." . . .

People think of vegetarianism as heavy and uninteresting. . . . Thus Greens' luncheon menus of pasta dishes, salads and sandwiches include desserts ranging from a yogurt ice cream sundae with strawberries and walnuts to triple chocolate cake. . . .

"It's wholesome, although it may be richer than the food in traditional restaurants. And it's organic as much as we can make it that way." . . .

While Greens tries to use mostly organic foods, getting them is a problem. The organic farming industry is so controversial . . . that you never know whether you're *really* getting organic food. . . .

Variety is Greens' solution to what it sees as less-than-perfect agricultural options. So [it] gets ingredients from a lot of growers and, in turn, offers a lot of options to its patrons.

"A vegetarian who eats a broad diet and listens to [his or her] body will stay as healthy as possible." . . . Greens tries to reflect that philosophy.

Restaurant profiles adapted from *Nutrition and the American Restaurant* by Patricia B. Kelly. Public Voice for Food and Health Policy, Washington, DC, 1983.

Appendix E

SELECTED RESOURCES

Government Agencies

U.S. Department of Agriculture
(USDA)
Agricultural Marketing Service
Agricultural Research Service
Food and Safety and Inspection Service
Washington, DC 20250

USDA, Human Nutrition Information
Service
Nutrient Data Bank
Hyattsville, MD 20782

U.S. Food and Drug Administration
(FDA)
Rockville, MD 20852

U.S. Government Printing Office
(GPO)
Superintendent of Documents
Washington, DC 20402

Federal Trade Commission
Washington, DC 20580

Bureau of Alcohol, Tobacco, and
Firearms
Washington, DC 20226

Consumer Product Safety Commission
Washington, DC 20207

Environmental Protection Agency
Washington, DC 20460

National Marine Fisheries Service
U.S. Department of Commerce
Washington, DC 20235

**Associations and Consumer
Organizations**

American Dietetic Association
216 W. Jackson Blvd.
Chicago, IL 60606

American Heart Association
7320 Greenville Avenue
Dallas, TX 75231

Center for Science in the Public Interest
1501 16th Street, NW
Washington, DC 20036

Food Marketing Institute
1750 K Street, NW
Washington, DC 20006

National Restaurant Association
1101 Connecticut Avenue
Washington, DC 20036

Public Voice for Food and Health
  Policy
1001 Connecticut Avenue, NW
Washington, DC 20036

Society for Nutrition Education
1700 Broadway
Oakland, CA 94612

Publications

Agriculture Handbooks No. 8-1 to 8-16
  (Revised Edition Series) and 456.
  Nutrient Composition Data.
U.S.D.A., Washington, DC

FDA Consumer
U.S. Food and Drug Administration
Washington, DC

Food Management
HBJ Publications
Duluth, MN

*Food Values of Portions Commonly
  Used* (Pennington and Church)
Harper & Row
New York, NY

Restaurants U.S.A.
National Restaurant Association
Washington, DC

Nutrients in Foods (Leveille and Zabik)
The Nutrition Guild
Cambridge, MA

Nutrition Action Health Letter
Center for Science in the Public Interest
Washington, DC

Restaurants and Institutions Magazine
The Cahners Publishing Co.
Newton, MA

Restaurant Business Magazine
New York, NY

*Tufts University Diet and Nutrition
  Letter*
Tufts University
Boston, MA

*University of California, Berkeley,
  Wellness Letter*
University of California
Berkeley, CA

Index